University Centre Barnsley

Banding Together

Banding Together

How Communities Create Genres in Popular Music

Jennifer C. Lena

PRINCETON UNIVERSITY PRESS

Princeton and Oxford

Copyright © 2012 by Princeton University Press

Published by Princeton University Press, 41 William Street,
Princeton, New Jersey 08540

In the United Kingdom: Princeton University Press, 6 Oxford Street,
Woodstock, Oxfordshire OX20 1TW

press.princeton.edu

Library of Congress Cataloging-in-Publication Data

Lena, Jennifer C.
   Banding together : how communities create genres in popular music / Jennifer C. Lena.
      p. cm.
   Includes bibliographical references and index.
   ISBN 978-0-691-15076-5 (hardcover : alk. paper)   1. Popular music—Social aspects.
2. Popular music genres.   I. Title.
   ML3918.P67L46 2012
   781.64—dc23

                                        2011018691

British Library Cataloging-in-Publication Data is available

This book has been composed in Minion and Myriad

Printed on acid-free paper. ∞

Printed in the United States of America

10 9 8 7 6 5 4 3 2 1

Dedicated to my parents, Hugh and Susan Lena

In loving memory of Richard "Pete" Peterson

Contents

Acknowledgments

As with many of you, music figures importantly in my memories. My parents played music all the time: folk rock and classical at home, Top 40 and classic rock in the car, doo-wop and soul at parties, and Paul Simon's *Graceland* while we washed dishes on Block Island. Willie Lee introduced me to the Doors, and I soon realized that each of my friends had thrillingly different music to share. I remember Jamie Hirsch playing Jane's Addiction, the Smiths, and the Violent Femmes in the basement of the performing arts building at Wheeler School, and Tyler Francis had an early copy of Phish's demo tape. I won a cassette tape of the Beastie Boys' first album at David Bedrick's bar mitzvah, just as rap joined the playlists at WPRO FM. During a semester I spent abroad in Ireland, the guys in the H Block introduced me to Portishead and Thievery Corporation, while Will Sandalls lovingly, patiently taught me about jazz and recording studio technology. Jon Dworkin's eclectic tastes—rap, funk, and jazz standards, and classical South Indian music—along with his deep, abiding respect for my opinions, catapulted me into my professional work on music.

In graduate school, at Columbia University in the 1990s, my research interests in music flowered under the mentorship of faculty who dabbled, to greater or lesser degrees, in the study of culture. Priscilla Ferguson and Jeff Olick helped to unlock the secrets of Pierre Bourdieu's theories of cultural taste and distinction, and Lynn Chancer led a phenomenal independent study course on the sociology of culture. My fellow students, both in my cohort and years ahead and behind, inspired me to work harder than I ever imagined possible, and to dedicate myself to ideas that matter. I took every opportunity to spend time with Harrison C. White during graduate school. A giant intellect, Harrison offered honesty and insight that have been critical to my development as a scholar. But in the end, it was a new faculty member, Peter S. Bearman, who took me under his wing.

He helped to subsidize my education, challenged my ideas, and patiently encouraged me to improve my writing. Although I didn't feel his influence until I was well into my dissertation process, he irrevocably shaped my tastes and interests.

I joined the Department of Sociology at Vanderbilt University in 2003. After several years cosupervising students and talking shop, emeritus Professor Richard "Pete" Peterson and I decided it was time to work on a project together. Pete passed along an invitation from Mayer N. Zald to examine the cultural dimensions of social movements. A paper on music genres eventually emerged and was published in the *American Sociological Review* in 2008. At the invitation of Tim Dowd and Susanne Janssen, we produced a second paper on political music that we presented at Erasmus University. During the research for and construction of these papers, I benefited from the support of a Research Scholar's Grant from Vanderbilt and a fellowship from the Center for Arts and Cultural Policy Studies, at the Woodrow Wilson School, Princeton University. Many colleagues were kind enough to provide feedback on various drafts of these manuscripts, including N. Anand, Shyon Baumann, Howard S. Becker, Andy Bennett, Daniel Cornfield, Paul DiMaggio, Jennifer Earl, Robert Faulkner, Scott Frickle, Simon Frith, David Grazian, Michael Hughes, Larry Isaac, Pierre Kremp, Steve Lee, Iván Orosa Paleo, Francesca Polletta, Motti Regev, Bill Roy, Ken Spring, Chuck Tilly, Jason Toynbee, and Ezra Zukerman. Claire Peterson generously provided her editorial services for two years, and was a patient caretaker of the project for much longer. In the fall of 2008, Brayden King mentioned our projects to the new sociology editor at Princeton University Press, Eric Schwartz. Eric asked whether Pete and I would consider writing a book-length argument, but we decided to take a break and work on other projects.

During the winter of 2009, Pete's health slowly declined, and he passed away on February 4, 2010. Less than a week later I wrote to Eric, asking whether he was still interested in the book. I suppose I know of no better way to mourn the passing of a colleague and mentor than to push his work forward. I hope that Pete would be proud of the book that I've written, and that he would see it as I do, as a memorial to a cherished friend. There is a lot here he would disagree with, but I think he would love to argue about it.

The construction of the book has been swift, and would have been unthinkable without the help and support of a team of people. First, Eric's wisdom, patience, humor, and unwavering enthusiasm for the project have made this process a pleasure. Janie Chan and Lauren Lepow were a great help in the preparation of the final manuscript and I am grateful for the encouragement and assistance of the anonymous reviewers of this text. I benefited from the focused attention of the graduate assistants I sent to and from the library in search of hundreds of texts; my thanks to Katherine Everhart and Carly Rush. Support, good humor, and much-needed distractions came from many other friends and colleagues, including Shyon Baumann, Zen Bowers and Matt Walker, Katherine Blue Carroll, Nita Farahany, John Wayne Janusek, Sean Kanousis, Eric Klinenberg, John Krinsky, Gabriela Lena Frank, Peter Levin, John Levi Martin, Gina Neff, Jonathan Neufeld, Mark Pachucki, Paolo Parigi, Mike Richman, Gabriel Rossman, Bill Roy, Justine and Keivan Stassun, Ben Tran, Tiffany Tung, Tim Vogus, Steve Wernke, and Fred Wherry. I remain honored and humbled by the support of David Grazian, fellow music-lover, culture expert, and a good friend who always remembers to call on my birthday. I would not have enjoyed the writing process nearly as much if I had not been working alongside Terry McDonnell. His comments and ideas helped me to improve every chapter of this book. I hope someday I will have his facility with prose, and I am eager to celebrate the publication of his wonderful book. Steven J. Tepper has been an extraordinary colleague, and I am in his debt in so many ways, not the least of which is for his suggestion of this book's title. The contributions of Tammy A. Smith are too numerous to mention and my gratitude to her is inestimable.

Like most books, this one has something to prove. This book is for my parents, who taught me that we make the road by walking.

Portions of this work are adapted from:

Jennifer C. Lena and Richard A. Peterson, "Politically-Purposed Music Genres," *American Behavioral Scientist*, Special issue: Globalization and Diversity in Cultural Fields: Comparative Perspectives on Music, Literature and Television 55 (2011): 574–588. Used by permission of the publisher.

Jennifer C. Lena and Richard A. Peterson, "Classification as Culture: Types and Trajectories of Music Genres," *American Sociological Review* 73 (2008): 697–718. Used by permission of the publisher.

Jennifer C. Lena, "Social Context and Musical Content: Rap Music, 1979–1995," *Social Forces* 85, no. 1 (2006): 479–495. Copyright © 2006 by the University of North Carolina Press. Used by permission of the publisher. www.uncpress.unc.edu

Banding Together

Chapter 1

Music Genres

I start every semester in my Sociology of Hip-Hop and Rap Music course by asking the students to tell me a story about the origins of this musical style. The collective narrative that emerges, cobbled together from episodes of VH1's *Behind the Music*, *Vibe Magazine* articles, and song lyrics, is that rap music's origins lie in the desire of inner-city, poor, black men to document their lives and critique the social order that blocks progress for our nation's minorities. In criticism of this, a second group of students argue that this political narrative is a smoke screen, masking and justifying the sexism, violence, and profligate lifestyle of rap songs and artists.[1]

The terms of this debate would have been totally foreign to proto–rap artists in the mid-1970s when they were performing DJ sets in courtyards, parks, and community centers. Oral histories reveal a group of young men and women seeking to make money and a name for themselves as disco DJs. According to at least one account, the first "rap party" was a celebration of DJ Kool Herc's sister's birthday, organized as a fund-raiser for school clothes for the siblings.[2] It was only years later that rappers began to bemoan the sacrifice of politics to profit. But the power of the political reading of rap has nearly obscured what early performers have said about this period, and about their goals in making music.

Evidence of the power of this account is found not only in my classroom discussions, or the popular media that teach students to view the music in this fashion, but also in the actions of canonizing organizations. For example, the first rap song added to the National Archive of Historic Recordings (in 2002) wasn't the first rap song performed, or even the first one recorded (an unabashed party song called "Rapper's Delight"), but instead was Grandmaster Flash and the Furious Five's 1982 single, "The Message." This song's staccato vocal track describes the living conditions and frustrations of those mired in urban poverty. It is neither the best-selling rap single of the period, nor the song with the most radio play, nor, I would argue, the best loved by fans. It is, however, the first rap track that exemplifies the lyrical conventions that characterize a strain of politically oriented rap.

That the canonization process would define political, or so-called Black Nationalist, songs as the characteristic style within a genre dominated by African American performers should not surprise any student of twentieth-century U.S. history. It should also not surprise us to know that there are multiple, conflicting accounts of rap's origins. The adage that "history is written by the winners" suggests how strongly our present circumstances color the knowledge and interpretations we make of the past. So-called revisionist histories are required when the desire to explain the present as the necessary outcome of past events blinds us to other events and explanatory factors.[3] Such thin historical accounts identify a small number of explanatory factors (think of "for want of a horse" accounts of King Richard III of England's death at the Battle of Bosworth) and prevent us from revealing "event structures" and the relationships that produce outcomes.[4] Thin histories are flawed not because they identify the wrong events and people, but because they focus on too few of them, and because the importance of events and performers is determined by contemporary values. The need to revise thin histories in light of new discoveries or shifts in political and cultural attitudes means that we never get an "authoritative" history; rather, we accumulate multiple accounts of history and its significance.[5] A thick account of history defocalizes the actions of individuals (e.g., charismatic leaders, kings and reformers, divisive wives) and shifts our attention toward social structures and collective action.

Music is particularly in need of thick histories. In most histories of music, the focus is placed on individual actors: genius performers, opportunistic promoters, or divisive wives. By attributing credit for bold innovations to single individuals, we have a fragile, thin explanation for the very complex worlds in which these innovators lived. Moreover, historians often identify and lay substantial credit at the feet of idiosyncratic events, serendipity, and luck (or their opposites).[6] By defining acts of invention or providence as outside of history, as the product of individual genius and serendipity, these accounts suggest that creativity and innovation operate despite societal influence and social interaction. But if we take a closer look, each of these "great man" accounts has a shadow history in which geniuses depend upon the social systems in which they create their magic. As sociologists have shown time and again, great American art is produced by collaborative links between skilled practitioners.[7]

If you've ever been a member of a music community—as a fan or performer—you know that it takes tens, scores, or even thousands of people to make that community work, for better or worse. Music is a participatory, community-based activity.[8] At different stages of development, music communities are organized to lend themselves to different forms of participation. To return to the rap example, it is only after the community was large enough to sustain many, and many different, performers and songs that it was even possible to argue about whether the music "should be" seen as a political expression. As we look across musical communities, we discover more evidence that debates over the political content of music is keyed to the scale of the community size. Debates over profit, authenticity, or politics are extremely common once any music community has reached a relatively mature state of development.[9]

Documenting and understanding the attributes of music genre communities that emerge during different stages of development is the objective of this book. In looking across communities and musical styles, we can discover something that is rarely offered in musical histories: an analysis of how music communities *in general* operate: what shared obstacles and opportunities creative people face, what debates tend to characterize different states of the field, and so forth. These patterns are the grammar that allows us to understand the cultural language of popular music. Ultimately, my goal is to use the study of shared attributes across musical communities to provide a model of sociocultural classification. I seek a model that can be used to analyze many different cases in which people collaborate to draw boundaries around groups of things: ideas, artworks, people, organizations, to name just a few.

Banding Together is a study of the ideological, social, organizational, and symbolic attributes of twentieth-century American music. Three questions guide the investigation: (1) What are the common economic, organizational, ideological, and aesthetic traits among contemporary music genres? (2) Do music genres follow any patterns in their development, and if so, what explains their similarities and differences? and (3) Using contemporary American musical genres as a point of reference, how can we discover new genre forms and trajectories? I explore these questions in music in order to offer a comprehensive view into both classificatory schema employed to organize sound and sociocultural classification systems in general.

To identify these uniformities, I begin by isolating the formal characteristics of twelve attributes found across styles of music. These organizational, economic, interpersonal, and aesthetic attributes are used to differentiate one musical style from another, and a given style from one moment in time to the next. Drawing from an inductive coding of histories of sixty American market-based musical forms from the twentieth century, I demonstrate patterns of attributes.

What Is a Theory of Sociocultural Classification?

Questions of symbolic classification have been central to sociology since its earliest days because distinctions between classes become the nucleus around which we develop identities, affiliations, hierarchies, knowledge, and conflict. Classifying rap as political, misogynist, or profit-oriented has enormous consequences for fans, artists, and promoters. Since the advent of their discipline, sociologists have generated systems of sociocultural classification for a diverse set of phenomena, including forms of organization, religious belief, fashion, gender, sexuality, art, race, and societies at large (to name a few of many examples). The sociological concern with systemic change in such classification systems is venerable, yet there is no robust and generalizable theory of dynamic change, though efforts have been made in domains including nation building, social movements, name-giving practices, and French cuisine.[10] In the case of music, stylistic distinctions (between jazz and blues, for example) organize people and songs within a system of symbolic classification. While numerous studies chronicle the history of specific styles of music, none seek to document recurrent processes of development and change *across* styles. The objective of this book is to generate a robust theory of musical communities, culminating in a system of sociocultural classification that can be applied to a wide range of phenomena. Such a theory of classification should produce thick histories.

I study music to illuminate processes of sociocultural classification for several reasons. First, and perhaps most importantly, my expertise lies in the sociological study of music, and rap music in particular. One of the reasons I chose to study rap music was that I found myself in an intellectually vibrant and progressive department during graduate school. While scholars in general were at pains to distinguish consecrated musical genres from "vernacular" ones, my colleagues encouraged me to disregard these distinctions and treat rap music as another case to which the tools of social science could be usefully applied. Second, I chose music because it helps me to have a lot of the right kind of company. Within the academy, music is a focus of experts across a number of fields, including those studying digital technologies, regulation and deregulation of industries, firm and market structure impacts on industries, taste, identity, history, censorship and surveillance, and authenticity.[11] While some scholars might seek to avoid densely populated research fields, I was delighted to discover a wealth of primary and secondary data sources on which I could rely. These many histories of musical communities have provided the data for this book. Since they document the numerous features of music communities potentially relevant to a theory of sociocultural classification, this is a final and critically important reason for my selection of music for this study.

After more than ten years of research and teaching within the field, it became obvious to me that formal similarities across musical communities exist. For example, there are clear and recognizable differences between a "garage band" and groups making music for mass audiences. In the case of the former, performers play in front of small groups, have no consistent access to performance spaces, meet and practice in private spaces like homes, and tend to be musically unsophisticated. Disagreements within these groups emerge when individual performers push their personal agendas—musical, social, political, and economic—on members of the small community. At the other end of the spectrum, popular musicians play in front of huge audiences, have difficulty getting booked in all but the largest performance venues, and meet and practice within formal organizational settings like recording studios. With the exception of lead performers, musicians cycle through a variety of groups because unanimity of

performance conventions makes individual instrumentalists relatively in-
terchangeable. As a result of widespread consensus over the conventions of
musical performance, disagreements are highly interpersonal and unique,
or technical. After noting that certain characteristics immediately differentiate moments in a musical style's trajectory, I began to document how the
social organization of musical production changes over time.

Creating an exhaustive list of these characteristics or attributes required
that I construct a conceptual template and then iteratively refine it. Identifying the attributes that characterize musical communities was a straight-
forward, but lengthy, process. First, there was the question of how to draw
boundaries around the case—that is, how to define what "counted" as data,
and what did not. These are common problems when scholars seek to produce "thick" histories of the sort I described in the chapter's opening pages.
The simplest solution was to cast a wide net while ensuring that the sources
of information are reliable. It was immediately apparent that music made
outside the United States, and before the early twentieth century, faced
drastically different circumstances during its birth and death, so I decided
to exclude such music from consideration. The more difficult problem was
to identify musical styles that could be properly analyzed as genres.

I define musical genres as systems of orientations, expectations, and
conventions that bind together industry, performers, critics, and fans in
making what they identify as a distinctive sort of music.[12] In other words, a
genre exists when there is some consensus that a distinctive style of music
is being performed. You will immediately notice that I do not use the word
"genre" to refer to musical idioms (e.g., polka or techno), and instead refer
to such idioms as musical *styles*. I believe my definition of genre facilitates
a deeply sociological approach to the subject, in that it focuses attention
on the set of social arrangements that link participants who believe themselves to be involved in a collective project.[13]

Genre communities draw together a diverse constituency of record
labels and other complex organizations; fans, listeners, and audiences;
musicians; and "historical legacies that come to us within broader social
formations."[14] Genre communities are art worlds: networks of cultural production, distribution, and consumption.[15] Art worlds include technologies
or artistic materials (e.g., cameras, brushes); regulatory systems (e.g., copyright law); distribution systems and display locations (e.g., compact discs,

galleries); reward systems (e.g., sales charts, awards); organizations (e.g., record labels); systems of appreciation and criticism (e.g., college curricula that convey art historical resonance); gatekeepers (e.g., talent scouts, newspaper critics), and audiences.[16]

Given this definition, genres are numerous and boundary work is ongoing as they emerge, evolve, and disappear.[17] That is, while genres need some degree of consistency for coherence, they also must change: "genres do not work by simply reproducing the same patterns over and over; such repetitive logic would likely have little appeal to popular music audiences."[18] The shifting boundaries of genres make them difficult to pin down. Musicians often do not want to be confined by genre boundaries, but their freedom of expression is necessarily bounded by the expectations of the other performers, audience members, critics, and the diverse others whose work is necessary to making, distributing, and consuming symbolic goods.[19] For example, "'heavy metal' is a term that is constantly debated and contested, primarily among fans, but also in dialogue with musicians, commercial marketing strategists, and outside critics and censors. Debates over which bands, which songs, sounds and sights get to count as heavy metal provide occasions for contesting musical and social prestige."[20] The genre within which particular songs, or performers, are positioned can change over time.[21] These debates serve not only to sort bands and songs into groups but also to identify those who are aware of current distinctions from those who are outsiders or hapless pretenders. Within the stream of electronic and dance music, for example, keeping up with the introduction of new styles—more than three hundred in just 1998 and 1999—is an accomplishment only the most diligent and committed fan could achieve.[22] The ongoing boundary work that characterizes music genres is therefore an attribute worthy of study, not a problem to be avoided in the endeavor of examining how genres work. In this book, I included every variant style, group, or performer that made a claim to a given genre community. Since my focus was on the formal attributes of music communities, there was no need to adjudicate the status of any particular band.

Musical styles vary widely by popularity and longevity. Some music forms, such as rock 'n' roll, become very popular and last over a long period of time. Some, like disco, are very popular and short-lived.[23] Some, like polka, thrive over many decades without becoming widely popular, and many, such as big beat, Northern soul, psychedelic country, and range rock, have only a transitory existence. Most evolve out of one or more earlier musical styles that develop in analogous sectors of society and share cultural characteristics. For example, there is a recurrent affinity of avant-garde art with art-oriented pop music. Late nineteenth-century French modernist artists' incorporation of popular music sensibilities into their work culminated in the appropriation of jazz elements in the 1920s. The process operated in reverse when bebop jazz musicians of the late 1940s asserted their work to be related to the latest avant-garde art of their time, a pattern to be repeated later by the Beatles and the Velvet Underground, among others.[24]

Some musical styles, over the course of decades, spawn a number of variants.[25] These families of music retain their coherence through shared institutions, aesthetics, and audiences. I call these sets of styles "streams" through which a number of genres may flow.[26] For a musical example, rock 'n' roll, drawn from rhythm and blues (R&B), country music, and pop, began to be considered a distinct style in 1954.[27] In the decades since, it has spawned numerous new styles, including rockabilly, glitter rock, punk, heavy metal, emo, and more, ultimately forming a rock stream.

What Are Genre Forms and How Are They Identified?

Reading histories of musical styles created in the twentieth-century United States, I began the iterative process of identifying the attributes that characterize different communities. I ultimately examined sixty domestic and four international styles, documented in over three hundred primary and secondary texts. I used a preliminary survey of works on bluegrass, grunge rock, rap, and bebop jazz to generate a list of attributes. I then brought this preliminary list to bear on the remaining fifty-six domestic genres, and proceeded to add, condense, or remove attributes as necessary. This process resulted in the template of attributes represented in table 1.1. Each of the twelve rows represents a dimension common to all sampled styles, and each cell represents specific attributes. During the construction of this list of attributes, it became apparent that there was an additional dimension of difference that roughly corresponded to the complexity of the musical world at a given time in its history. Particular attributes of the musical community tended to accompany other attributes. And so, for example, communities with very few members lacked regular access to performance venues, and often did not even have a name they used to describe their emerging musical style. Also, music that attracted national or international

Table 1.1. Genre Forms and Dimensions

Dimension	Genre Forms			
	Avant-garde	Scene-based	Industry-based	Traditionalist
Organizational form	Creative circle	Local scene	Established field	Clubs, associations
Organizational scale	Local, some Internet	Local, Internet linked	National, worldwide	Local to international
Organization locus	Homes, coffee shops, bars, empty spaces	Local, translocal, and virtual scenes	Industrial firms	Festivals, tours, academic settings
Sources of income for artists	Self-contributed, partners, unknowing employers	Scene activities, self-contributed	Sales, licensing, merchandise, endorsements	Self-contributed, heritage grants, festivals
Press coverage	Virtually none	Community press	National press	Genre-based advocacy and critique
Genre ideal or member goals	Create new music	Create community	Produce revenue, intellectual property	Preserve heritage and pass it on
Codification of performance conventions	Low: highly experimental	Medium: much attention to codifying style	High: shaped by industry categories	Hyper: great concern about deviation
Technology	Experimentation	Codifying technical innovations	Production tools that standardize sound	Idealized orthodoxy
Boundary work	Against established music	Against rival musics	Market driven	Against deviants within
Dress, adornment, drugs	Eccentric	Emblematic of genre	Mass-marketed "style"	Stereotypic and muted
Argot	Sporadic	Signals membership	Used to sell products	Stylized
Source of music name	Site or group specific	Scene members, genre-based media	Mass media or industry	Academics, critics

audiences was plagued by debates over the expertise of performers. In order to capture these similarities, or clusters of attributes within dimensions, I created four genre forms: Avant-garde, Scene-based, Industry-based, and Traditionalist. These types are represented as columns in table 1.1. Thus genre types are characterized by constellations of dimensional attributes. For example, in the upper-left-corner cell of table 1.1, "creative circle" is the representative organizational form of Avant-garde genres.

The entries in a column of the table represent an ideal-typical construction of a genre type and so do not operate like those of the periodic table of elements or the genetically based taxonomies in biology. This is because each specific attribute is neither necessary nor sufficient for a musical style to be coded as having a particular genre form. The table of dimensions and types should be considered a conceptual tool for understanding genre. Had I made more detailed distinctions among attributes, it would have been possible to create more than twelve of them, and perhaps, more than four genre types. For example, I could have chosen to break "press coverage" into two dimensions: one that captured the size and demographic attributes of readers, and one that reflected the content or character of specific articles. While it is possible that readership and content do not work in concert, there is substantial evidence to suggest that these attributes are correlated. In considering the inclusion of new dimensions, I sought to ascertain whether they meaningfully distinguished musical genres from one another. Ultimately, the four-genre type by twelve-dimension resolution was the most parsimonious.

Organizations and Money

Over time, musical communities experience particular organizational forms, produce and distribute works for differently sized audiences, and operate within certain kinds of organizations. These dimensions—organizational form, scale, and locus of activity—are the first three rows in table 1.1.

Each phase of a musical style exhibits a typical form of social organization: a circle, a scene, the diffuse actors moving in and around formal organizations, and a fourth state in which participants are fractured across all three forms of social organization.

Musical communities can range from the hyperlocal to the global, and I refer to this dimension as organizational scale. Genres can be housed in neighborhoods, nurtured by a local scene, or supported by the massive machinery of global enterprise. The center of activity is a musical community's organizational locus. For example, doo-wop groups in the late 1940s often performed in the same two clubs: the Royal in Baltimore and the Howard in Washington.[28] Performers, fans, record label talent scouts, and anyone else interested in the style found their way to those spaces. The form, scale, and locus of doo-wop in the 1940s was local, Scene-based music. Similarly, in Seattle, during the years when Sub Pop Records sought to create a market for the so-called Seattle sound (later dubbed "grunge rock"), promoters showed their resourcefulness by creating new bars, clubs, and other performance venues in a city where such spaces were rare, particularly if one sought to attract an underage crowd.[29] In these examples we see both that genres depend upon existing music performance spaces, and that they can create the organizational locus for the music from raw materials. In their Scene-based phase, several music styles relied upon a group of venues spread across cities, in which they found local audiences for the music. In black musical styles, performers traveled the "chitlin circuit," salsa performers gigged on the "cuchifrito circuit," and Jewish entertainers played the "Borscht Belt," while Reverend Dorsey and fellow Chicagoans created the "gospel highway."[30] In the Traditionalist genre form, community members rely on formal organizations, both large and small, to support their activities. Fans and performers create clubs and associations that distribute information on the history of the style and the current activities of its members. But Traditionalists also draw resources from large organizations designed to serve the needs of larger or diverse groups. Museums and universities often provide physical space and financial resources that allow genre members to write histories, host conferences, air radio programs, and mount performances. Record labels devoted to the production of contemporary music may agree to produce one or a small number of remastered or rerecorded albums. Although these organizations are not dedicated to serve the genre community, their support is key to the vibrancy of Traditionalist genres.

It is extremely important to analyze the spaces in which music is experienced because spatial arrangements impact the form and nature of community engagement. The size of the venue, the amount of distance and interaction between musicians and audience members, and the volume of the music in the space all guide participants as they figure out how to act and interact, and determine what they should expect about the other "rules of the genre."[31] For example, contemporary punk music often occurs in venues with raised stages above dance floors to accommodate the pit slam dancing of fans. The combination of collision and mutual protection among punk fans within the pit reflects the blend of individuality and camaraderie that characterizes the rebellious attitudes in contemporary punk music.[32] In contrast, classical music and opera are typically performed in venues that are filled with tightly locked rows of chairs and provide no space for dancing. This conveys the expectation that these styles are designed for passive, thoughtful consumption, and not for other forms of physical engagement.

The organizational form, scale, and locus of a musical genre reflect several other features of production and consumption. Clusters of these attributes may predict the nature of a music community's relationship with the state. Smaller, hyperlocal circles that don't generate much attention or profit may not be exposed to tax policies on income or business ownership, but members may be especially vulnerable to police supervision if they are seen as dangerous elements within the community. Only those musics with a relatively advanced division of labor are likely to pursue government subventions to cover the production of works.

These examples also reveal that organizational form, scale, and locus reflect the status and role structure of the group. We should not expect a small musical community to develop a bureaucratic infrastructure, for example. Patterns in the organization of the music may also influence the means of communication employed by group members, such that smaller groups rely on person-to-person contact, and larger groups rely on Web pages, newsletters, and other mass media technologies that reach beyond face-to-face interaction. For example, as I discuss in more depth in chapter 2, most heavy metal styles survive through the circulation of music and information through "distros," or distribution lists. Lists such as these nurture the growth of death metal, as members share not just music, but also information and advice. For example, many groups (including Nasty Savage, Death, and Morbid Angel) relocated to Florida in order to record with Scott Burns and his staff at Morrisound Studios, based on the recommendations of fellow musicians.[33] This suggests that the arrow of causality points both ways: the means of communication within a community is both produced by, and can produce, the music's primary location in physical space. Since relations with the state, the degree of bureaucratization, and communication media are consistently associated with attributes of a music's organizational form, scale, and locus, they were not included as distinct dimensions in table 1.1.

The sources of income available to artists largely reflect the organizational form, locus, and goals of the genre, and have been of specific interest to scholars working at the intersection of political economy, urban social dynamics, and cultural production.[34] There are no studies that exhaustively document the amount and kind of income that musical artists earn, although contract negotiations, financial hardships, and cross-platform branding strategies feature in most profiles of music producers, label heads, and bands.[35] However, we know that the kinds and amounts of funding available to groups of artists determine, to a large extent, the size and diversity of the public that hear their music. Conversely, the size and diversity of the fan base for a musical style determines, to some degree, the kinds and amounts of funding available to artists.

At the Avant-garde stage, music producers require meager resources: really just the time and space to experiment. In music scenes, the sources of practical support are the most diverse of across all genre forms: artists often rely on family members, friends, and nonmusical employment to support their creative labor. For example, most singers in doo-wop's Scene-based phase held "straight" day jobs in the community with businesses that formally and informally supported the music community: performers were allowed to work on a part-time or ad hoc basis to accommodate tour schedules. Alphonso Feemster of doo-wop group the Four Bars of Rhythm explained that in the group's early days: "I'm singing, still singing, working day job at Morton's [Department Store], right. Eddie Day worked at an old mattress factory around the corner from Morton's. Melvin worked in there with him. We were all in the same area."[36] Baltimore and Washington, D.C., businesses sponsored radio programs for doo-wop music, sold records, and sometimes sponsored or managed talent shows, contents, or even groups themselves.[37] In Industry-based genres, artists no longer need to rely on family, friends, and nonmusical employment to earn a living, but this is an exceptional achievement for musicians. Musicians earn income from recording contracts, concert ticket sales and appearances, merchandise sales, and sponsorship agreements. While many organizations involved in Traditionalist genres are nonprofit businesses supported by donations and grants, universities also play an important role, supporting musical styles by hiring historians and musicians to teach courses on the subject.[38]

The nature of media coverage is differs substantially among the various genre forms. In the Scene-based period of many musical styles, local media will carry sympathetic and informed pieces on the emerging community. In grunge rock's Scene-based period, local Seattle radio stations like KCMU and KJET included the music on their playlists, and locally operated, alternative press outfits like *Backlash* and the Seattle *Rocket* published stories on the music.[39] Of course, scene members can use the media instrumentally to advance the popularity of the music. In grunge, Sub Pop record label owners Pavitt and Poneman hired a London press agent to promote the bands in the United Kingdom (believing the British music press's endorsement would build interest in the genre), and paid for *Melody Maker*'s Everett True to cover Seattle's "grunge phenomenon." After influential British DJ John Peel began to positively review Sub Pop's music, the rock press caught on and Seattle bands were soon described as "the saviors of rock."[40] Grunge quickly became an international popular sensation, propelling the scene into an Industry-based genre.

In contrast, the Industry-based phase is often dominated by poorly informed and critical feature pieces in the national media. While some of the better music periodicals will seek out performers and produce stories on the politics and lifestyles of musicians, major news media tend to sensationalize Industry-based music, spinning the lifestyle as a danger to its fans, or claiming a danger is posed to society by its "lawless, anti-social, and hedonistic" fans.[41] In Traditionalist genres, the media focus on the music as material to review, not as a news story. These media support the goals of such genres: to preserve the history of the Scene-based phase, to introduce new fans and performers to the music, and to adjudicate claims of authenticity among the community. And so, for example, in the 1960s and 1970s, the rock press didn't write pieces analyzing the vocal approaches of older groups, or their instrumentation, but instead "concentrated . . . on finding the 'true auteurs' of the groups, usually the composers or the producers."[42] Thus the focus ceases to be on the music itself and shifts toward an authentication process that only loosely addresses sound. Characterizing the scale and nature of press coverage is an important tool in identifying a musical style's genre form.

Genre Ideals and Style

Genres are defined not only by features of the organizational environment and institutional practices that arise within it, but by attributes of the artists and the music they play. These dimensions include the genre ideal, performance conventions, technology, boundary work, codes of dress and speech, and the source of the genre name.

Genre stakeholders have a set of target goals, or "a set of preferred changes toward which [they claim] to be working," not unlike social movements. I call these target goals the *genre ideal* of the group; these are, specifically, a group of preferred changes the genre members seek to enact.[43] Genre ideal bears a strong similarity to the sensitivities of "critical communities," where a group of critical thinkers cultivate a sensitivity to some problem, and develop consensus about its causes and a shared sense of how it should be addressed or solved.[44] In music, these often emerge out of grievances with the status quo. For example, Avant-garde grunge artists developed a genre ideal built from their shared objections to the hair metal, pop, and rock of the time. Grunge was antimacho and antimainstream, a reaction against both the "fluff" of pop singers Madonna and Paula Abdul and the big hair and "beef cake posturing" of hair metal bands like Mötley Crüe, Poison, and Bon Jovi.[45] Grunge vocals were simple, often unintelligible, because singers avoided the operatic voices of hair metal. The emergence of a new artist, school, party, or movement is marked by the facts that it poses problems for other artists, and that its arguments become the focus of conversations and struggles.[46]

Even when a genre ideal is not expressly stipulated, group members come to share a sense of what changes they seek to make in existing music. As the genre ideal matures, however, community members turn their focus toward the preservation of a historic or earlier style. When doo-wop reached its Traditionalist phase, in the late 1960s, the British invasion was drawing a large, middle-class audience to rock 'n' roll. Doo-wop aficionados, in fanzines like *Big Town Review* and *Record Exchanger*, lamented the ignorance of the new rock audience, and especially their lack of understanding of doo-wop's role in the invention of the popular style.[47] Since Traditionalist genres have less fan support than most contemporary, popular music, they often ennoble their tastes through implied kinship with artistic forms characterized by unimpeachable aesthetic credentials and a small, discerning audience. For example, jazz player Bob Wilber said of the 1990s: "I think it's maybe the most important movement in jazz in the next decade, the restoration of early jazz. . . . In other words, we play Mozart today and it isn't considered old-fashioned. Why not play Jelly Roll Morton, King Oliver, early Duke Ellington, Benny Goodman, and Charlie Parker?"[48] The comparison of early works in several jazz styles with Mozart is meant to reframe the nadir of jazz's popularity as a harbinger of canonization to come.

Genre ideal is used to refer to a set of performance conventions adopted by the group so that players know what to expect of each other. These vary widely from being very open and experimental to being rigidly codified. To show that they are part of the scene, fledgling musicians must show that they understand the coalescing genre performance conventions. Innovators or stars within the community are produced when artists are able to introduce or modify performance conventions in ways that meet with approval. Of course, most conventions are borrowed from other genres in the music stream, but some are modified or unique to the style-in-formation. Conventions governing audience behavior are also consolidated over time.[49] In addition, conventions concerning the evaluation of performance develop and become the center of critical discourse in and around the genre.[50] While smaller groups tend to prioritize innovation, and local groups seek to nurture a community of support, other genres seek to produce revenue, or to preserve heritage.

The demonstration and innovation of performance conventions is often dependent upon the availability and mutability of technologies required for the music's production. Changes in technology often augur the emergence of new musics. Such was the case when rap musicians discovered a means by which two turntables could be linked together and synchronized so that music from one or both decks could be heard. Without this innovation, the modern art of "turntableism" and the live performance of rap would not have evolved as they did. Genre forms are differentiated based on the use to which technology is put: as an experimental tool or in the form of conventional instruments designed to standardize musical sound.

Members of musical communities seek to identify themselves, more or less strongly, with the group, and so nomenclature, fashion, and slang are characteristics that evolve with the community. Genre members identify who belongs within the community and who does not, using distinctive dress, adornment, drug use, and argot. Some of these identifiers are demographic: for example, members are of the appropriate age, gender, ethnicity, and body type, and come from specific geographic places. Generally none of these is essential, but they make it easier to meld into the community. In addition, identifiers based in elective affinities may include any or all of the following: clothes, accessories, dancing prowess, distinctive language, hair management, body work, sexual norms, drugs of choice, expressive values (white power, flower power, urbanity, rusticity, religiosity, alienation), and other lifestyle elements.[51]

Style is a central symbolic resource that genres (like subcultures) employ in order to identify their relationship to the status quo, particularly in cases where they seek to undermine cultural hegemony.[52] But there is not always a direct correspondence between different "styles" and musical difference; it has been argued that riot grrrl, straight edge, anarcho-punk, and white power music differentiate their communities by political and philosophical, not stylistic or musical, distinctiveness.[53] However, there is no mistaking the correspondence between creative modes of dress and speech and new musical communities, just as the relationship between mass producers and marketers is evident in the case of mature, popular musics. Artists often identify their style as an extension of their group's ideology; consider Chinese rock musician Geo Qi:

> [Our style] represents our attitude, and also had a psychological value. When you have your hair down to your shoulders, everybody looks at you on the street. It naturally draws attention to you. It sounds superficial, but in the Chinese tradition you're supposed to be reserved and discreet, and we need to break through this restriction.[54]

Since rock musicians in China often voice criticisms of CCP (Chinese Communist Party) censure of individual expression and creativity, styles of dress are a simple way to embody their critique.

In other cases, musical communities adopt styles of dress as a form of critical engagement with stereotypes. Doo-wop group the Ink Spots wore clean and pressed white suits with flowers in their lapels. During performances, the group members used sharp, precise movements and a formal posture. In doing so, they adopted a different stature from that of most other black artists, or from the stereotype of black artists, and their "shuck . . . jive . . . and blackcrobatic dancing for white Hollywood. The Ink Spots were not stereotype."[55] The group used their style as a form of political critique and genre affiliation.

In the Industry-based genre, a music's style is mass-marketed, and often appears across multiple formats as firms seek to profit from the sale of as many consumer products as possible. As signatures of the Industry-based phase of grunge, a popular movie was released that was centered in the Seattle music scene (*Singles*), and the alternative rock festival Lollapalooza sold out stadiums across the country.[56] Soon, "alternative," a descriptor applied to grunge bands from Seattle, was being used to sell consumer products like Budweiser (the "alternative beer") and to describe an MTV video program (*Alternative Nation*); the "grunge aesthetic" inspired designer Marc Jacobs to incorporate flannel shirts, wool ski caps, and Doc Marten boots into the centerpieces of Perry Ellis's 1992 spring collection. The Style section of the *New York Times* ran a front-page story titled "Grunge: A Success Story."[57] The editor of men's style magazine *Details* was not alone in observing that the packaging of grunge as style is ironic, in much the same way that punk music's mass merchandizing was ironic: "the thing about grunge is it's not anti-fashion, it's unfashion."[58] Of course, part of the mass appeal of both grunge and punk was its presumptive sincerity.

Specific slang and argot function to draw a boundary around musical communities, but names durably define the group. The chosen name can be used to distinguish musical types and reveal processes of collective memory and discursive structures that link nomenclature to genre forms. These names emerge from many different sources, and at different stages in any music's development. It is frequently the case that disc jockeys and critics are viewed as the progenitors of the names of musical styles: disc jockey and television personality Alan Freed is famously credited with popularizing the term "rock 'n' roll."[59] Often multiple individuals lay claim to having invented the name that sticks. For example, while Venezuelan radio disc jockey Phidias Danilo Escalona used the term "salsa" to denote Latin dance music in the early 1960s, New York publisher Izzy Sanabria claims to have invented the term.[60] Performers and fans sometimes reject particular names that are seen to have been invented by firms seeking to profit from the music, designating these terms as inauthentic. For example, when band leader Rubén Blades was asked, "What is Salsa?" he responded, "I never liked that adjective. It was used for identifying a series of rhythms coming from the Caribbean area in order to sell it to North Americans and the rest of the world. That is to say, to simplify a form of musical information that is really complex. . . . It came to obtain the pejorative acceptance of a spoiled genre in the most hidden part of Latin American culture."[61] Indeed, some genre designations have been created by fiat by powerful elements of the music industry, as when, on June 25, 1949, *Billboard* magazine introduced the "Rhythm and Blues" (R&B) chart to represent the best-selling records in the diverse and contending genres in the field of popular black music. The invented term R&B replaced an earlier term, "race records," also invented (by the Okeh Record Company) to refer to music created by and for African Americans.[62] Race records included sounds now associated with diverse styles including gospel, blues, black vaudeville, spoken-word texts like sermons, and some jazz. Like the earlier term, R&B is more a marketing category than a description of a cohesive set of aesthetic traits. *Billboard* similarly created a chart called "country and Western" (C&W) to encompass hillbilly, honky-tonk, western swing, cowboy music, folk, and country jive. Finally, the term "world music" was created by record labels seeking to sell folk music, primarily that recorded by African musicians, to Western consumers.[63]

These twelve dimensions of musical communities organize or describe four characteristic genre forms: Avant-garde, Scene-based, Industry-based, and Traditionalist. The four genre forms can be used to describe any of the sixty U.S. genres at any one moment in time. Given a description of the organizational form or locus of a musical community, the clarity of its dress codes, or the degree of consensus over musical conventions, any musical style can be sorted into one of these genre forms. The forms provide a shorthand to illuminate the obstacles and opportunities faced by community members.

What Genres Are Not

Not all commercial music can be properly considered a genre in my sense of the term. Music crafted for specific types of venues or alluded to by reference to a commercial category should properly be considered nongenred music. Examples include Tin Pan Alley, Broadway show tunes, and commercial music that is crafted for a specific demographic and designated by a commercial category (e.g., middle-of-the-road (MOR), music for lovers, dance music, easy listening music, world music). One early problem case is Tin Pan Alley music. The designation is used to describe music created in the early years of the twentieth century on Twenty-eighth Street in New York City by a network of music publishers and theaters. It is not so much a genre as a set of arrangements involving several organizational levels with an elaborate and strict division of labor, and attitudes designed to produce songs with hit potential.[64] Songs in the Tin Pan Alley songbook resemble one another aesthetically, but that similarity derives from artists' desires to emulate other hits; it is "a much more homogenous style than had ever before been the case in the history of song in America."[65] Most importantly, Tin Pan Alley music evolved gradually and without the clear breaks that would have necessitated the evocation of a genre designation.

Much the same argument holds for pop and teen music. At its core, pop music is music that is found in *Billboard* magazine's Hot 100 Singles chart. Songs intended for the pop music market typically have their distinguishing genre characteristics purposely obscured or muted in the interest of gaining wider appeal.[66] Artists making such music may think of their performances in terms of style, but the organizations that assist them in reaching the chart most certainly do not. Songs are created to attract an audience, but not necessarily "fans" who discriminate on the basis of genre distinctions and conventions. In addition, while aspiring artists within genres think of their music as working within the conventions of a set of musics, artists making pop music sample from different styles to keep their music fresh. The performers who work exclusively within pop music, and no other musical idiom, are typically industry creations. For example, artist development expert Lou Pearlman played a vital role in creating the "boy band" sensation of the late 1990s (e.g., Backstreet Boys, O-Town, and 'N Sync) by drafting performers who answered casting calls. Such star making is a fascinating and underresearched topic. Music from genres can transform into pop music; consequently, the pop charts are a mix of "pure" pop (that is to say, a succession of hits that are marginally different) and songs derived from genres that are popular at the moment, such as rap or punk. Accordingly, pop is best considered as a chart, a way of doing business, or a target demographic, and not as a genre.[67]

World music provides a final example of a commercial music category that should not be confused with a genre. According to a guide that purports to present the "basics" of world music, the term is most often used to describe traditional, folk, or roots music that is played by indigenous musicians, and that may incorporate other musical forms, including influences from global popular forms like rock or jazz. "Indigenous" folk musics that are not fairly described in these terms include rock 'n' roll, R&B, jazz, soul, Broadway show tunes, classical, heavy metal, country music, blues, disco, karaoke, and rap, although exceptions are allowed in the final case.[68] Artists chosen from the domestic repertoire of a variety of countries and regions (e.g., Bulgaria, West Africa, Peru) are repackaged and relabeled as world music, and customers buy it as such. Thus "world music is clearly not music from the 'world,' but a narrow selection of sounds from somewhere else in the world."[69] This convoluted logic suggests a misspecification of the style. It indicates that we should consider world music to be music crafted for a global audience by reference to a commercial category. In fact, the category of "world music" was invented following a meeting in London in 1987 of staff from several small record labels who sought to create a market for music "variously labeled as 'ethnic,' 'traditional,' or 'roots,' which was increasingly in popularity."[70] World music is a marketing category invented to expand the audience for African popular music.[71] World music has no distinctive stylistic or idiomatic features, and the label was created to sell musical styles that were seen to have an underdeveloped market potential.[72] World music should properly be considered nongenred music.

In this book, I focus on twentieth-century music genres from the United States and exclude such nongenred music. I also restrict myself to music created in the commercial marketplace and thus eliminate from consideration the many "classical" and "art" musics. Genres that function in nonprofit or grant-based economies have different creative, organizational, financial, audience, and critical support mechanisms from those of commercial musics.[73] The types and trajectories of genres among nonprofit musics therefore take on forms distinct from those that are the focus here.[74]

It is my intention to use genre as the unit of analysis, and thus to distinguish my work both from those who treat consumers as the object of interest (as in studies of taste), and from work that treats genres as unchanging. There are comparative studies of musical styles, but within these, music consumers are typically used as the unit of analysis, and a reception perspective is employed in the examination of how groups of consumers use available genres to express their social identity or status.[75] Since these studies are frequently based on the analysis of survey data, the "genres" employed (e.g., rock, MOR, classical) are typically very inclusive, closer to what I mean by "stream," and what others mean by "field."[76] They are not, however, much akin to the units of consumption as defined by consumers. Instead, my approach assumes that genres are constituted and changed by the choices individuals and organizations make. Thus I examine the evolution of self-defined collectivities. My approach is guided by the simple observation that it is the case not only that fans of bebop in the 1940s differ from contemporary listeners, but also that bebop as a style has changed as well. Although the music nominated by fans in the two periods may be largely the same, and may share a common history and lineage, the social environment in which the genre is organized has been transformed.

Outline of the Book

The objective of *Banding Together* is to explain processes of music genre development, exploring why some styles gain mass popularity and others thrive in small niches. This requires that we examine the attributes and activities of music communities, looking beyond legendary performers and events. Rather than seeking to influence your tastes, my objective is to ask you to question how your tastes in music are instruments of power, limiting and encouraging certain social boundaries, between those who are "like you" and those who are not. More generally, my goal is to construct a broad theory of how classification schemes develop. My argument is that in doing so, we reveal the structure of cultural organization, a structure that goes to the heart of social organization. The argument proceeds as follows.

Chapter 2 uses three case studies—bluegrass, bebop jazz, and rap music—to explore in greater depth how genres cohere, that is, how styles, conventions, and goals are crystallized so as to define musical communities. I also focus on debates and key moments when such consensus breaks down or changes. I note that particular attributes of each musical community tend to accompany other attributes. And so, for example, communities with very few members lack regular access to performance venues, and often do not have a single adjective or title they use to describe their style. Similarly, music that attracts national audiences is often plagued by debates over the expertise of performers. In order to capture these clusters of attributes within dimensions, I created four genre forms: Avant-garde, Scene-based, Industry-based, and Traditionalist. In Avant-garde genres, music practitioners come together to share their concerns over the state of the music, but often do so without conceptualizing a set of goals or identifiers for the group. While most Avant-garde genres wither or merge with other genres, a few grow in size and develop a more focused and coherent group identity in the Scene-based phase of development. A very few Scene-based genres are successful and visible enough to draw the attention of commercial interests that transform them into Industry-based genres, during which musics draw the attention of national media and retailers and fuel a rift within the community between "old heads" and "tourists." This rift reaches its apex in the fourth phase, the Traditionalist genre, in which the community seeks to preserve the music of the Scene-based period. Since the objective in chapter 2 is to demonstrate the utility of these genre types for understanding musical communities, I do not present the history of any style from birth to the present. Instead, I show how groups of attributes characterize musical styles at each genre stage.

To prevent the confusion that would result from the scattershot use of examples from sixty different musical styles, I rely on only three: bluegrass, bebop jazz, and rap music.

In matching musics to these four genre types, I discovered that there are characteristic arrays of musical genres that I call "trajectories," and the two common trajectories for music genres are the focus of discussion in chapter 3. The three styles explored in chapter 2 (bluegrass, bebop, and rap) share a trajectory with the majority of musical styles examined for the book. This AgSIT genre trajectory (I coin the term by abbreviating the sequence of four genre forms) characterizes fifty-one of the sixty musics examined for this study. Some eight musical styles manifested a variation on this trajectory because they originated as Scene-based genres. A final group of nine musics started as Industry-based genres, and then developed Scene-based and Traditionalist genre forms, and this second trajectory is therefore abbreviated IST. The first objective of chapter 3 is to identify these two trajectories and illustrate them with examples from several musical styles, including gospel and funk. While these two trajectories provide robust explanations of genre trajectories, almost 58 percent of musical styles did not pass through all the genre forms in their trajectory. For example, grunge rock did not develop a Traditionalist genre, although it had all the characteristics of a musical style traveling the AgSIT trajectory. I find three causes for the blocked emergence of particular genre forms: (1) the absorption of musical styles into other styles and streams, (2) racist exclusion, and (3) aesthetic and social factors that prevent the expansion of the musical scene to new audiences and performers. In the second half of chapter 3, I explore these three mechanisms of inertia that produce incomplete musical trajectories across genre forms. My exploration focuses attention on several musical styles, including Laurel Canyon, grunge rock, house, techno, New Orleans jazz, South Texas polka, and tango.

Thus far, the focus has been on documenting genre forms and attributes in the twentieth-century United States. In chapter 4, I expand the focus to include music produced elsewhere. A preliminary survey of the popular music of countries with widely differing political economies, music cultures, and levels of development revealed that the four genre forms do exist, to a greater or lesser degree, across the globe, but there proved to be another widely distributed form that was not found in the U.S. sample:

the Government-purposed genre. Musics in this genre receive substantial financial support from the government or oppositional groups with a direct interest in the ideological content of popular music. I find two major types: those sponsored directly by governments, which benefit from national distribution and legal protections, and an antistate type supported by an opposition party or constituency. I examine four nation-cases to advance the argument: the People's Republic of China, Chile, Serbia, and Nigeria. In China, we witness an evolving history of central government action where active promotion of propaganda music is temporarily challenged by the anti–status quo power of rock, only to be co-opted by the machine of nationalization and repression. Chile's *nueva canción* is a Government-purposed genre developed by extragovernmental actors and used to fight a repressive dictatorship and to critique Western culture and global media. Nigeria's rich musical heritage gave birth in the mid-1960s to Afrobeat, a globally popular antigovernment genre, whose charismatic leader was subject to repressive surveillance and violence by the state. Like *nueva canción*, this music was also employed to critique global media as modern imperialist powers. Finally, in the former Yugoslav republic of Serbia, ethnic nationalist groups and entrepreneurs created turbo-folk, but the music has now transformed into a multicultural pop phenomenon. This chapter explores a rarely examined and poorly understood phenomenon in popular music, and demonstrates the flexibility of these analytical tools for addressing additional cases of cultural categorization.

In the concluding chapter, I discuss classification systems that exist within music and its peer culture-producing fields. I emphasize the role of power in setting boundaries around categories and defining these categories as legitimate. I consider the application of this model of classification to the sociological study of science and collective memory. Finally, I address the future of music, and close with a consideration of the link between music categories and taste.

By the end of the book, I hope to have shown that music genres can be best understood not as the invention of autonomous geniuses, and not as a succession of musical innovations aligned in an orderly and predetermined lineage, but instead as trajectories of genre forms made of just twelve social, organizational, and aesthetic attributes. For lovers of music, the book should provide a unique perspective on the characteristic social forms of music communities. Fans intuitively understand that there are differences between garage bands and global pop music, but I hope that presenting those differences systematically and using a huge sample of music styles will enrich their intuition. The similarities among seemingly quite different music communities is striking, and I hope the book can function to facilitate a kind of mutual recognition and respect among artists and fans of popular music.

Chapter 2

Three Musics, Four Genres: Rap, Bluegrass, and Bebop Jazz

Music histories are full of hints that there is a pattern to the evolution of communities of sound. In an early history of bluegrass music I find one such allusion:

> [bluegrass] Musicians . . . share certain characteristics. Growing up in areas which were the source of mountain music, the men were taught to pick and sing by friends and neighbors. Some first gained reputations over local radio shows, then moved to larger stations, and finally found national prominence. Timing played a crucial part in success: being at the right time at the right place led to joining "name" bands and obtaining radio and record contracts when they decided to go out on their own. . . . None of these people has become wealthy from string-band music, yet all express a strong feeling of satisfaction over being able to entertain with and perpetuate the kind of music they care so much about.[1]

In this description, note the transition of the musical community from an Avant-garde genre composed of peers, into a Scene-based genre where local radio stations play a key role in uniting a local constituency for the music. In some cases, artists are "at the right time . . . [and] place," attract attention from the mass media, and are propelled into an Industry-based genre form. Although many of these artists do not reap enormous financial rewards from their musicality, they establish a Traditionalist genre form in which musical preservation unites musicians and provides "a strong feeling of satisfaction."

In this chapter I examine in detail the progression of three musics through the four genre types and focus on the changing mix of the resources they use. These resources include organizational form, scale, and locus; the sources of income and press coverage for artists; the codification of genre ideal, performance, and technological conventions; boundary work; styles of dress, adornment, drugs, politics, and argot; and the invention of a name for the style. In order to focus on the attributes that characterize genre forms, I chose not to present the history of any single music. Rather, I selectively present examples from three musical styles: bluegrass, old school rap, and bebop jazz. It is my hope that focusing on examples from a sample of musics will highlight the features of genre types and their attributes without producing unnecessary confusion.

Rap is a rhythmic, electronically based music combined with spoken, rhyming lyrics and sometimes sung choruses.[2] Though rap has since developed into a stream, or a group of joined musical styles, I consider its early development as old school rap, a period that lasted from the mid-1970s to the middle of the 1980s.[3] Bluegrass evolved into a style within the stream of country music between the mid-1940s and the 1970s. It is characterized by the harmonizing sounds of the banjo, fiddle, and mandolin, with bass and guitar providing rhythmic accompaniment and the notable absence of drums, bass, woodwind, or electrified instruments.[4] Bebop is a form of jazz that arose in the early 1940s. Played by a small combo of musicians on acoustic instruments, and usually led by a saxophone and trumpet, it is characterized by a series of fast extended solos improvised on a song's harmonic structure rather than on its melody, employing chords that routinely include flatted fifths, flatted and raised ninths, and augmented elevenths, with these notes being emphasized, often, as melody notes.[5]

Avant-garde Genres

Music, like other forms of taste, changes slowly and incrementally.[6] Nonetheless there are junctures when performers, fans, and commentators point to cumulative changes significant enough to distinguish it from earlier forms of music. Music performers always have some dissatisfaction with contemporary music or their place in it, and fans are looking for novelty, so there is a consistent, if inchoate, desire for change. Avant-garde genres are formed when music practitioners come together and share their concerns over the state of music in their field of action and reinforce each other's desire to do something about it.[7] Avant-garde genres are quite small, having no more than a dozen active participants who meet informally and irregularly, and are often conceived in spaces like coffee shops and basements. Borrowing a term from fine arts, such creative groups are called "circles." They attract virtually no press attention, performance conventions are not codified, and there is typically little consensus over how members should dress, talk, or describe themselves as a group.

Avant-garde circles are leaderless and fractious and consequently typically unravel in a matter of months from lack of recognition, or because a subset of the circle participants gain wider recognition. The objective of Avant-garde genres is to play informally together, share recorded music, and air complaints about the hegemonic music in the relevant stream of music. The genre ideal, and specifically the musical ideas that are central to it, may emerge from members taking lessons, carefully listening to records, and playing with different kinds of musicians. Alternatively, Avant-gardists may assert that prevailing musical styles have become predictable and emotionless and, flaunting the fact that they are not able to play instruments in conventional ways, make what others see as loud and harsh sounds. This was the experience of both the thrash metal and punk Avant-garde genres.[8] In crafting music that is "new," Avant-gardists may combine elements of musics that have been treated as distinct.

The desire to produce a new music drives the group to engage in experimental practices, including playing standard instruments in unconventional ways, creating new musical instruments, and modifying objects that heretofore have not been employed in the production of music. For example, in early shows of the Avant-garde punk band Iggy and the Stooges, group members "played" a food blender filled with water and a microphone; they made rhythm by dancing on a washboard wearing golf shoes, and by drumming on fifty-gallon oil drums using hammers as drumsticks.[9]

Such circles typically meet face-to-face, but this may be changing in the era of the Internet.[10] Circle members need spaces to meet where they can freely discuss and cement their shared investment in musical innovation. The difficulty of securing space for discussion and practice is sometimes eased by the existence of music venues used by musicians playing another musical style, or bars and restaurants that serve a large and diverse community of artists. Max's Kansas City, a nightclub once located at 213 Park

Avenue South in New York City, played this role for a generation of artists including Andy Warhol, Jim Morrison, Lou Reed, Patti Smith, Robert Mapplethorpe, and Iggy Pop. Owner Mickey Ruskin sought to create an artist's bar that would imitate the Cedar Tavern, a pub in the Village that played host to the literati in the 1950s. According to Danny Fields, a former music industry insider (he comanaged the Ramones), "Max's was where everybody got consolidated. . . . You had all these changes in art, music, sex, the way people dressed, what they thought, how they lived, and you had to have someplace where you could go to figure it out."[11] Max's was where that happened. Similarly, Ralph Ellison captured the importance of Minton's Playhouse in Harlem, New York, to avant-garde bebop musicians:

> They were gathered here from all parts of America and they broke bread together and there was a good feeling and promise, but what shape the fulfilled promise would take they did not know. . . . Yet it was an exceptional moment and the world was swinging with change. . . . For they were caught up in events . . . [including] a momentous modulation into a new key of musical sensibility; in brief, a revolution in culture.[12]

Alternatively, Avant-garde genre members may be pushed out of particular spaces even if music is made there. For example, DJ Disco Wiz, who performed with rapper Grandmaster Caz, remembers that "everybody was going with this disco trend, but we wasn't feeling it. It wasn't for us. We weren't socially accepted at disco joints; we were pretty much segregated," and so Wiz, Caz, and other rappers started holding parties in parks and houses in which young, African American, Latino, and Caribbean teens were welcome.[13]

What later became known as rap music began as a form of disc jockey practice in New York City in the early 1970s. Young men and women combined the rhyming slang of mobile radio disc jockeys, the dance orientation and energy of disco club DJs, and the DIY (do it yourself) aesthetic found in most youth cultural movements. In the early to mid-1970s, they held dances in public parks, local clubs, and event spaces owned by the Police Athletic League or housing developments. Performance groups ranged from one to several DJs who performed collaboratively or competitively.[14] These early DJs communicated with and copied one another, and the intensity of their competitiveness is illustrated in the practice of soaking off the identifying labels on the records, a practice designed to protect a DJ's discovery of particularly prized music.[15] The DJs played music from a range of styles, including rock, R&B, blues, German electronic music, punk, and reggae. Some DJs used microphones to talk to the audience, while others remained silent behind the turntables.

In the 1930s, a number of country string bands experimented with perfecting a style in which instruments playing interweaving melodic lines played fast, much like the New Orleans jazz bands of the time.[16] The Georgia Wildcats, Monroe Brothers, Blue Sky Boys, and Delmore Brothers, among others, experimented with up-tempo instrumental and vocal harmonizing. At the time these "hot" hillbilly bands of the Great Depression period were not distinguished from other hillbilly bands and gospel groups. Like the others, they played on the radio, occasionally made records, and performed music, did comedy, and sold products at medicine shows, tent shows, rural schools, fairs, and store openings. What did distinguish these hot string bands is that they focused on sonic and rhythmic complexity rather than highlight the lyrics, as was the common practice in country music.[17]

During that decade, swing played by large dance bands using written arrangements was the most popular style of jazz. Frustrated by the melodic and harmonic restrictions of the form as well as by the hierarchical working conditions, young musicians, some trained in music theory, began experimenting with alternative ways of expressing themselves. Several were able to develop their ideas while working as soloists in swing orchestras. This was most possible in Kansas City, where three hundred clubs with live musical entertainment thrived.[18] In other environments, soloists were more likely to be admonished to keep close to the written score and derided for what most swing musicians saw as a lack of discipline or signs of insanity. This view of Avant-garde bebop players is reflected in their nicknames: John Burks Gillespie is better known as "Dizzy," and drummer Kenny Clark was also known as "Kook-a-Mop."[19] Experimentalists worked with other like-minded players, developing their ideas by "woodshedding" in informal practice sessions, as well as jamming in after-hours clubs and at private parties.[20]

The experimental ethos of Avant-garde circles is often expressed through the idiosyncratic grooming, dress, demeanor, and argot of members, but these are not (yet) consolidated into a distinctive style. Photographs and accounts of early rap music illustrate the range of styles worn by fans and DJs, including various gang-related costumes and the flashy polyester outfits most associated with the disco aesthetic.[21] The performing attire of early bluegrass players varied from bib overalls and gingham outfits to planter's outfits and formal clothes.

In Avant-garde genres, circle members contribute resources, and they also get resources from others attracted to the musical experimentation. Partners contribute nurturance, financial support, and a home; other musicians and music industry people act as informal advisers and critics; by supporting new music, bar owners get customers on off nights. As a rule, Avant-garde genre members do not receive remuneration for their participation in music-related activities. They earn money for performing conventional styles of music and from nonperformance employment. Thus many Avant-gardists live with little recognition and many privations. These harsh conditions may retrospectively be romanticized as bohemian, but they contribute to the demise of many Avant-garde genres. Recounting stories of hard living in the Avant-garde period fuels heroic tales if the genre achieves notoriety. The experiences of Lou Reed in his years as an Avant-garde punk musician are not atypical:

> [The members of Velvet Underground lived] in a thirty-dollar-a-month apartment and we really didn't have any money, and we used to eat oatmeal all day and all night and give blood, among other things, or pose for these nickel or fifteen cent tabloids they had every week. And when I posed for them, my picture came out and it said I was a sex maniac killer that had killed fourteen children and tape-recorded it and played it in a barn in Kansas at midnight.[22]

These privations are exacerbated by the tendency of some Avant-garde musicians to consume quantities of drugs and alcohol.

The music and the people making it receive virtually no press coverage, which makes it exceedingly difficult for us to find accounts of Avant-garde genres that failed to progress into another genre form. Numerous appellations are given to the new music, which also contributes to the difficulty in identifying musics that do not survive the Avant-garde period.

Musics can remain in the Avant-garde period for a long time or may quickly transition into Scene-based genres. The key features of this transition are these: relatively stable aural and visible identifiers of the group emerge; artists begin to seek resources that allow them to perform their music for a larger public; and the group identifies a set of goals for action—in the case of musical styles, I define these goals as actions or ideas that are seen to be solutions to the complaints the group has about status quo music.

Scene-based Genres

It appears that most Avant-garde genres wither or merge with other musical styles early on, and only a few begin to draw more substantial resources and a larger cluster of devotees and evolve into Scene-based genres. Scene-based genres are characterized by an intensely active, but moderately sized group of artists, audience members, and supporting organizations. For more than a decade the concept of "scene" has been used by scholars to refer to a community of spatially situated artists, fans, scene-focused record companies, and supporting small business people.[23] Such local scenes may also be in communication with like scenes in distant locales whose members enjoy the same kind of music and lifestyle. In recent years, we have acknowledged the importance of virtual scenes composed of devotees who interact via the Internet, or traditional postal correspondence, as with the "distros," or photocopied letters promoting metal rock merchandise for sale or trade.[24] Scene-based genre members earn money from activities within the community, including music making, especially once they attract the attention of the local or specialty press. Much attention is paid to codifying performance conventions, technological innovations, and the dress, adornment, drugs, and argot of group members. Members are also concerned with distinguishing themselves from rival musics, especially those that share the same performance spaces or fans. Most Scene-based genres acquire a name for their group that is invented or announced in the Scene-based media.

Scene-based genres have a loose organizational form characterized by nested rings of groups characterized by varying levels of commitment to the community. At the center are clusters of those most responsible for the distinctive characteristics of the music, including many members of the Avant-garde genre. Then there is the ring of committed activists whose identity, and sometimes means of employment, are tied to the scene. Outside of this is the ring of fans that participate in the scene more or less regularly. The outer ring is made up of "tourists" who enjoy activities within the scene without identifying with it. Such distinct rings are characteristic of mature scenes like the Chicago blues in the 1990s. While newer scenes exhibit similar rings of commitment, their structure is much more fluid.[25]

Stylistic innovations and the charismatic leaders who promote them play a key role in developing the consensus around genre ideal. This consensus marks the transition from the Avant-garde to the Scene-based genre. The two artists recognized at the time as the prime exemplars of the newly emerging bebop style were Charlie Parker and Dizzy Gillespie. Parker was the brooding genius of harmonic innovation who used reeds harder than anyone else to create sounds never before heard on a saxophone, and Gillespie was the well-schooled theorist, showman, and promoter for the emerging music.[26] In bluegrass music in the mid-1940s, Bill Monroe sought to create a string band equivalent of Chicago-style jazz from the late 1920s. Dubbed by folklorist and promoter Ralph Rinzler "the father of bluegrass music," Monroe is said to have had a vision of the sound and style of bluegrass before he found the instrumentalists who could play it. By 1946, Monroe assembled a band to play his high, lonesome sound, including Lester Flatt, Chubby Wise, and Earl Scruggs. This sound was built on tight harmonizing, instrumental ensemble play punctuated by virtuoso solos: "hard-driving and tight playing and singing, combining elements of brother duets, fiddle breakdowns, church harmonies and jazz."[27] He pressed his band to play every tune faster than other bands. To get a sharper tone, he played songs in keys unfamiliar to country fiddlers and had band members tune their instruments a halftone higher to get a louder and brighter sound.[28] Finally, in rap music, key stylistic innovations were linked to each of the style's three "grandfathers." Kool Herc contributed large bass-heavy PA systems for DJ parties; Afrika Bambaataa, the "King of Records," used his large and diverse music collection to craft vibrant landscapes of sound; and Grandmaster Flash created an electronic mixer to allow DJs to extend the instrumental breaks that would later form the backdrop for rap's spoken word lyrics.

Technological innovations can also change the balance among elements of the music during the Scene-based genre. Rap provides a strong example of this feature, as the technical ability to connect two turntables via a mixing device allowed DJs to craft a continuous loop of sound from two copies of the same vinyl album without any audible disruption. This refocused crowd attention on the rappers, whose spoken exhortations became more elaborate. Groups increasingly employed rappers who stood in front of the DJ and rapped complete sentences with end-rhymes; this came to be seen as a key feature of the music.[29] Thus rap was importantly shaped by the increasingly standardized electronic equipment used by artists. Likewise, the development of powerful, portable, and relatively compact sound amplifiers in the late 1930s was important to making possible both bluegrass and bebop. Swing bands of the early 1930s succeeded in projecting sound to large and noisy audiences by increasing the number of brass instruments, but the much smaller combos forming the bebop genre in the early 1940s relied on the new portable sound amplification systems. Guitar and mandolin performers in the bluegrass scene moved toward a microphone during their solos in order to be heard over the banjos and fiddles.[30] Thus the transition between Avant-garde and Scene-based genres marks the introduction of both technological and live performance conventions that in turn affect conventions in the recording studio in later periods.

Social conventions, including styles of clothes and adornment, body type, argot, and "attitude," are codified in Scene-based genres. These allow fellow travelers to identify scene members. In rap music, performers and avid fans began to wear distinctive jewelry ("door knocker" earrings, "dookie" chains), athletic or casual clothes, and particular hats (e.g., Kangol caps, professional sports teams caps) to signal their membership in the community. This attire made a strong statement of informality and youth identity that marked a difference from disco and R&B; Run D.M.C. declared their identity in lyrics, proclaiming, "No leather suits and no homo boots," a caricature of disco garb. Instead, they were "tougher than leather," which was the title of one of the group's albums, their collective autobiography, and a semibiographical movie made about their lives. The attire of bluegrass musicians in Bill Monroe's band provided a contrast with the class origins of the style's musicians and fans. In the early 1940s, bandleader Bill Monroe dressed his band in tailored outfits, including jodhpurs, riding boots, and small-brimmed Stetson hats, the traditional dress of the Kentucky gentleman horse-breeder, or a "cavalry remount platoon."[31] This trope is particularly interesting because through their accents, nasal singing style, and song lyrics, bluegrass musicians and fans identify themselves as Appalachian mountain people, set off against the modern urban-industrial world.[32] Bebop musicians used their style to draw comparison to other artists, especially French bohemian artists: Dizzy Gillespie, among others, wore a black beret. While dress was important, the prime symbol of bebop group allegiance was the development of an elaborate vocabulary to describe themselves, swing players, ignorant fans, demanding managers, varieties of drugs, and the authorities. This rapidly evolving argot enabled them to deride outsiders in their presence, and made its way into a number of bebop songs. In each case, the negative reactions of "square" people and authorities serve to confirm scenesters' sense of their importance and have the effect of bolstering scene solidarity.[33]

Scenes, musical and otherwise, commonly emerge in so-called bohemian neighborhoods where rents are low, police supervision is lax, multiple opportunities for low-skill labor exist, concentrations of other artists are found, and residents tolerate diversity of all kinds.[34] Such neighborhoods nurture the scene, and the lifestyle growing around it, by fostering constant interaction among scenesters without attracting unwanted attention from the wider community.[35]

These neighborhoods include local businesses that support the Scene-based genre, including coffee shops, clubs, dance halls, record stores, churches, small recording studios, and independent record labels. Business entrepreneurs, often drawn from the ranks of scene participants, become music promoters, club owners, and band managers. Some found independent record companies, Scene-based fanzines, and Internet sites, while local newspapers, radio stations, and criminal elements arrive in the area to support the scene and to derive profits from it.[36] In the cases of old school rap and grunge music, for example, independent record labels like Enjoy and Sub Pop Records recorded and promoted the Scene-based bands, and were often located in the neighborhoods that performers frequented.[37] Supportive businesses often include venue owners offering time on weekday or off nights for live performances, as was the case for bebop and rap.[38] As a Scene-based genre, bluegrass depended on gaining notice via the many radio "barn dances" of the time, most notably the Grand Ole Opry in Nashville and the National Barn Dance in Chicago. These live radio appearances led to invitations to tour and make phonograph records. Bebop was centered in several small Harlem clubs, and clubs on Fifty-second Street in New York, where primarily white audiences were first introduced to the music. Radio was not important because there were no radio stations devoted to serious jazz, and dissemination via phonograph records was blocked in the early 1940s by the wartime shortage of shellac to make records and a ban on recording enforced by the American Federation of Musicians' union.

Scene musicians and ancillary creative people often are not able to support themselves entirely from the music. They typically take low-skill service jobs in the community and also depend on money and other support from partners, family, and friends. As scenes develop, these neighborhoods draw both more casual scenesters and merchandisers of elements of the genre lifestyle, hastening the end of the intensely local genre form.[39]

Genre-based media begin to develop in Scene-based genres. The strong and relatively coherent complaints of genre members against the status quo often attract attention from niche media, who provide the clearest, most nuanced and positive portrayals of the scene. These include fanzines, Internet sites, blogs, small-circulation magazines, and often the local free weekly entertainment guide. Collectively they serve to define, explain, promote, and critique the music and its associated lifestyle. There were a number of periodical magazines devoted to jazz, such as *Down Beat*, that created an ongoing debate about the emerging music, and the men's fashion magazine *Esquire* did occasional articles on the bop scene. This brought bebop to the attention of jazz lovers and those who wanted to be trendy. Likewise, journalists Nelson George and Robert Ford wrote sympathetic and informed pieces about rap music that appeared in the *Village Voice, Billboard,* and other publications friendly to new music.[40] The PBS documentary *Style Wars* sympathetically documented the poverty and cultural richness that fueled early rap music and graffiti culture. It also criticized municipal and city authorities who were cast as responsible for urban social dysfunction and unable to fix any problem except through the imposition of more and more extreme forms of surveillance and punishment.

Because these writers try to talk about the coalescing style, they have to find a name to describe its musical aesthetics. Thus begins the formulation of the collective memory about the history and founding heroes of the music. The chosen name is sometimes an onomatopoeic representation of the genre's sound, as with "bebop" and "doo-wop." Rarely, the genre name will derive from a band's name, as was the case when "bluegrass," used to refer to the style of ex-sidemen of Bill Monroe, came to characterize a more general style of music. More often it has to do with sexuality (e.g., "jazz," "rap," "funk," "rock 'n' roll," and "straight edge"). The term "rap" originally referred to romantic or sexual verbal exchanges, but it was later broadened to describe any form of verbal exchange characterized by "strong, aggressive, highly fluent, powerful talk," and it is believed that this word was chosen to refer to the emerging genre over the alternative term "hip-hop" because of its combination of connotations—both romantic and competitive.[41] However, hip-hop argot that was commonly used in early lyrics survives today, and critics and fans still defend its use.

In Scene-based genres stakeholders have only a few contacts with the world outside the scene, but those they do have are important in building the solidarity within the community. First, there is usually bitter antagonism between proponents of the new music and representatives of the status quo in the relevant field. The most notable examples include the British beachside fights between the mods and the rockers; the "Disco Demolition Derby," when rock fans dynamited disco records halfway through a baseball game in Comiskey Park; and the verbal duel between heavy metal and punk that played out on the pages of *Creem Magazine*.[42] Fighting against a shared antagonist often builds solidarity within Scene-based genres. Second, the operation of the scene in marginal facilities with opportunistic promoters means that scene participants are regularly exposed to what they identify as dangerous conditions, and they may be liable to arrest for violating ordinances concerning dancing, noise abatement, fire, and decency, as well as laws controlling liquor and drug use.[43] For example, in 2000, the Chicago City Council put new regulations and licensure in place to control rave music dance parties after the press linked the scene to sex, drug use, and danger. The new regulations placed responsibility for any violation of the law not on the drug dealers or users, but on the DJs who performed at these events.[44] Collective complaints or collective action against these threats can bond Scene-based genre participants. In the Chicago case, scene members were unable and unwilling to fight moral and legal regulations, but a similar rave community in Toronto was more successful in defending themselves. Toronto ravers campaigned for, and achieved, the reversal of the ordinance banning raves from city property. Finally, symbols of inclusion/exclusion also serve to identify scene members to outsiders who may be alarmed, upset, or simply bemused. These three sources of censure all serve to build scene solidarity. As importantly, they typically lend the genre an oppositional political cast.[45]

In addition to their musical complaints, Scene-based genre members will often critique large social injustices, although they may target their critique within the local environment (e.g., a neighborhood, even a specific politician). Lyrical content often incorporates aspects of this oppositional stance.[46] In the Scene-based period, rap music songs like Grandmaster Flash and the Furious Five's single "The Message" employed descriptions of everyday life in New York City slums as a means to critique politicians, social service agencies, and a society that would leave a generation stranded in urban poverty.[47] The introduction of large portable radios called "boom boxes" or "ghetto blasters" allowed rap fans to drown out other music (often that of ethnic minorities) and thus functioned as a form of identity politics in interracial urban neighborhoods. When "political" songs were played, this magnified the threat rap intended to pose to the status quo.[48]

Insertion of politics into the scene's identity is an indicator that the music has entered a mature phase of the Scene-based genre. From the outset, some of the bebop musicians and many of its devotees, having experienced searing racial hatred and discrimination, were committed to black pride and black power in the music.[49] Most bop songs were purely instrumental or punctuated with spoken-word jive talk, but not lyrics. Some of these simply mocked the status quo, but some were explicitly political. For example, Charlie Mingus's "Fables of Faubus" is a cacophonous, mocking song about Orville Faubus, the governor of Arkansas, who barred the entry of black students into Little Rock's Central High School. Many more bebop song and album titles said, in effect, "Black is beautiful." The politics of bluegrass came to be typical of those in the country stream and are clearly inflected by class (in addition to race): lyrics expressed resistance to urban ways and wistfulness for a simpler rusticity.[50] The music valorizes a return to traditional communities and values, morality and simplicity, honesty and loyalty and stability, all of which are seen to be in decline.[51] Experts describe country fans as having "the adopted pose of rustics resigned to the march of time," and acting like "exiles in their own homeland, painfully holding on to closeness in a world that has already deserted them."[52]

An additional aspect of scene members' political identity project is that they begin to defend the borders of the group and differentiate between what are acceptable lifestyle choices and what are not. In bebop, rap, and bluegrass, these disputes were highly visible and contentious. The early boppers had huge fights with swing musicians and critic-advocates of the older style.[53] Dizzy Gillespie was famously thrown out of Cab Calloway's top-notch swing band for musical insubordination.[54] Ornette Coleman, a later innovator, had his specially made instrument crushed by fellow musicians who felt upstaged by his complex and aggressive way of playing hard bop.[55] Rap musicians turned against the Sugar Hill Gang, performers of the first commercial rap single, "Rapper's Delight." Genre community members claimed that the group had been "manufactured" by record label head Sylvia Robinson, and was thus an inauthentic representation of the style.[56] These rappers' shock at the commercial success of the single was equaled by their surprise that an unknown act would be the first to put the music on wax.[57] The success of "Rapper's Delight" sparked competitive resentment, and in short order other rap artists would sign to new and old record labels in an effort to get out of the underground and onto the radio.[58] In bluegrass music, Bill Monroe trained and lost a large cadre of musicians, many of whom went on to form similar bands of their own. Monroe feuded with these others, claiming that they were stealing his sound, and indeed the Blue Grass Boys' distinctive ensemble sound was increasingly seen as the bluegrass style of music available to all who could master the demanding techniques.[59]

Many Scene-based musics wither or merge into streams. This has been the experience of alternative country music, a genre that emerged in the 1990s and had considerable success. It lost momentum soon after 2000 when many of its most successful artists and groups moved toward the production of rock. Meanwhile, mainstream country music and Americana music moved in the direction of alternative roots music and absorbed much of the alternative country-music fan base.[60] For those styles that transition into an Industry-based genre, the key ingredient is that the scene attracts the attention of major music producers seeking to develop new music and new markets.

Industry-based Genres

Industry-based genres are so named because their primary organizational form is the industrial corporation. Some of these are multinational in scope, but others are independent companies organized to compete directly with the multinationals.[61] Along with industrial firms, the prime actors in these genres include singers and musicians who contract for their services, targeted audiences, and a wide array of ancillary service providers from song publishers to radio stations and retail outlets. Artists generate income from sales, licensing, merchandise, and product endorsements, and this often drives aesthetic decisions. Performance conventions are highly codified, driven by industry categories and the production tools that standardize sounds. The attire of performers is adapted for the mass market, and made widely available to fans, along with any argot, adornment, or features of lifestyle that can be monetized.

The goal for members of Industry-based genres is to produce revenue by selling musical products to as many consumers as possible. There are several means employed to increase sales. Efforts are directed toward codifying, simplifying, and teaching the genre conventions. Tablature for guitars and other instruments and transcriptions of the lyrics are widely available, and musical teachers and mentors are in plentiful supply in most places. Firms train new artists to work within highly codified performance conventions, and record producers regularly coach songwriters and artists to make music that is simple and clearly within the style so it will appeal to the mass audience. Over the past century, technological innovations have also served to standardize and simplify the production of music in order to satisfy the needs of mass production. The classic example is the emergence of the (relatively) unbreakable, seven-inch vinyl record that played at 45 rpm, a format cheap and durable enough for small labels to produce, which enabled companies like Sun Records to create the first rock 'n' roll records.[62] Additionally, "contact men" working for the firm conscript music critics and disc jockeys into promoting new works and artists.[63] Trade magazine–produced weekly charts of song sales help to guide industry decisions about the relative success of individual songs and whole musical styles.[64] The otherwise highly competitive multinational entertainment conglomerates collectively fight the unauthorized use and distribution of their copyrighted music, and do whatever they can to frustrate the development of spin-off styles.[65]

A common feature of the transition from the Scene-based to the Industry-based genre is the assertion of market dominance by major record corporations that gain control from the independent labels that had dominated the Scene-based genre. Enterprising independent label heads understandably seek to increase the visibility of their artists and the sales of their records, but insofar as they are successful, the major companies may buy out artist and label contracts. For example, at the start of rap's Industry-based genre, major labels asserted an oligopoly over charting singles and albums, primarily by buying artist contracts and record labels that had proven successful.[66] Likewise, in the case of bebop, by 1945 record companies had rushed to sign all performers who seemed to be drawing a following. The story of bluegrass was a bit different because, from the start of the Avant-garde genre in the 1940s, Bill Monroe had a contract with RCA Victor, the premier phonograph company of the day, but by the middle of the 1950s record companies were rushing to sign other bluegrass acts.

Sales success is a strong indicator of the presence of an Industry-based genre. Sales success is gauged according to codified performance conventions that are governed by industry categories, although they may sometimes be recognized as novel and added as a shelving designation, a type of sales chart, a division of a record company, and so forth. The popularity of bluegrass music is suggested in the fact that between 1959 and 1965 only three of sixteen Flatt and Scruggs singles did not chart among *Billboard's* top Country Music Singles.[67] In 1965 their theme song for the TV program *The Beverly Hillbillies* ("The Ballad of Jed Clampett") was on the country music chart for twenty weeks and was number one for three weeks. In addition, it reached number forty-four on the *Billboard* popular music chart.[68] While the situation was different in the 1940s and 1950s when bebop and bluegrass became established, today a major indicator of a genre's becoming established is its recognition by entertainment industry groups, including trade magazines and trade associations.[69]

Artists working in Industry-based genres generally earn their income exclusively from work performed for large organizations. However, it is a common misunderstanding that sales revenue is sufficient to provide artists with an extravagant lifestyle, or that record sales are the major source of income for artists working in such genres. In fact, artists selling their first album, or even multiple, successive albums, must invest a substantial proportion of their "advance on sales" to pay for the production and promotion of each album. Until artists "recoup" this advance (by earning enough from record sales to pay back the advance), they are indebted to their employer. Given the high cost of video production and touring, and the fact that artists earn only 5–10 percent of the profit from each record sold, most contemporary artists never do recoup.[70] Industry-based genre artists profit more from merchandise sales, concert ticket sales, and performance royalties (from live and recorded performances of their songs).[71]

In the process of absorption into multinational corporations and mass production systems, genre names become more clearly fixed. If a name emerged in the Scene-based period, producers and journalists may continue its use, as was the case with rap music. Curiously, it sometimes happens that new styles are melded into the music category—issuing not in a new name for the music, but in the expansion of its aesthetic content.[72] For example, the term "bluegrass" was first used in print in 1957, but two years later, when folklorist Alan Lomax described it as "folk music in overdrive," after which the music was bracketed with folk rather than country music.[73]

Like the music, elements of dress, adornment, and lifestyle are exaggerated and mass-marketed to new fans of Industry-based genres. While the leading artists of bluegrass and bebop nurtured an oppositional stance well into their Industry-based genres, many leading rap artists played an important part in commercializing the rap look and lifestyle and earned a great deal of money in the process. The most famous early example is found in rap group Run D.M.C.'s single praising their shell-toe, fat-laced sneakers, called, "My Adidas." The company cosponsored the group's 1988 *My Adidas* tour, and the group reportedly signed a $1.5 million sponsorship contract. A decade later, rap mogul Sean "Puff Daddy" Combs would open his own apparel company, Sean John. Clothes and accessories associated with rap became de rigueur for millions of American teens and influenced celebrity attire.[74]

The financial resources and promotional expertise of major companies will often propel Industry-based genres into the national media.[75] In most cases, national media coverage of the genre will be ill informed about the music, and will depict the musicians as the Pied Pipers of deviance.[76] For example, in the late 1940s, the national press began to regularly report on bebop music, and these stories focused on the zoot suit fashions, argot, racial mixing, juvenile delinquency, and drug taking.[77] The danger of

Industry-based genres is framed in three contradictory ways. Journalists may portray the genre lifestyle as innocent fun and feature its colorful surface aspects; they may spin the lifestyle as a danger to its fans; or they may claim a danger is posed to society by its "lawless, anti-social, and hedonistic" fans.[78] All three readings were made of psychedelic rock at the time of the Woodstock and Altamont festivals of 1969.[79] The media may also ignite a "moral panic" in which genre spokespeople, police, political authorities, religious leaders, parent groups, teachers, and moral pundits of all sorts provide the willing press with lurid quotes.

Press coverage of these moral panics often highlights racist, classist, or sexist tropes. For example, in 1943–44 bebop jazz was blamed for the widespread white-on-black race riots at military bases and in northern industrial cities.[80] Forty years later, rap music was similarly blamed when riots erupted in Los Angeles following the Rodney King trial.[81] Tensions over race, class, and gender also emerge within Industry-based genre communities. For example, when large numbers of more educated, liberal, northerners flocked to the bluegrass community in the 1960s, they were characterized as "drug-taking freeloving pinkos," to which they responded by describing working-class, southern bluegrass fans as violent racists. The added attention to the genre is likely to draw even more fans.[82]

An extended example from rap music may best serve to illustrate how mass production, media coverage, and racial (or classist, sexist, or other) stereotypes combine in the case of many Industry-based genres. In 1984, a film called *Krush Groove* was released to theaters, a release accompanied by violence. The film featured rock and rap performers, but strictly followed the conventions of a musical comedy. Media reports of film showings documented stampedes, brawls, and crowd violence, and framed the events as episodes of "racial violence." One such description quoted a victim who claimed, "It was clear-cut [that the violence against me] was a racial thing." Other community members were quoted in the press asserting that the movie was "attracting a black crowd to a white town," which "means trouble, especially because they come out of the movie all psyched up."[83] Such claims of racial antagonism were linked to the fact that the heroes of the movie performed "the music of a particular black community"—rap music.

The members of rap group Run D.M.C. were featured in the movie, and they soon became the lightning rod for public concern about the relationship between rap and violence. In September 1986, the group earned rap music's first platinum album for million-dollar sales of their third LP, *Raising Hell*. But critics claimed that this achievement was the result of support from the same black gangsters responsible for *Krush Groove*'s violent reception.[84] D.M.C.'s summer promotional tour was marred by violence, vandalism, and muggings. In the most serious incident Run D.M.C. was prevented from taking the stage after gang members alleg-edly started a "rampage" that left more than forty people hurt. Accord-ing to *Newsweek*, the provocateurs were not D.M.C. fans; however, "the incident sparked a new wave of speculation about the relationship be-tween violence and rap, the terse black pop that features rhymed lyrics punched out over choppy rhythm lines."[85] Responding indirectly to the incident, Tipper Gore explained that "[disillusioned kids] unite behind heavy-metal or rap music, and the music says it's OK to beat people up."[86] Antirap crusaders like Robert H. Bork described the music as a "knuckle-dragging sub-pidgin of grunts and snarls, capable of fully expressing only the more pointless forms of violence and the most brutal forms of sex."[87] References to unrestrained violence or sexual activity were clearly coded references to racialized stereotypes endemic to the moral panic around inner-city drug use and social service abuse (e.g., the "Welfare Queen") that dominated American politics in these years.

Despite the level of conflict that often accompanies the Industry-based genre, hard-core scene members often spend this period complaining that the sense of being oppositional and hip has been lost. In bebop and blue-grass, hard-core scenesters accused artists of "selling out" by mixing in pop music elements so that the resulting product would have greater popular appeal. In rap music, even (financially, critically) successful producers like Rick Rubin asserted the purity of the music's precommercial phase:

> At the time that I started it was still kind of a pure thing . . . [peo-ple] were doing it out of love for it. And I think that changed to people thinking they could get something from it. And when that happened the art kind of went away, and it became commerce, and people trying to put records together to sell. And that's what really ruined it for me.[88]

In Rubin's comment, he acknowledges that the introduction of commer-cial interests into the community affects the music that is made, but he neglects to note that these forces also impact artists who have survived from the Scene-based genre. The threat posed by the popularity of music created in the Industry-based genre encourages the hard-core scenesters to cleave to a reductionist notion of the genre ideal.

While bluegrass music never achieved the same level of mass popularity or sales as bop or rap, its connection to the folk music revival of the late 1950s and early 1960s drew many northern middle-class young people to the music. Thanks to bluegrass's inclusion at the Newport Folk Festival, and Mike Seeger's albums *American Banjo Scruggs Style*, and *Mountain Music Bluegrass Style*, a generation of young fans was exposed to performances and texts that presented an uncontestable history of the music, and they were invited to join the revival. But older fans resented their involvement with the music, and believed that this attention compromised the genre ideal in order to increase record sales and festival attendance. This Traditionalist genre emerged after a decade in which bluegrass's popularity receded, overtaken by the success of rock 'n' roll performers who drew attention away from bluegrass by adapting standard tunes to the new sound, as Elvis did with Monroe's "Blue Moon of Kentucky." "That was the problem for Monroe and other traditional performers: much Rock 'n' roll was flamboyant, brash, and loud"; while some artists, like Sonny James, successfully transitioned into rock artists, others, like Monroe, waited a decade until the folk revival sparked an interest in music of the Scene-based genre.[89]

Supporters of the Scene-based phase of the music are especially put off by the large number of "tourists" joining the ranks of the music's fan base in the Industry-based phase. New recruits argue over what constitutes authenticity in music, musicians, and signs of group affiliation,[90] and committed older, longer-term fans and performers engage in a discourse about authenticity lost.[91] This tension is sometimes divisive enough to propel some genre members into forming an Avant-garde genre, while the others create a Traditionalist genre.

Traditionalist Genres

Musical styles that have experienced the explosive Industry-based phase of development tend to suffer a crisis as their many casual fans find a new distraction, and a style's mass popularity wanes. Major record companies looking for the "next big thing" no longer promote the music, and the media see it as music to review rather than as a lifestyle that is the source of news. Resources shrink as players, performance space owners, and fans move on to other music interests. The massification of musical styles and growing friction between hard-core musicians and scenesters against outsiders fuels the fracturing of music into numerous distinct styles.[92] For example, the growth of R&B music and the rise of rock drew fans away from bebop. Not surprisingly, the general media reduced its coverage of bebop, and the major record companies reduced their marketing and financial support of artists or terminated their contracts altogether.

Traditionalist genres emerge when committed players, fans, and genre-supporting business people decry what they identify as the adulterating consequences of the commercial exploitation of the music in the Industry-based genre. They focus on purifying the music by eradicating the excesses of the Industry-based genre and reenacting a version of what the music was like in its Scene-based period. They seek to preserve the community's musical heritage and inculcate in a rising generation of devotees the performance techniques, history, and rituals of the style. Fans and organizations dedicated to perpetuating the music put great effort into constructing its history and highlighting exemplary performers who embody the collective memory of the genre they construct. Hard-core bebop fans who had been dismayed by the adulterations made in the Industry-based genre, and by the hordes of touristic fans, set about trying to re-create bebop as it had been in the glory days as a Scene-based genre. And, increasingly, bebop was being interpreted as a modern art form worthy of scholarly attention and preservation in the major conservatories of classical music.[93] The February 28, 1964, issue of *Time* magazine, for example, featured Thelonious Monk on its cover and reported his eccentricities as signs not of madness but of creative genius.

Traditionalist genres are discussed in academic or lay treatments of music, are performed at conferences and festivals, and rely on small-scale or nonprofit organizations. In bluegrass, fans' interests were served by two periodical magazines, *Bluegrass Unlimited* and *Muleskinner Blues*, and the International Bluegrass Music Association and Hall of Fame. The genre-oriented press publishes schedules of events, recounts recent events, prints articles on performance techniques, profiles both venerated and rising artists and groups, and reviews new and remastered records. As was the case with *Bluegrass Unlimited*, this press can host debates over questions of critical importance to preservationists: "What is bluegrass? Who started it? Is it ever all right to use amplified instruments? And, when bluegrass artists start selling lots of records outside the field, should purists hate them?"[94]

Many archival music compilations are released, and a small industry is devoted to remastering and rereleasing old albums. Traditionalist bluegrassers are exceptional in this regard: at least thirty-five small record companies (e.g., Rounder Records, Flying Fish, Rebel Records) have been formed to rerelease a number of recordings from the 1940s and 1950s that are identified by scholars as "canonical,"[95] and Lester Flatt released a number of reunion albums with other canonical bluegrass performers.[96] This canon is sometimes paid tribute by artists working in other genres: for example, James Carter's 1995 CD release *Jurassic Classic* acknowledges his debt to earlier bebop performers.

At the start of the Traditionalist genre, a scholarly literature emerges that strives to preserve, codify, and organize the field, as was the case in Mayne Smith's 1965 article "An Introduction to Bluegrass," published in the *Journal of American Folklore*. Scholars and lay historians are often preoccupied with the quest for the true or authentic, complete history of a musical style, and this preservationist spirit is precisely what strongly differentiates Traditionalist genres from other genre types. Musicians and promoters often play a key role in defining the field, particularly if they were active during the Scene-based genre form. For example, Mike Seeger contributed liner notes to his 1959 album *Mountain Music Bluegrass Style* and precisely defined its roots: "the term came into use in the early 1950s, originally referring to the music of Bill Monroe. . . . Bluegrass describes a specific vocal and instrumental treatment of a certain type of traditional or folk-composed song."[97] The codification of a musical style's history and significance is the core activity of Traditionalist genre members.

In rap music, this literature emphasized the music's roots in black oral practices and its importance to urban, poor, black neighborhoods.[98] It situated rap music as the locus of political identity and action in a consumer context.[99] Rap lyrics were seen to focus "on features of ghetto life that whites and middle-class blacks would rather ignore," and it is for this reason that Chuck D designated rap music "Black Folks' CNN."[100] Rap's politics were inflected with religious or Black Nationalist sentiments.[101]

The selective emphasis placed on the politics of rage (even if sublimated into religious rhetoric) demonstrates a core set of values shared by rap Traditionalists, and their willingness to silence or eliminate other popular themes from within Scene-based rap. As I suggested at the start of chapter 1, these alternative accounts of rap's significance include its role as a dance and party music.

Members of Traditionalist genres meet in clubs and at gatherings of musical associations, academic conferences, and festivals; they communicate at a distance through newsletters, academic journals, trade magazines, and discussion sites on the Internet. In fact, new communication technologies may allow members of Traditionalist genres to fabricate and promulgate a history for musical styles, as was the case with the so-called Canterbury sound.[102] The groups associated with this musical scene, including Caravan and Wilde Flowers, were not based in Canterbury (instead, they lived in London), the aesthetic similarities among works are weak at best, and the term "Canterbury sound" had only recently (in the 1990s) been adopted by local record shops to sell (otherwise unmarketable) music. All of the "scene writing" was accomplished by online participants at a Web site devoted to the style, and is essentially unimaginable in real, as opposed to virtual, space. Traditionalist genres are populated by dedicated fans, semiprofessional and experienced musicians, and academics from a variety of disciplines. Academic classes in the music and its history often become available, but much instruction in musical technique and genre lore is received via one-on-one interaction with established performers and other aficionados.

Performers and promoters commonly rely on employment outside the musical community. Festivals and tours often provide the greatest percentage of music-related income to Traditionalist performers, in combination with income from selling records, musical instruments, and music-related ephemera. Many fans sing, play an instrument, or act as promoters of events, so there is a less distinct division of labor among fan, artist, and industry than in Industry-based or fully developed Scene-based genres.

Members regularly travel to conferences and festivals, collect and display records and memorabilia, raise money for ailing artists, and build organizations dedicated to perpetuating the music. Festivals are extremely common among Traditionalist genres, and are critical to their momentum and cohesion. Famed Traditionalist genre festivals include the Newport

Folk Festival, the Country Music Association's Festival (FanFair), Merle-fest, Kaustinen Folk Music Festival (Finland), Rocktoberfest, the Montreal Jazz Fest (Canada), the Montreaux Jazz Festival (Switzerland), the Cambridge Folk Festival (UK), and the Lakeside Blues Festival (Finland). Festivals play a key role in codifying and legitimating a single genre ideal.

Bluegrass music is one of those musics that rely upon the multiday festival to sustain the Traditionalist genre. A three-day festival held near Roanoke, Virginia, in 1965, set the model many others would follow. The music of the festival was chosen to illustrate "The Story of Bluegrass," which had been scripted by Ralph Rinzler, by then Bill Monroe's manager. The festival opened with Monroe and the Blue Grass Boys playing the "Mule Skinner Blues," the first number Monroe had played on the Grand Ole Opry, in 1939. The script mentioned all of the significant sidemen who had gotten their tutelage from Monroe, by way of introducing the groups. The current assemblage of Blue Grass Boys opened the finale; then Monroe invited his old sidemen up, one by one, and they finished with the assembled aggregation singing the gospel anthem of remembrance and healing, "Will the Circle Be Unbroken." That same year, Rinzler edited the first Decca Records release of Monroe originals, and, in 1967, Rinzler produced the first of several Festivals of American Folklife at the Smithsonian Institution in Washington, D.C.[103] In the years following, and until the mid-1980s, bluegrass festivals proliferated, especially in the southeastern United States. For example, the March 1983 issue of the fan-oriented *Bluegrass Unlimited* lists 490 events.[104] Because it was possible for fans to spend the summer months going from festival to festival, Bob Artis titled his chapter on this period "The Endless Summer."[105]

Members of Traditionalist genres tend to resemble one another in dress, adornment, and argot. They wear muted, somewhat stereotypic styles of the aging artist or academic and may often use verbal expressions seen by others as out-of-date. They may also resemble stereotypes of a Scene-based performer. This is demonstrated in dramatic fashion in Chicago's blues clubs, where performers are "overblown caricatures": "generally uneducated American black men afflicted by blindness, or else they walk on a wooden leg or with a secondhand crutch; as they are defiantly poor, they drive beat-up Fords and old Chevy trucks, and usually cannot read or write their own name."[106] The dedication of bluegrass legend Bill Monroe to his traditional performance style was so great that he refused to book "longhairs" at his festivals, effectively filtering out any progressive elements from his concerts in the early 1970s.

Committed Traditionalists expend a great deal of energy fighting with each other about the models they construct to represent their music and the canon of its iconic performers. They argue over which instruments and vocal stylings are appropriate, and they may even battle over the place and time when the music originated. We witness this in the censure of "crossover" rap artists of the 1980s like Vanilla Ice or Digital Underground, who are derided for having "made rap palatable to white, suburban youth across the country."[107]

The test of authenticity is often taken to be the race, class, educational attainment, and regional origins of performers. So it is said that to play bluegrass a musician must be white, working-class, rural, and preferably from the Appalachian Mountains; you must be young, white, and an underachiever to perform punk music; and all salsa musicians must be Latin American.[108] Even journalistic and academic accounts of Traditionalist genres engage in such demographic profiling.[109] These outsiders often conflate stories of a musical style's exotic origin with its present Traditionalist form, and these stereotypes influence tourists who want to know something about the musical style. For example, well-meaning blues fans come to Chicago expecting to find the music played by "uneducated American black men afflicted with blindness or some other disability, playing in ramshackle joints that are dimly lit, unbearably smoky, and smelling as funky as their music sounds."[110]

Scholars documenting Traditionalist genres in which racial minorities, women, and the poor play a dominant role often conflate the behavior of individual performers with the culture of people of shared attributes.[111] Popular culture and music specifically are reduced in these accounts to "coping mechanisms," rituals, or oppositional action that groups use to mitigate poverty, racism, and sexism. Accordingly, artists' legitimacy can be judged on the basis of both their demographic attributes (e.g., you are not a real rap artist if you are not African American) and the extent to which their behavior aligns with stereotypic behaviors of that group.

While there have been a smattering of reunion tours, reissues, and musical reactions against the elements within rap music, Traditionalist performers have not been as conspicuous there as in bluegrass. This may be due to rap's more recent development and shorter life span, but I do note the appearance of a Traditionalist sentiment in a growing scholarly literature, as I noted above. It is fair to say that there is no coherent revivalist tradition of bebop. Some musicians began to explore new ways to revitalize the genre ideal, and new Avant-garde genres emerged from their efforts. Bebop artists helped to spawn hard bop, cool jazz, free jazz, psychedelic jazz, and third stream musical styles. At the same time jazz history is taught in heroic terms, and bop music is seen as the foundational music style for serious jazz musicians ever since.

After the Tradition

Most research on music traces the development of one style, and there has been surprisingly little research on the interconnections between musics over longer periods of time. These studies are quite diverse because each follows the contours of a specific historical case.[112] In this final section of the chapter, I wish to illustrate several examples of how new music is hived off from the old. While I will return to a more extensive discussion of such "germinal" genres in later chapters, I here offer a short description of this process in rap, bebop, and bluegrass.

Industry-based communities often disband with the drift of casual fans to new musical distractions and the consequent twilight of mass popularity. The crisis within the community is focused on a debate between the nascent Traditionalists, who seek to preserve the music performed in the Scene-based phase, and those who focus on continuing the aesthetic development characteristic of the Scene-based period and living out the creative spirit of the music through innovation and hybridization. This second group often forms a new Avant-garde genre. In punk music, for example, Traditionalists defined punk as a particular style of music developed in a specific time period that they sought to preserve. Avant-gardists defined punk as the spirit of any music based in the DIY aesthetic and defiance of norms, both musical and cultural. The first may go on for decades, but the latter is generally short-lived because a new musical designation emerges to describe the movement. That is, Avant-garde genres can be considered to emerge out of the Traditionalist genre of another musical style. I hesitate to describe this process as a "cycle" because the system does not return to the same starting state, as in calendar cycles, most crop rotation cycles, astrological cycles, and so forth. Instead, it perhaps more closely resembles the cell cycle, at least in cases where mitosis (cell division) includes nontrivial modifications in the replicated DNA.

Avant-gardists revolt against the popularizing tendencies of the Industry-based genre, and those who write about them begin to use the evaluative discourse of art, evoking images of genius and creative quest.[113] Some find inspiration from unusual meldings of music in cooperation with other creative artists working in other musical styles. The discourse of creative genius helps the musicians to distance themselves from the demands of fans of the style from which they have hived off. Like all Avant-gardists, they must rely on sympathetic independent record companies, promoters, and venue owners. Avant-gardists also tend to distance themselves from Traditionalist artists and fans.

Jazz as a stream has been committed to competition, innovation, and, increasingly, an arts aesthetic, so it is no surprise that Avant-gardism grew directly out of the successes of the Industry-based period. The numerous creative musicians following in the wake of Parker and Gillespie—including Thelonious Monk, Charles Mingus, Miles Davis, Roland Kirk, Jerry Mulligan, Archie Shepp, Ornette Coleman, and especially John Coltrane—continued to expand the jazz sound. The word "bop" was abandoned, and a number of new terms including "hard bop," "progressive," "cool," and "newthing" came into use to describe these developments. Thus bop became the progenitor of a number of Avant-garde musics in the jazz stream.

The massification of the music and increasing internal dissatisfaction similarly fueled the fracturing of rap into numerous, distinct Avant-garde genres.[114] In 1989, activist Daniel Caudeiron forecast the future of rap music:

> A few years ago the major record companies wouldn't touch most rap groups with a barge pole. But now we're getting second, third and fourth waves of signings; if you're rap, you can do no wrong. Of course it's going to make for a lot of internal debate on what is or isn't rap. Historically, any time a music begins as something radical, innovative and closely tied to race and the inner city streets, questions are raised over what is valid once it hits the mainstream. It happened with jazz, blues and disco. Why should rap be different?[115]

Toronto promoter and DJ Ron Nelson had a more critical response: "We are in a slump. For the first time in five years I'm scrambling to find enough good rap to play on my show. The fear now is that rap could go the way of the dinosaur. I'm studying the trends and I'm wary. There is a huge transition happening, and it hasn't focused in a new direction yet."[116] Traditionalists like Nelson were overlooking a large and vibrant set of Avant-garde genres growing within rap. One of the earliest grew out of Los Angeles and was later dubbed "gangsta rap" for its lyrical content and the antigovernment statements made by its leading practitioners.[117] Later "jazz rap" emerged in opposition to the "negativity" of gangsta rap, and performers built their political stance upon middle-class black or "Afrocentric" identities.[118] In total, twelve styles of rap music have been documented since the start of a Traditionalist genre, making rap one of the largest musical streams in U.S. recording history.[119] In addition, substantial rap scenes developed in France (especially among the *pieds noirs*), Germany, Canada, Great Britain, Holland, Japan, New Zealand, Senegal, South Africa, Russia, Croatia, India, and elsewhere.[120]

The Traditionalist stage of bluegrass music was marked by an increasing mix of musical elements, and by the early 1970s the community began to fracture into two different camps. On the one hand, some artists and fans sought progressive transformations of bluegrass, while Traditionalists sought to reconstitute the music as it had been in its Scene-based period. Among the former, many instrumentalists worked with new ways of playing and began to bring music from other genres into bluegrass. The band New Grass Revival, formed in 1972, provides a good case in point. Their first album was titled *New Shades of Grass* and included covers of rockabilly songs such as Jerry Lee Lewis's "Great Balls of Fire." It also featured lengthy improvisational solos, and electronic pickups for greater volume and tone control. Other bluegrass groups covered folk rock and country rock numbers. The New Grass Revival and other newgrass groups represented "a kind of progressive cult."[121] In the same period, the Byrds, Gram Parsons, the Flying Burrito Brothers, the Grateful Dead, and other West Coast bands pushed the boundaries of progressive bluegrass even further. The three-album set *Will the Circle Be Unbroken* featured the Nitty Gritty Dirt Band, and invited guests from bluegrass and country music to perform.[122]

In short, one feature of Traditionalist genres is that they are capable of inspiring the creation of Avant-garde genres in new musical styles. To the extent that these hived-off musics are linked to their parents, musical styles conjoin into streams. The development of streams, and the social structures that support them, may offer distinct advantages to new musical styles progressing through the genre forms. For example, the development of heritage and preservation organizations may offer relatively young music communities resources like awards, induction into Halls of Fame, and coverage in industry magazines. Record companies that recognize the location of new musical styles in existing streams may transfer production and promotional strategies, modeled after those used on other musics within the stream, with better or worse results. Streams thus function as a kind of meta–genre form, organizing, to a greater or lesser extent, the progression of music across genre forms. In the conclusion, I will return to this idea to speculate about the causes and consequences of stream development.

Conclusion

Drawing upon the analysis of several hundred music histories, I introduced a scheme of genre dimensions and attributes in the previous chapter. As we fit different styles to these dimensions, what emerges are four genre forms, or distinct stages in the array of these attributes. Emerging musics experience analytically distinct phases, and the form and activities of genres change from phase to phase as they face differing challenges and require discrete sets of resources. In this chapter, I detailed the progression of three musical styles, bebop jazz (1938–60), rap (1972–95), and bluegrass (1938–80), across these genre forms.

The most perplexing problem, at least with respect to the study of Avant-garde genre forms, is how to identify them in their formative stages. Most Avant-garde communities are not identified as such until long after their dissolution, once group members and outsiders have had time and space for retrospection. The search for these musical communities will inevitably produce a lot of "noise," since Avant-garde genres are easily confused with other social formations, including circles of friends and nascent political parties. The study of nascent state phenomena has been largely confined to social psychological research and really hasn't impacted the study of music or culture.[123] An intensified focus on identifying the coalescing features that operate in the formative stages of social groups will have wide utility. If music genre activity is easily confused with the creation of a political movement, for example, then the opportunity can be seized to develop even better understandings of the resemblance of these two sociocultural processes.

The comparison of political movements and music communities may also provide a greater understanding of why some musical styles attract interest from consumers while others do not. New audiences for particular styles may appear unexpectedly, as was the case when middle-class college students and young, unmarried, working college graduates joined lower-middle-class housewives as fans of soap operas in the late 1970s. In this case, the plot characteristics (overlapping, tenuously related plots, periodic crises, depictions of cohesive suburban communities) appealed to both the traditional viewer and the new, middle-class viewer's desires for excitement and titillation.[124] Producers seeking to attract and retain new viewers transformed the soap operas to include younger characters, more upscale and exotic locations, and an emphasis on adventure and mystery themes. In this case, the work was adapted to appeal to new consumers' tastes, which unexpectedly emerged. In other examples, such as bebop jazz or rock 'n' roll, the perception of new tastes led to the creation of a novel form of work.

While there is more to learn about the source of new tastes among consumers, we know comparatively more about how organizations adopt them within Industry-based genres. The adoption of innovations by major record labels follows a well-researched pattern by which "contact men" (including those working in Artist and Repertoire [A&R] divisions of companies) identify popular Scene-based musics, and encourage the firm to engage them. They do so in one of two (related) ways: by signing development contracts with successful artists and bands, placing them within style-based divisions of the firm, or by buying the independent record companies that have nurtured the genre and operating them as subcontracted units of the firm.[125] The financial resources and promotional expertise of the major companies can then propel the music into the national limelight, marking the start of the Industry-based form. Research has shown that major labels are increasingly subcontracting with successful labels from Scene-based genres rather than absorbing them into the central firm. Scholars might collect and analyze the relatively quantifiable data that firms employ in the acquisitions process in order to identify features of this process, to understand the transformation from Scene-based to Industry-based music. For example, it would be important to discover whether having highly codified genre conventions is a key element pushing a community into the mass market.

The development of a musical style is marked by increasing codification of its genre ideal, performance conventions, and fashion style, and the establishment of a single name used to identify the music and its performers, fans, and organizations. This process requires that group members engage in decision-making and consensus-building activities, but there is very little empirical research on these activities in music genres. However, the study of other small groups, their discourse and organizational processes, may provide some starting points. For example, there are several theories of decision making that may guide our study of music communities. Groups may be engaged in unconscious planning; they may be dominated by a legitimated leader; they may use reflexive monitoring (where group members evaluate previous experience to shape future conduct) or practical consciousness (where experience influences action in a more informal way).[126] Most of this research has been done on small groups within organizational contexts, however, and it is possible that the study of emergent genre ideal consensus would illuminate decision-making processes that are unique to nonorganizational contexts. But if we could identify genre communities that employ similar decision-making processes, we may seek to include a new genre dimension in table 1.1, and find that decision-making style is linked to other attributes of the group. For example, genres that are dominated by a legitimated leader may be more likely to merge with a stream or less likely to attract "tourists." If one person exerts control over the group, this may lead to more effective strategic planning but may discourage the casual engagement that characterizes those fans and musicians in the outer circle.

Over time, as the genre ideal becomes more focused, collaboration sessions are less likely to stall on debates over technique, and members use knowledge of these conventions and ideas to differentiate insiders from hapless pretenders. The degree of codification of performance conventions is quite high once the group achieves an Industry-based genre, and is enforced by the extensive distribution of instructional manuals and tablature, and widespread awareness of canonical performances. This is the period when instructional courses begin to be offered, as was the case in tango and in disco, at least once the Dimples Discotheques School of DJing opened and began to regulate the playlists graduates could present at parties.[127] But does this codification process resemble that found in other fields of collaborative endeavor?

Conversation analysis offers some useful starting points, as research into "institutional talk" has demonstrated a link between interactions and entitlements that issue from formal roles.[128] In music communities, members who are fluent in genre talk may be granted the authority to innovate, to set new terms for collaboration, or to speak to outsiders on behalf of the group. In social movement studies of "claims making," we find another model of how to conceptualize the choice of performance conventions. One exemplary study can be found in Tilly's consideration of the parliamentarization of British politics, in which he shows how the nature of claims making shifted from spontaneous protest toward formalized grievance mechanisms pursued by political parties and organized social movements.[129] The accretive process by which ideas and identities are expressed by political parties may be a model for transitions in the performance conventions of musical communities.

I addressed at some length the importance of style to Scene-based genre members who seek to identify insiders, which later leads to the mass production of a simplified version of this style within Industry-based genres. I am less certain of the process of styling that occurs within Traditionalist genres, as many forsake stylistically specific forms of dress and adopt a generic style often associated with the intellectual elite. This may be a result of the Traditionalist's desire to emphasize the music over the lifestyle of the group. It may also be a function of the occupational and class status of many Traditionalists, and their age. Many are employed in teaching and research professions that support the scholarship on Traditionalist genres, and may assimilate to local occupational norms rather than genrespecific codes. Although scholars have expressed an interest in analyzing the style of youth cultures, Scene-based music communities, and other contexts in which there are synergies between music and fashion, there is no study of the style among Traditionalists.[130] Since Traditionalists lack both a centralized system of fashion production and a network of designers, trend forecasters, and magazine editors devoted to organizing and diffusing innovation, it is unclear how innovation and diffusion practices work within these communities.[131] Do practices spread through information cascades where people conform to local leaders, or because there are sanctions in place that punish deviance within the community?[132] Do members recognize a common style, or are they conforming to fashion expectations in some other field? In short, what causes lie behind the tendency of Traditionalists to dress alike?

The names I have chosen for the genre forms reflect their dominant organizational character: the scene, the entertainment industry, and the clubs and associations devoted to preserving traditions. It is possible that the forms taken by music communities are a function of isomorphic pressures within the environment. Isomorphism is a constraining process that encourages each organization to resemble others that face the same set of environmental conditions.[133] In punk music, the organizational and institutional dynamics of the music industry frustrated the desire of some bands to operate on a democratic basis, and they were forced to remain Scene-based or assimilate to the dominant, bureaucratic model.[134] In addition to isomorphic pressures, it is possible that genres assume particular organizational forms because they are in competition with other styles to serve audience needs. If this is the case, we could compare music genres to other organizational ecologies. For example, New York City social welfare agencies during the Progressive Era competed with one another, making claims to use the same technologies to treat the same types of social problems.[135] The consequence of this niche competition was that settlement houses lost the battle to become the primary delivery organization for social welfare services. In music, it appears that classes of nonprofit, collectively owned artist organizations commonly lose their bid to be primary providers of cultural content within Scene-based genres. How might we use insights drawn from the study of organizational ecologies to understand how genre organizations compete by making jurisdictional claims?

In my discussion of boundary maintenance in chapter 1, I noted the tendency of musicians and fans in Scene-based and Avant-garde genres to define their community in opposition to the established genre within the field. Processes of boundary maintenance are also directed toward other musics contesting for resources in the same niche. Notable examples of this include the street fights between mods and rockers in the early days of rock 'n' roll in the UK; the homophobic rock fans of the 1970s who loudly declaimed that "disco sucks"; and rival rap "crews" that contested for dominance in the mid-1970s and again in the mid-1990s. One such battle was played out on the pages of rock magazine *Creem* throughout 1979 and 1980, pitting punk and metal fans against each other in a war of words. Punk fans declared themselves to be more intelligent and sophisticated listeners and accused metal fans of fascism. Metal fans claimed that punk performers were talentless hacks. Because metal received far more press and sold more albums, punk fans claimed that their affinity for less popular artists was actually a sign of their superior tastes.[136] Metal fans were described as if they had no ability to discriminate but rather followed popular tastes, leading punks to conclude that metal fans relished inauthentic music.[137] Definitions of masculinity were also at stake in this debate, and metal fans articulated bigoted, homophobic descriptions of punks' style, while punks cast doubt upon the musical talent of hard rockers, given their tendency to attract "unsophisticated" female listeners. The two groups differed in how they framed the significance of music history: while metal fans sentimentalized the rock stream of which their music was a part, and celebrated its durable appeal, punk fans valued novelty over tradition and associated the latter with obsolescence.[138] In this rendering of events, it appears as if the genre ideals of the two groups were inevitably bound to conflict, especially since *Creem* reviewed the music of both scenes. But there's good reason to question the assumption of inevitability. After all, sometimes genres competing for resources within the same niche are able to produce a kind of dynamic, productive tension, in which one acts as a "countergenre" for the other.

This leads me to question the circumstances that facilitate productive or destructive competition between musical styles. When do musical styles encourage the survival of other styles by providing alternative values, and when do they ensure mutual destruction? Is it ever the case that such conflict, ceteris paribus, results in some institutional or organizational changes within the community? Are there cases in which the "losing" style withers, is absorbed by another style, or consolidates its strength as a Scene-based genre and survives in a semiunderground existence? This last appears to be the case for UK goths and the country balladeers of Austin, Texas.

A second form of competition pits musical communities against local residents. When scenes are embedded within residential areas, locals may object to the rising tide of nighttime visitors attracted to the clubs, bars, and restaurants that support Scene-based genres. For example, early

Scene-based disco clubs annoyed residents of New York's SoHo neighborhood (some say because of the large black and gay presence) and provoked the City Planning Commission to initiate a campaign against dance venues in August 1974, "declaring that they exploit the 'energy of the art center' while contributing 'nothing to its growth.'"[139] In this case, the city was unsuccessful in shutting down the clubs, and soon a handful of dance establishments were opened in the area, most hosting more than a thousand partiers on weekend nights. The colocation of scene participants is keyed to the evolution of the group's genre ideal, but organizations and clusters of organizations have varying levels of success in sponsoring Scene-based music. Business owners, particularly the local, independent entrepreneurs who often sponsor innovative music, will benefit greatly if we can analyze the management and promotion practices that are most effective in Scene-based genres, and expand our knowledge about those practices within Industry-based genres.[140]

Claims about unfair competition from copyright violations and digital music distribution are increasingly common in the media, and important to understand. Debates over copyright regulations in music tend to focus on two issues: sampling, parodies and other reuses of intellectual property, and the unauthorized reproduction or distribution of works. With respect to the last, record industry leaders often argue that digital music file exchange is adversely affecting CD sales. However, the data suggest that this is not the case. During the heaviest period of file exchange (via Napster, one of the early industry leaders), CD sales were at an all-time high.[141] In part, these discussions focus on producer legitimacy: who is authorized to produce and profit from particular works? As such, discussions over copyright are discussions about the boundaries of a class. Thus copyright debates fit within the boundary work of genres, extending this work beyond that which I've discussed earlier: competition between musics within niches, between members of a community seeking to define conventions, between moral crusaders and genre members.

There's one additional aspect of boundary work that I have not yet discussed: the issue of censorship. As I noted earlier in the chapter, new media tend to sensationalize music communities and their music at the start of the Industry-based period. The media deploy particular frames in these articles, viewing the lifestyle or the fans as a danger to society. We saw evidence of this in media treatment of psychedelic rock at the time of the Woodstock and Altamont festivals of 1969, to name one of many examples.[142] Media debates over the dangers of popular music do focus on the vulnerability of the young to sexually explicit and violent content. One notable case involved the attempt by the Broward County, Florida, sheriff to ban the sale of rap group 2 Live Crew's album *As Nasty as They Wanna Be*. Sheriff's officers visited more than twenty record stores, proffered a copy of Judge Mel Grossman's advisory opinion that the album was obscene, and required that they remove the album from sale. Although these stores and many others across the country did remove the album from their shelves, a district court suit against the sheriff found that the action imposed "unconstitutional prior restraint on the plaintiff's right to free speech," and albums were replaced on the shelves.[143] However, the issue was taken up by the Parents Music Resource Center (PMRC), one of several religious and politically conservative citizen groups who lobbied to have music publishers voluntarily apply obscenity labels on albums, a practice that continues today.[144]

While Americans appear to be concerned about the morality of musical content consumed by youth, the British journal *Index on Censorship* found that most incidents of censorship were reported in the Middle East and North Africa, and the motives were more likely to be political than aesthetic or moral.[145] Moreover, while censorship drives in the United States tend to emerge during a music's Industry-based period, those in other countries appear to impact music communities in all four genre forms. This leads to the question of whether the two processes share any similarities beyond the impulse to censor music. Are the claims for and against music made differently, or by different constituencies, across the globe? Are imported musics censored differently from domestic forms? What organizations or groups play a role in these debates, and to what degree are they integrated into a music community? While there is some excellent work being done on censorship and art, what remains is to link incidents of censorship with the capacity of particular genre forms to attract or contest these intrusions.[146]

Although I have not focused close attention on the overlap of genre forms within a musical style, it is clearly the case that such overlap exists. Scene-based communities for particular musical styles almost always persist despite the adoption and production of some of the music by major recording companies, in an Industry-based genre. The Seattle grunge scene continued active musical production during and after the mass popularity of groups like Nirvana. Similarly, Traditionalist genres may emerge before the music experiences its Industry-based phase. This was the case in bluegrass, where the emerging Industry-based genre was stalled by the introduction of a competitor music, rock 'n' roll: "As Rock 'n' roll flourished, bluegrass wilted," says one music historian.[147] While most bluegrass artists worked only in local venues and on radio shows in the 1950s, artists like Bill Monroe strove to consolidate local scenes and build a canon for the music; these are the threads that were later woven together to form a Traditionalist genre. It was not until the 1960s that folk revivalists spurred national interest in bluegrass and propelled the music into its Industry-based phase.[148] In fact, the survival of local scenes may be key to maintaining broad interest in Industry-based genres, particularly in cases where the popular artists offer concerts that are prohibitively expensive to attend, or that are not scheduled in or near particular communities.

The boundaries between phases of genre forms are defined by a shift in the amount and kind of resources used by musical communities. As I noted in the introduction to this chapter, these should not be considered necessary or sufficient conditions for development. It may be the case that particular musical communities acquire resources at different rates. However, it is more likely that additional musical examples will affirm the central tendency and indicate the relative importance of resources on genre development. That said, it appears that some resources are more critical to the advancement of musics through genre forms than others. For example, in the Scene-based form it appears that generating major label record contracts for some artists is a critical resource that propels the music into its Industry-based phase. There is no evidence that a shift in dress, or the availability of sheet music, have been instrumental to this transition. Similarly, the emergence of two different genre ideals in the Traditionalist form—one that emphasizes the preservation of music, and the other emphasizing the spirit of innovation—predicts the evolution of a new Avant-garde genre in a new musical style. I have resisted the urge to stipulate the relative importance of genre dimensions in driving transitions across forms because these assessments should be determined by purposive sampling of active musical creation. I have sought to avoid the tautological application of the discovery of genre dimensions and forms as predictors of musical change.

There are several genre dimensions that may be underspecified in this model. Such underspecification may lead us to overlook important differences between musical styles that might ultimately result in the identification of a fifth genre form. For example, music historians place great emphasis on the importance of charismatic leaders in Avant-garde and Scene-based genres; given that art worlds are collaborative productions, these claims appear apocryphal. However, the long-term strategies leaders may enforce for the survival and health of the community may make the music better adapted to its circumstances. If leadership strategies could be specified and measured, we may seek to add this as a further genre dimension, as I have already suggested.

The objective in this chapter was to apply genre forms to three musical styles in order to illustrate their operation. In tracing these histories, I have discovered that genre forms are ordered into trajectories that lead these musics from Avant-garde to Traditionalist genres. While musical styles like bluegrass and bebop represent a dominant type of trajectory in American music, there are important variations upon it. Some styles fail to achieve one of the genre forms, "skipping" it, while following the same general pattern of progression. Others "stall out," remaining in one genre form for a great many years. Still others have radically different originating conditions. A study of these trajectories is the focus of the following chapter.

Chapter 3

Music Trajectories

Musical communities take on differing characteristics as they ebb and flow, and these changes are directly related to the range of problems or opportunities the group encounters. To bring these characteristics into sharper focus, I have demonstrated that there are four analytically distinct genre forms. In the Avant-garde genre, music practitioners come together to share their concerns over the state of music, but do so often without conceptualizing a set of goals or identifiers for the group. While most Avant-garde genres wither or merge with other genres, a few grow in size and develop a more focused and coherent group identity in the Scene-based phase of development. Now and then a Scene-based genre is successful and visible enough to draw the attention of commercial interests; such interests push it to become an Industry-based genre, during which musics draw the attention of national media and retailers and fuel a rift within the community between "old heads" and tourists. This rift reaches its apex in the fourth phase, the Traditionalist genre, in which the community seeks to preserve the music of the Scene-based genre.

This progression of a musical style across these genre forms can be described as a trajectory. Trajectories are "a cumulative, rather than repetitive, sequence of linked events, suggesting a certain directionality to change."[1] Music histories depict trajectories in the form of influence flowcharts, time lines, dynastic phases, and other visual and interpretative frameworks for organizing important events. For example, we can consider heavy metal music as a succession of album releases, and community-defining events produced by artists and critics of metal. In one "complete headbanging history," a flowchart time line of dates and events begins with the February 13, 1970, release of Black Sabbath's debut album. It includes "turning events" like the spring 1985 formation of the Parents Music Resource Center (which would promote the censorship of heavy metal sales and airplay), and community-defining events, like the January 1982 midperformance decapitation of a rubber bat by Ozzy Osbourne.[2] Similarly, an authoritative history of funk includes a list of band names within each of the five "dynasties" of the style.[3] Music historians emphasize the actions of particular bands in order to illuminate the meaning of a sequence of events, or a history. Sometimes, music historians prioritize the succession of stylistic characteristics as bands acquire the properties or attributes the author deems central to a style. For example, one text opens with a table containing the five stages of doo-wop, with cell values indicating the character of music according to eight criteria: use of nonsense syllables, presence of falsetto, and lyrical content are just three of these.[4]

Instead, we can now consider the history of American music in terms of each style's trajectory across genre forms, rather than through particular events or musicological stages. By demonstrating the similarities across musical styles, we learn something sociological rather than musicological about music history. This approach illuminates the deviations certain bands and styles make from the path traced by other groups. As we consider how particular musical styles transit through sequences of genre forms, we are able to see how attributes of the community impact trajectories. Drawing us away from "great man" theories that highlight the influence of individuals, the sociological study of music trajectories can bring into clearer and sharper focus differences among groups, and why they matter.

In mapping sequences of sociological phenomena, like music communities acquiring genre forms, scholars attend to the construction of typical paths, and the causes and consequences of different paths.[5] In this chapter, I explore the trajectories of musical styles across genre forms by engaging in what are called "parallel comparisons," in order to show how several musical styles follow (or do not) the same patterns. I do not, however, engage in Millian contrast, positing independent and dependent variables.[6] While it may be possible in the future to provide evidence of the necessary and sufficient conditions for musical styles to progress across genre forms, it just isn't sound to rely on case studies pursuing other objectives when assessing or comparing the influence of various factors or variables on trajectories.

In this chapter, I describe two primary trajectories taken by musical styles across the four genre types. I have already introduced the first of these because it characterizes the three musical styles explored in chapter 2: rap, bluegrass, and bebop jazz. This is also the most common trajectory among the sixty musical styles examined in this book. Forty-eight other musical styles progressed across the four genre types in a trajectory abbreviated AgSIT, for a progression from Avant-garde, to Scene-based, then Industry-based, and finally Traditionalist genre forms (see table 3.1). A second trajectory, abbreviated IST, describes the transit of nine musics that started as Industry-based genres, then inspired a Scene-based genre form, and acquired a Traditionalist following. The first objective of this chapter is to identify these two trajectories, and to illustrate them with examples from several musical styles.

While these two trajectories describe the development of these musics accurately, thirty-five musical styles—almost 58 percent—did not acquire all the genre forms within their trajectory. For example, grunge rock did not develop a Traditionalist genre, although it has all the characteristics of a musical style traveling the AgSIT trajectory. There are three causes for the blocked emergence of particular genre forms: (1) the absorption of musical styles into other styles and streams, (2) racist exclusion, and (3) aesthetic and social factors that prevent the expansion of the musical scene to new audiences and performers. In the second half of this chapter, I explore these three mechanisms of inertia that produce incomplete musical trajectories across genre forms.

The authors of the music histories on which I rely for data did not intend to capture the genre dimensions, forms, and trajectories revealed here. In fact, most historians identify idiosyncratic reasons for the development (and termination) of the style. These include the loss of musicians to drugs or suicide, opportunistic promoters who doom a music style to irrelevance, or the failure of a charismatic leader to emerge and shape the community's future. Since my objective in this chapter is to illuminate the trajectories that characterize the organization of musics into genre forms, I must formulate principles from these accounts. The inductive nature of the enterprise means that I seek both to convey the particular history of each musical community and to generate principles from those histories. For this reason, I focus on selected musical styles to illuminate both trajectories and inhibiting factors on musical change. Given that I focused on rap, bebop jazz, and bluegrass in chapter 2, in this chapter I consider a different set of musics, including the singer-songwriter style of Laurel

Table 3.1. AgSIT Genre Trajectories

	Avant-garde	Scene-based	Industry-based	Traditionalist
Bebop jazz	x	x	x	x
Bluegrass	x	x	x	x
Chicago jazz	x	x	x	x
Folk revival	x	x	x	x
Folk rock	x	x	x	x
Gospel	x	x	x	x
Heavy metal	x	x	x	x
Hillbilly	x	x	x	x
Honky-tonk	x	x	x	x
Old school rap	x	x	x	x
Punk rock	x	x	x	x
Rockabilly	x	x	x	x
Rock 'n' roll	x	x	x	x
Salsa	x	x	x	x
Urban blues	x	x	x	x
Western swing	x	x	x	x
Alternative country	x	x	x	
Disco	x	x	x	
East Coast gangsta rap	x	x	x	
Grunge rock	x	x	x	
Jazz fusion	x	x	x	
Jump blues	x	x	x	
Psychedelic rock	x	x	x	
Thrash metal	x	x	x	
West Coast gangsta rap	x	x	x	
Delta blues	x	x		x
Doo-wop	x	x		x
New Orleans jazz	x	x		x
Chicago polka	x	x		x
Cleveland polka	x	x		x
Milwaukee polka	x	x		x
Black metal	x	x		
Country boogie	x	x		
Death metal	x	x		
Free jazz	x	x		
Garage	x	x		
Grindcore	x	x		
Hard bop	x	x		
House	x	x		
Jungle	x	x		
South Texas polka	x	x		
Techno	x	x		
Laurel Canyon	x			
Swing		x	x	x
Contemporary Christian		x	x	
Conscious rap		x	x	
Contemporary gospel		x	x	
Humor rap		x	x	
Reggae		x	x	
Soca		x	x	
Tango		x	x	

Canyon, grunge rock, gospel, house and techno, New Orleans jazz, funk, South Texas polka, and tango. I begin with a summary of the two trajectories and musics that typify each.

Two Genre Trajectories

Rap, bluegrass, and bebop jazz all experienced an orderly progression across the genre forms (Avant-garde, Scene-based, Industry-based, Traditionalist), and so their histories reflect the trajectory I've abbreviated AgSIT. Forty-eight other musical styles followed this sequence, making this the most common trajectory among twentieth-century American popular music styles (see table 3.1). Readers will note the irregular pattern some musical styles take across genre forms. Starting with alternative country, nine styles lack a Traditionalist genre, six are missing an Industry-based genre, eleven develop only Avant-Garde and Scene-based genres, and one, Laurel Canyon, attained only an Avant-garde genre. Of those eight styles that start as Scene-based genres, all but one lack a Traditionalist genre. These irregularities are the subject of the second half of the chapter. I focus here on those musics that achieve all four genre forms.

Since I have already described in some detail the development of rap, bluegrass, and bebop jazz, I turn next to a religious musical style known as gospel. The choice to examine gospel in more detail illuminates the ways in which quite distinct styles, even religious and secular music, evolve in much the same fashion.

Gospel, also known as "Black gospel," emerged in Chicago under the leadership of Reverend Thomas A. Dorsey.[7] Gospel synthesizes several musical traditions, including blues, choral music, shape note music, and hymns, to create what was first known as the "Dorsey song."[8] Most historians of the style note that Dorsey's career began in vernacular music, particularly within the blues idiom. It was only after two years battling a debilitating depression, grieving the death of a close friend, and making his religious recommitment that Dorsey set about writing religious music, first penning the hit song "If You See My Savior Tell Him That You Saw Me" in 1926.[9] The popularity of Dorsey's songs, in combination with his bluesy arrangements of the existing hymnal, his emotional displays, and his interaction with the audience attracted the attention of parishioners and local clergy, many of whom had recently migrated from the blues-saturated south to Chicago, in the Great Migration.

Dorsey was recruited by the pastor of the Ebenezer Church to form a Baptist choir there in 1931, although he had written only four songs and his new musical style was not yet called "gospel." He reached out to choir directors at other churches, who were intrigued by his ability to draw new congregants, and by August 1932 a Scene-based circle of gospel choruses had gathered together at the Metropolitan Community Church in Chicago for an informal musicale. This group would later become the powerful National Convention of Gospel Choirs and Choruses.[10] With his companions, singers Sallie Martin and Roberta Martin, Dorsey visited churches and auditoriums around the area, offering performances and training sessions, and selling their sheet music. The increasingly large circuit of churches in the Midwest and South that hosted gospel performances would come to be known as the "gospel highway."

Sallie Martin's noted organizational skillfulness (much superior to her singing abilities, it was said), and Dorsey's captivating performances, led to an explosion of sheet music sales. Dorsey's publishing house soon became the largest in gospel, and the most profitable black-owned business in the recording industry.[11] The Industry-based period of gospel depended upon not only sheet music sales and concerts, but also adoption by the mainstream (white) entertainment companies of performers and songs from the style. Mahalia Jackson, one of Dorsey's "discoveries," first recorded in 1937 on Decca Records, and soon thereafter Chicago's WLFL began weekly broadcasts of Dorsey's University Gospel Singers.[12] In 1939, Clara Hudmon, the "Georgia Peach," performed at both Radio City Music Hall and the World's Fair.[13] Two large publishers of white church music, Stamps-Baxter and R. E. Winsett, anthologized Dorsey's music in the late 1930s.[14]

By 1950, gospel music suffused urban, black neighborhoods.[15] Mahalia Jackson became an enormous star, starting with her 1946 recordings on New York–based Apollo Records. By 1954, her radio and television programs, and the promotional campaign launched by her new record label, Columbia, caused white audiences to identify her as the quintessential gospel singer.[16] She was later featured in *Time magazine*, befriended Martin Luther King, Jr., and sang at John F. Kennedy's 1961 inauguration and King's funeral.

Starting in 1968, gospel acquired all the features of a Traditionalist genre. In that year, James Cleveland gathered black choir members for a convention in Detroit, during which he offered performances, classes, and seminars designed to help singers, choir directors, radio announcers, and musicians craft their skills in accordance with the musical conventions of gospel. Other cities soon hosted Cleveland, including Philadelphia, New York, and Los Angeles. Performers who had been central to the Scene-based genre, including Sister Rosetta Tharpe, the Ward Singers, and Mahalia Jackson, toured the country, performing at famous venues like the Apollo Theater and the Newport Folk Festival.[17] By 1977, the Traditionalist genre of gospel was plagued by debates over origins and authenticity. One history from 1977 relates that, "during the last few years, gospel musicians have been confronted with many questions pertaining to its true meaning and origin. There have been various discussions on the subject at conventions, workshops, and informal gatherings. Many people, especially those who are just recently discovering and exploring gospel music, have challenged authorities on the matter of its heritage."[18] These debates about the boundaries of appropriate performance and expression are characteristic of all Traditionalist genres.

Gospel evinces the characteristics of the AgSIT trajectory. As musical styles transition from an inchoate state into an Avant-garde genre, previously individual opinions, styles of performance, and complaints about status quo music begin to coalesce. This coalescence occurs as a result of increased interaction among artists in specific locales, as happened in the black churches of Chicago at the start of gospel music's history. Genre ideals emerge from elements of distinct musics just as Dorsey famously combined blues elements with hymns and group harmonies.

Music communities can remain in the Avant-garde form for a long time, or may quickly transition to Scene-based genres. The key features of this transition are the emergence of relatively stable aural and visible identifiers of the group, the acquisition of resources to support larger and more frequent performances, and a growing consensus around a set of goals for action. In gospel, Dorsey relied on existing spaces and congregations to build a "gospel highway" in which his music could be performed and sold. The sale of sheet music at these performances boosted profits and facilitated the spread of the music, as new and smaller churches used the scores to imitate Dorsey's sound. That Dorsey and his collaborators chose to create and maintain their own publishing company is perhaps the key decision that saved gospel from remaining a regional, Scene-based music. The stylistic differences between gospel and other religious sheet music would have prevented white-owned companies from engaging in its sale, and there were no existing black-owned entertainment companies that could manage production and distribution of the scores.

The evolution of consensual signals of inclusion and exclusion among genre devotees (or styles of dress, argot, adornment, even drugs) is a key feature in the transition from an Avant-garde to a Scene-based genre. Although gospel performers' sedate and formal style did little to differentiate them from other performers within the praise music stream, their style of performance—an emotional display where improvisation, crowd involvement, and dancing were introduced into the religious context—demarcated the boundaries of their genre community. Another feature of group identity that marks this transition is the identification of a genre name. The term "gospel" was generally in use by the late 1930s, although some continued to define it as the "Dorsey song" style while others later qualified the music as "Black gospel." Once musical communities have distinctive musical conventions, a particular style, and a name, they are better able to defend the borders of the group from those who do not belong, just as they simultaneously direct criticism toward some power or authority that is seen to persecute group members. While bebop lyrics contained a great deal of racially marked political speech, and rap and bluegrass combined political lyrics with visible and contentious disputes with outsiders, it is hard to find evidence of such political content in gospel until much later in its development.[19]

As I have already noted, gospel's organizational locus and scale were key to its development, particularly the "gospel highway," the National Convention of Gospel Choirs and Choruses, and Dorsey's large and profitable sheet music publishing company. These organizations supported the music for a decade until the start of the Industry-based period. By the early 1940s, gospel singers were widely heard on radio and television broadcasts, at fairs and festivals—including those featuring nonreligious music—and Mahalia Jackson had graced the cover of *Time magazine*. In other musical communities, performers rarely overcome the limitations of the existing organizational environment in the Scene-based phase. Typically, circles of artists are supported by local organizations that exist for other purposes, including the provision of community space, or other styles of performance. Such businesses will offer performers in new styles stage time on weekday or off nights for live performances, but do little to help artists develop the resources that could propel them into an Industry-based genre.

Gospel's Traditionalist period, starting in 1968, largely resembles that of other styles, in that members focused on conferences, reunion tours, and fund-raisers for ailing artists. James Cleveland's conventions had a specific aim: educating singers, choir directors, radio announcers, and musicians in the music's style. Young musicians recruited to the genre tried to recapture the spirit of the Scene-based period, while old-timers were "rediscovered," venerated as founders, and expected to perform à la mode whatever their current musical passion might be. Performers like Sister Rosetta Tharpe, the Ward Singers, and Mahalia Jackson extended their careers, playing festivals, Las Vegas casinos, and even a USO tour in Vietnam. Artists who have survived from the Scene-based period are repeatedly asked to describe the music, the performers, and the scene of that earlier moment. Some withdraw from the newfound attention, most develop pat answers to the conventional questions, and a few spin stories that exaggerate their contributions to the style.

Out of gospel's Traditionalist period grew an Avant-garde genre of contemporary gospel, influenced by the slick, smooth sound of R&B and disco. While "traditional" gospel continues to have some limited appeal to white audiences, "those black performers who have whites buying their albums can often find they have lost their black audience."[20] This is largely the result of the racist distribution system that makes Black gospel available in independently owned record stores in African American neighborhoods and on black radio stations. In contrast, the large and more "centrally" located Christian bookstores stock mainly "contemporary Christian" music, which emerged from the Jesus Revolution in the 1960s, and resembles popular, secular music. A change in stylistic focus typically accompanies the move into white points of sale, or this is perceived to be so by black audience members who cease to be fans.

I have employed the history of gospel as an example of the AgSIT trajectory, the most common pathway followed by American music. Within the group of musical styles that follow this trajectory, a small minority began as Scene-based genres. While the consequences of a musical style's starting conditions are not entirely clear, I explore the characteristics of such styles in the following section in order to begin to understand the differences between music that starts as an Avant-garde genre, and that which begins in the Scene-based stage.

Scene-based Origins

Eight of sixty American musical styles began as Scene-based genres and evolved an Industry-based form, and represent a minor but important variation on the AgSIT trajectory. I note this variant type because it is unclear what consequences flow from a musical style's originating genre form. However, the causes of these differences are clear. Musical styles that begin as Scene-based genres, like the eight discussed here, inherit performers from proximal styles including non-U.S.-based musical communities. The five musical styles that grew out of existing domestic Scene-based genres (swing, contemporary Christian, conscious rap, contemporary gospel, and humor rap) were all hived off from other musical communities. By the time these musicians initiated a new style, members of the group were relatively proficient on their instruments, and there was significant consensus on the genre ideal. The three musical styles imported from abroad and that took on distinctive identities here (tango, reggae, and soca) had their origins in a community of fans and musicians with relatively mature notions of the music and how it should be played, and a network of local institutions that provided resources to the community. Although these styles transformed as performers worked and audiences listened and danced in their new home, they retained many characteristics that had developed abroad. In this section, I examine tango as an example of such immigrant music, both because it was imported early in the century and thus provides an interesting comparison case to more contemporary styles, and because it was almost immediately adopted as a popular style owing to its rather unusual reliance on a dance craze.

Tango began as strictly instrumental music in early twentieth-century Argentina. The style employed violin, flute, guitar, and a German accordion known as a *bandoneón*. The Argentine tenor saxist Gato Barbieri argued that the sound of the tango "is very European harmonically, and the melodies are almost operatic. The rhythm, sure, that was born in Buenos Aires."[21] The tango was a popular sensation in the café culture of Buenos

Aires, and by 1912 it was welcomed as the dance music of formal functions; this was also the first year in which it was recorded.[22] In 1917, orchestras began to add vocal accompaniment, and Carlos Gardel became the style's most famous singer.

The tango was introduced to the United States in Paul Rubens's musical comedy *The Sunshine Girl*, which opened at the Knickerbocker Theater in New York on February 3, 1913. Within a year, performer Vernon Castle and his wife Irene started teaching the tango at the Castle House School of Dancing, which they soon franchised across the country; classes with the Castles popularized the dance (along with several others, including the turkey trot).[23] Restaurants and clubs specializing in *les dansants* played host to many early tango performances, including Bustanoby's Domino Room (on Thirty-ninth Street and Sixth Avenue in New York), where Rudolph Valentino was a *danseur mondain* "(or less politely, gigolo)."[24] New hotels like the McAlpin and Sherry's were the first to cater to American elites' fondness for the dance. Older places held back, but in 1914 the Waldorf allowed patrons to dance between courses. Interestingly, tango is among the very few American musical styles whose development appears to have depended upon the popularity of a dance style, at least in its early stages.

Like other musics that transitioned from a Scene-based to an Industry-based genre, tango attracted a great deal of press attention, both positive and negative, and both fed its popularity. One Mrs. Ethel Fitch Conger was in the news because she claimed she would seek legislation to ban a step called "the dip" after breaking her leg dancing the tango. A high school student died in a trolley car accident after dancing for seven hours, and the headlines read, "Death Attributed to Tango." In 1914, Yale University made the front pages by banning the tango from its junior prom, and Harvard made the news saying it would allow the tango.[25] Moralists objected, suggesting that the dance led to immorality and forms of lewdness. Society matron Mrs. Stuyvesant Fish asked for, and got, the Castles to invent a desensualized tango.

The tango affected North American music profoundly in several ways. Not the least of these was that it increased the influence of U.S. publishing house E. B. Mark, which used a part-time salesman in South America, Milton Cohen, as a source for sheet music. The Argentine tangos and Brazilian *maxixes* that Cohen shipped north, and that Mark sold to the U.S.

sheet music market, dramatically increased the diversity of styles available to musicians. The tango thus influenced stride piano players, and made a famous appearance in W. C. Handy's "St. Louis Blues" in 1916. The filmic tango, danced by Rudolph Valentino in silent film *The Four Horsemen of the Apocalypse*, gave many cinema pianists—some of them jazz players—a chance to work with blending North and South American musical styles. Tango's impact was felt outside the immigrant Argentine community almost immediately in the many hybrid forms of Latin music to emerge in twentieth-century American culture (e.g., the mambo, salsa, reggaeton). While some argue that Latin music has been used only "as a seasoning," and that many styles (including the samba and bossa nova) have "given rise to fairly frivolous and nonsensical spinoffs that have obscured both their importance and their dignity," it is still the case that all our major musical forms (e.g., stage and film music, jazz, country, rock) have been given a Latin flavor, to some extent.[26]

Styles that begin as Scene-based genres, like tango, represent an important variation on the AgSIT trajectory. Instead of emerging from a community of audiophiles with inchoate but vigorous complaints about the state of music, these musical communities emerged among semiprofessional or skilled musicians, with significant consensus about their stylistic direction. They also began with an existing community of supportive fans and local organizations, grounded in an immigrant enclave, or hived off from proximal musical communities. It is unclear what consequences this variation on the AgSIT trajectory may have for such musical styles. As I will discuss in the conclusion to this chapter, these musical styles may be better able to withstand changes or challenges because they emerge from a more established community, even if they do not develop an Industry-based or Traditionalist genre form. Born in circumstances that are not as disorganized as AgSIT musical styles, SIT trajectories also do not appear to be as bureaucratic as those that emerge within Industry-based circumstances; I turn to these trajectories in the next section.

IST Trajectories

The second trajectory found among twentieth-century American musics was perhaps my most surprising discovery. These musical styles conspicuously share a source in the pooled efforts of a few creative musicians paired with arrangers, producers, and industry marketers working in the field of Industry-based music. Most readers would be surprised to find that musical artists are able to be inventive—generative—while working within the labyrinthine bureaucracy of large record labels. Most of us see the profit-motivated decision making of record labels as antithetical to the aesthetically motivated creativity of musical innovation. Most sociologists of music share this point of view, and this has driven them to investigate the conditions under which musical innovation takes place.

Initial research into the organizational conditions for musical innovation led scholars to conclude that large bureaucracies like record labels are terrible at sponsoring innovation. The music made by major record labels, particularly during oligopolistic periods (where majors own the preponderance of successful music), was described as bland and undifferentiated.[27] During those brief periods when independent labels usurped control from the majors, as they did in 1954 at the advent of rock 'n' roll, scholars argued that the diversity of music on the charts was substantially greater. That is, corporate oligopoly dissolved when emergent styles of music (and the artists who performed them), recorded by independent labels, became popular.[28] Competitive periods ended when major labels offered contracts to the most successful of these independent labels or artists, and the future success of these acts allowed majors to reconsolidate control over the market for recorded sound. However, major label management was no better at maintaining diversity than it was at creating it, and newly acquired artists would soon produce bland music, starting the cycle of competition and reconsolidation over again. It is this pattern that had led us to see major record labels as bad incubators of creativity.

This cyclical theory (that music markets shift from periods of concentration and homogeneous music, to competition and diversity) was challenged by scholars who studied music production after the 1960s. In the modern era of musical production, firms changed their production process into what is called the "open system." The open system decentralizes production so that creative activities are buffered from the corporation's administrative center by semiautonomous divisions or "label groups."[29] Divisions are run by freelance producers, or "creatives," who are accorded professional status and delegated responsibility for the creation of music, limited only by the budget set by the front office.[30] Influenced by a report from Harvard University, most of the large labels instituted the open system starting in the early 1950s.[31] By the 1970s, decentralized production attenuated the negative effect of oligopolistic markets on musical diversity.[32] That is, after the 1960s, large labels began to produce innovative music in a more continuous fashion by acquiring independent labels and artists but keeping creatives in charge of production. The combination of factors provides a robust explanation for the inability of large firms to offer consistently diverse music before the 1960s, and their remarkable ability to do so thereafter.[33] It begins to reveal the reasons why the links between musical innovation and organizational locus are deep and complex.

Given that we now understand more about the conditions under which innovative music can be made by artists working with major record labels, a more detailed consideration of the IST trajectory is in order. In this section, I review the nine musical styles that were invented as Industry-based genres (see table 3.2). These musics are fairly evenly split between the two production styles discussed above: the contemporary, open system that uses label groups and other decentralized production and management techniques, and the closed system of the pre-1960s. The musical styles include cool jazz, movie cowboy, soul, and southern gospel in the latter category, and new jack swing, Nashville sound, nu metal, and outlaw country in the former.[34] I chose to explore funk music, both because its creation precisely coincided with this transition into the open system of production, and because it was an enormously popular style during the 1970s.

Cool jazz, soul, new jack swing, and nu metal all emerged from the efforts of successful artists working with industrial record company producers or arrangers.[35] Funk also began as an Industry-based genre. Its an-

Table 3.2. IST Genre Trajectories

	Industry-based	Scene-based	Traditionalist
Cool jazz	x	x	x
Funk	x	x	x
Movie cowboy	x	x	x
New jack swing	x	x	x
Soul	x	x	x
Southern gospel	x	x	x
Nashville sound	x	x	
Nu metal	x	x	
Outlaw country	x	x	

tecedent styles include the gospel of Mahalia Jackson, the southern soul and R&B of Stax artists, the blues and rock of B. B. King and Chuck Berry, and the jazz of Sun Ra and Miles Davis.[36] Bass-heavy and polyrhythmic, funk's aesthetic focuses on speed, asymmetry, dissonance, and repetition, and more than to any other element, funk musicians commit to grooving on "the one: the downbeat, or the first pulse in the four-beat bar used in most Western music. Playing on the one produces a choppy, bouncing energy to the music, and it is the signature sound of funk.[37]

Most funk bands are very large, including a horn section, several guitars, multiple percussionists, and a lead singer. Some songs are structured with a single bridge, while others closely resemble free-form jazz with a central theme around which instrumentalists and vocalists improvise.[38] Fred Wesley, trombonist and bandleader for James Brown, George Clinton, and Bootsy's Rubber Band defined the funk song:

> If you have a syncopated bass line, a strong, strong, heavy back beat from the drummer, a counter-line from the guitar, or the keyboard, and someone soul-singing on top of that, in a gospel style, then you have funk. So that if you put all of these ingredients together, and vary it in different ways, you can write it down, you can construct the funk.[39]

In funk, melodic lines are often created by rhythm instruments, vocals can be instrumental, and few other styles of music rival its sonic complexity. Both James Brown and Sly and the Family Stone are credited with funk's invention, and the style matured to include extremely popular and prolific artists during the first half of the 1970s, like George Clinton and his musical collectives (Parliament and Funkadelic); Earth, Wind & Fire; the Ohio Players; Kool and the Gang; and others.

Some scholars, perhaps inspired by funk master George Clinton's hyperbolic claim that "In the beginning there was funk," trace a long tradition for the music, reaching back to West Africa, the Middle Passage, and antebellum ring shouts, and reaching forward to touch the blues, gospel, and then jazz and rap.[40] Particular uses of the word "funk" can be found in the earlier musical record, including boogie-woogie piano player Professor Longhair, also known as "the Originator of Funk and Rock 'n' Roll," and New Orleans cornetist King Buddy Bolden's signature tune, "The Funky Butt."[41]

Most of the major innovators of funk music were already successful performers working in various styles of jazz, R&B, and soul who used their expertise, contacts, and access to performance and recording facilities to develop funk. Instrumental and R&B backing bands in the late 1960s began to improvise with the rhythmic themes that would later characterize the funk style, but were at the time referred to as "dance bands" or "black rock," or simply collapsed into soul or R&B. Playing as a backing band for the Falcons and Wilson Pickett, the Ohio Untouchables struck out as a solo group renamed the Ohio Players and signed with Westbound Records. After playing backup for Stax Records stars Otis Redding, Rufus Thomas, and Sam and Dave, among others, Booker T. & the MG's also struck out as an independent funk group. While working as Chess Records' house band and for the pop-jazz Ramsey Lewis Trio, drummer Maurice White formed Earth, Wind & Fire from performers playing for other groups (including New Birth, Friends of Distinction, Friends & Love, and Charles Wright & the Watts 103rd Street Rhythm Band). The hiving off of musicians from existing performance groups resembles the history of musical styles in the SIT trajectory, but the massive resources and immediate popularity of these idioms mark them as Industry-based genres from the very start.

James Brown, already an accomplished soul and R&B artist, played a critical role in the development of funk. Had he not negotiated the right in 1964 to supervise his own recording sessions without the presence of an A&R man (who would otherwise have selected tunes and coordinated the sessions), funk's history would have been significantly different. According to one historian, "this revolutionary act allowed . . . [Brown] to quickly establish [his] own distinctive stamp in the studio and on stage, creating a sound that is immediately identifiable."[42] After firing his backup band over a labor dispute, Brown hired brothers William "Bootsy" Collins and "Catfish" Collins. The new band redirected Brown's style toward funk, emphasizing the polyrhythmic nature of his late-sixties compositions, and focusing compositions on "the one." With the Collins brothers, James Brown emerged as an innovator of the funk sound. Their first collaboration resulted in the song "Sex Machine," now considered to be one of the earliest funk singles. Brown spin-off groups—including Maceo and the Macks, Lyn Collins, Bobby Byrd, and Marva Whitney—would carve a legacy in funk.

A second funk band, Sly and the Family Stone, also started with a record contract with Epic Records. The group "literally willed into public consciousness the idea that the band's makeup"—both men and women, white and black—"was revolutionary."[43] This made Sly Stone "the first black rock star to be packaged by the corporate music industry."[44] The band would also be credited with crafting the blueprint for the funk album with *Stand!* (Epic Records, 1969).[45] Funk's focus on an album-length recording marked a significant departure from other styles' exclusive focus on the single as the hit-making format. Starting in 1970, the Industry-based genre lasted until a flowering of Scene-based funk became popular in the late seventies and early eighties. The Industry-based genre was populated by the many performers who circulated through the bands led by James Brown, Sly Stone, and George Clinton.

While James Brown was the most renowned performer to work in the funk idiom, George Clinton was seen to be its most proficient practitioner. George Clinton's first band aspired to be a successful doo-wop group on Revilot Records and scored their first hit with "I Wanna Testify" in 1967. The Motown-affiliated Revilot label soon shuttered its doors, and Clinton lost the rights to the group's name, but he penned several songs used by the label's artists (including "I'll Bet You" for the Jackson 5 and "Something I Can't Shake a Loose" for Diana Ross). Clinton signed a new group, Funkadelic, to Westbound Records, with the Parliaments as backup singers; he decided to perform as the lead singer.[46] The band released their first full-length album in 1970, a self-titled release with the first track broadcasting the question "Mommy, What's a Funkadelic?" In the same year, Clinton reconstituted the Parliaments as Parliament, and began to campaign for radio airplay and sales by saturating the market with P-Funk (Parliament and Funkadelic) material: "He began to release albums on different labels using the same band but different names by creating what he deemed 'two distinct identities for one band—the mystical voodoo of the Funkadelics and the stabbing, humorous fun of Parliament.'"[47] Clinton assigned harder and heavier guitar-based songs to Funkadelic, and market-friendlier, brass-based songs to Parliament. In doing so, he discovered that he could keep the musicians' work satisfaction and productivity high by allowing them to experiment under the Funkadelic rubric, while engaging a mainstream market using the Parliament moniker.[48] The P-Funk collective would spin off other performance groups, including Bootsy's Rubber Band, and two all-female bands: the Brides of Funkenstein and the Parlets. The groups benefited from staging concert events during which the many associated bands would appear on one bill. The result was that the P-Funk collective (including Parliament, Funkadelic, and Bootsy's Rubber Band) was one of the top fifteen live acts for 1977.[49]

Wacky wordplay and costume are central to the aesthetic of funk performance. Including the many permutations and compound words crafted from "funk," members of the P-Funk collective took street slang and non-sense words and created a playful lexicon. Performers adopted a similarly eclectic stage attire: capes, sequins and glass jewels, Afros, and sunglasses, although deviations from this style were common and comical, including Garry "Diaperman" Shider's habit of wearing a diaper on stage, Cynthia Robinson's red trumpet, and George Clinton's early practice of cutting a hole through a hotel bed sheet to create an impromptu muumuu. Bootsy Collins put a lot of work into crafting an image for his "Star Child" persona, including custom-made star-shaped sunglasses and bass guitar.[50] Of the style of Parliament, he noted, "First we were straight. Straight suits and clean. Then, when the hippies came, we took it to exaggeration. We wore sheets, we wore the suit bags that our suits came in. And it was funny to us, 'cause we come from a barbershop [the Silk Place, owned by Clinton and the original meeting spot for the band], we knew how to make you look cool, so we never felt uncool. We had fun doing it. Plus, I knew Jimi Hendrix did it."[51]

The high-water mark of funk probably came in 1975, with the nearly simultaneous release of two albums by Parliament: *Chocolate City* and *Mothership Connection*. The cover art for *Chocolate City* depicted the Lincoln and Washington memorials, the Capitol Building, and the White House melting "under the heat of black Technofunk and the increasing 'chocolate' character of the nation's capital."[52] On the song "Chocolate City," Parliament invited blacks and those living in "Vanilla Suburbs" to enter the "Fourth World," led by Clinton's alter ego, Dr. Funkenstein. The lyrics suggest that a transformation to the highest levels of political leadership is possible:

> Now don't be surprised if [Muhammad] Ali is in the White House,
> Reverend Ike [Turner], Secretary of the Treasure,
> Richard Pryor, Minster of Education,
> Stevie Wonder, Secretary of Fine Arts,
> And Miss Aretha Franklin, the first lady.

Appearing onstage in the Funkenstein persona, Clinton emerged from the Mothership Connection spaceship, promising concertgoers transport to a better, funkier future in space.[53] Clinton would temporarily retire in 1980, while facing the economic pressure of the group's enormous expenses and the declining market for music in America. He was arrested, with Sly Stone, the following year for possession of cocaine.[54] The band was officially released from their Warner Brothers contract after the 1981 album *The Electric Spanking of War Babies*.

The heyday of funk included bands like the Bar-Kays, Brick, Cameo, the Isley Brothers, and spin-off bands from the first period, including Bootsy's Rubber Band. Some band members, like Walter "Junie" Morrison, moved from group (Ohio Players), to solo act (Junie), back to join a group (the P-Funk Mob), making hits at each stage. With the rising success of this second generation of funk bands, the music evolved several derivative styles, including the jazz-funk of Grover Washington, Jr., and Roy Ayers, the funk-soul of Earth, Wind & Fire, and, most significantly, the dance funk of K.C. and the Sunshine Band and Chic. Scene-based funk communities sprang up, particularly in "chocolate cities" across the United States, including Dayton, Ohio, leading Brown to call the city "A Land of Funk."[55] Bands hailing from Dayton include the Ohio Players, Slave, Lakeside, Roger, Zapp, Sun, Faze-O, Platypus, Dayton, Shadow, Junie, and Heatwave. The music would have an influence on a range of media, from television shows (Sanford and Son, Soul Train), to movies (e.g., Melvin Van Peebles's *Sweet Sweetback's Baadasssss Song*, which featured a soundtrack by Earth, Wind & Fire), humorists like Flip Wilson and Richard Pryor, and even poets, including Gil Scott-Heron, and writers like Ishmael Reed (and his 1972 novel *Mumbo Jumbo*).

The ascendance of disco was perhaps the largest factor in the demise of funk's creative period. Evidence that funk bands felt challenged by the rise of disco's popularity surfaces in songs like "The UnDisco Kidd" and "Anti-disco." Many funk bands changed their sound, speeding up the tempo and shortening songs to assimilate to the radio-length form; among them were James Brown, who declared himself the "Original Disco Man," the Ohio Players, the Isley Brothers, and Earth, Wind & Fire, each releasing disco singles.

By the 1980s, funk music continued to influence artists but ceased to exist as a viable marketing category within pop music. Funk returned to prominence as an important part of the musical bricolage that forms the backdrop for so much contemporary rap music. James Brown, Sly and the Family Stone, and Parliament/Funkadelic are by far the most sampled artists in rap, all of them funk music superstars.[56]

On Genre Trajectories

Based on the initial case studies of bebop jazz, bluegrass, and old school rap, I expected that all musical trajectories would grow from Avant-garde circles, but just forty-three of the sixty styles began this way, and only sixteen experienced the full AgSIT trajectory. While the three case studies examined in chapter 2 illustrate this trajectory, gospel was explored here as an exemplar case. Next, I analyzed the eight musical styles that began as Scene-based genres and represent an important variation on the AgSIT trajectory. The first five grew out of preexisting domestic Scene-based genres, and the other three were imported from abroad and took on distinctive identities here. I explored tango as the exemplar of the SIT variant trajectory. Finally, nine of the sixty genre trajectories began as Industry-based genres, developed Scene-based genres, and most experienced Traditionalist phases. This sort of trajectory was unanticipated, but a number of cases seemed to manifest this "anomaly." On close inspection I found that most of these genres conspicuously shared their source in the pooled efforts of a few creative musicians paired with arrangers, producers, or industry marketers working in the field of industrial music. Funk was used as an illustration of this pattern.

I noted my surprise at the counterintuitive discovery that several twentieth-century musics emerged as Industry-based genres (IST), which suggests the importance of more carefully analyzing the role of corporations in genre formation and development. Multinational corporations often inhibit musical innovation, because firms constrain artists to produce only marginally different aesthetic content in order to sustain firm profits.[57] How does the increasing role of multinational corporations in the early stages of musical innovation impact the incubation of musics in Scene-based genres?[58] Those in the industrial sector may "prematurely" harvest Scene-based genres in order to profit from them as Industry-based genres. What are the consequences for the aesthetic content and trajectory of such music? It is entirely possible that, in the twenty-first century, corporate control of the music industry may stifle the development of autonomous genres of the sort that flourished in the twentieth century. It is also possible that the myriad technological changes stimulated by digitalization, together with the radical restructuring of corporate organizations, may provide the opportunity for the development of new genres.

In studies of trajectories, scholars often focus on the pace, or number of events during an interval of time, and duration, or the amount of time that elapsed during an event or between events. Both pace and duration are assessed objectively (as a matter of "clock time") and subjectively, as participants perceive duration and event frequency. Further theoretical work should be done on the factors influencing the pace of music development. Does the pace of developing musics have any relationship with the features of the genre form? Is one genre form typically shorter or longer than the others? What are the consequences for a musical style if it remains in one genre form for an unusually long or short period? For example, one might hypothesize that a long period of isolation in a Scene-based genre can allow community members to craft a stronger sense of community—one that they later utilize to sustain control over the genre ideal after large businesses enter the scene. I earlier made this suggestion with respect to tango, and it may hold for other styles within the SIT trajectory. On the other hand, a long period of incubation may suggest that the group does not have the resources required for expansion. Similarly, wide-ranging technological innovations such as digitization or changing institutional arrangements of the entertainment field, such as increased vertical and horizontal integration within the industry and the degree of concentration within the industry, may quicken the transitions between forms or result in the homogenization of cycles across musical styles.

While the pace of development may be one important factor determining the achievement of particular genre forms, the data reveal evidence that three other forces produce deviations within trajectories. As can be seen in table 3.1, nine musics in disparate streams (including alternative country, disco, gangsta rap, jump blues, psychedelic rock, and thrash metal) experienced Avant-garde, Scene-based, and Industry-based genres but have not formed a Traditionalist genre.[59] Three musics, delta blues, doo-wop, and New Orleans jazz, developed a Traditionalist genre without ever having become an Industry-based genre. Eleven musical styles evolved lively Scene-based genres, but never became Industry-based genres nor formed a Traditionalist genre. In the remainder of the chapter, I explore possible causes for the blocked emergence of genre forms.

Inhibiting Factors on Musical Trajectories

As I have noted, a large minority of musical styles did not acquire all the genre forms within their trajectory. Instead, many of them stalled or skipped a genre form. In the remainder of this chapter, I seek to understand the forces that inhibit, derail, or otherwise modify a musical style's transitions within a trajectory. Again, the objective is not to identify necessary or sufficient conditions or to consider counterfactuals, but instead to identify mechanisms of inertia within genre trajectories. Across the many styles of music, I find three significant impediments to trajectory sequences: (1) the absorption of artists into other styles, and musical styles into streams; (2) various forms of resistance to expansion, including both planned obsolescence of some styles and the incompatibility of a style's genre ideal with the promotional machinery of the U.S. record industry, and (3) racist exclusion. I consider each of these in turn, using a different musical style to illustrate each.

Absorption into Other Musics, Other Streams

One of the primary inhibiting factors on the emergence of genre forms is the inclination of musical styles to fold into one another. In some circumstances, the labels, performers, and fans of a style are drawn into a proximal style. Although this tendency did not spell the demise of gospel, many of its performers began to compose soul songs, and later transitioned into major disco acts. Performers working in styles within the electronic/dance stream actually make a habit of leaving behind the genre ideal of older musics in favor of new styles. In this section, I explore the singer-songwriters who lived in Laurel Canyon, California, in the l960s, as they illustrate an extreme example of how such musical migration takes place. The singer-songwriter style of that time and place never developed past an Avant-garde genre because performers were pushed to initiate or join new musical styles.

While most Avant-garde genres wither or develop scenes, from time to time an Avant-garde circle explodes, spawning several new genres. Commonly such Avant-garde genres are labeled by the place they came together, and this was true of the loose collection of singer-songwriter-musicians who gathered in the bucolic canyons above Los Angeles in the late 1960s.[60] Musicians working in and around Los Angeles were drawn to Laurel Canyon for its beauty, affordability, short driving distance to the Sunset Strip, and creative milieu. According to theater and movie producer Judy James: "[The area] had gotten rundown and cheap before us, a lot of garages turned into one-room thises and thats, so there were always actors and musicians. There was a sense of hanging-outness, of finding out what was going on in the music business if you walked up and down Ridpath [Lane]."[61] While scene member singer-songwriter Jackson Browne described the scene as an "amazing tribal life," and Crosby, Stills, Nash & Young singer Graham Nash compared it to "Vienna at the turn of the century or Paris in the 1930s," because "there was a freedom in the air, a sense that we could do anything," most of the artists were either living in houses supported by record labels, or working under contract with one.[62] Many of these artists were represented by Lookout Management, with David Geffen serving as their agent. His business acumen was a critical component in the success of these artists: "generational solidarity was part of the equation, but the company's percentage of its clients' gross compensation was equally compelling." Ron Stone, Joni Mitchell's manager at Lookout Management, said, "During this period of time that this hothouse environment in Laurel Canyon is nurturing all these new and young artists, we were kind of reinventing the business to become more artist-friendly."[63] They did this by relying on album, not singles, sales, by extracting better royalty rates, and by negotiating more creative control for their artists.

Musical artists living in the Canyon in the mid-1960s included the members of the Doors; the Mamas and the Papas; the Byrds; Crosby, Stills, Nash & Young; the Full Tilt Boogie Band; Big Brother and the Holding Company; and solo artists including Joni Mitchell, Jackson Browne, Linda Ronstadt, Leonard Cohen, and Frank Zappa. Living was communal, and music, sex, politics, philosophy, and drugs united members of the community. Like all Avant-garde genres, the artists associated with Laurel Canyon were quite eclectic, but they were united in their dislike of the music of the day and in their determination to, as Judy James put it, "communicate what they were feeling, whether in music or in lyrics."[64]

The blend of sexual, social, and musical politics in Laurel Canyon is typical (if exaggeratedly fecund) of Avant-garde genres, and histories note the embeddedness of artists in networks of love, friendship, and music. One often-recounted chain of associations begins when Elektra Records studio engineer John Haeny awoke one morning to a nude Judy Collins posing for the cover shot of her album *Wildflowers* in the backyard of his Ridpath Lane house. Collins had just broken up with rock journalist Michael Thomas, and Haeny had recently introduced her to singer Stephen Stills. Collins's album included several songs penned by Joni Mitchell, who visited the Haeny house often with her boyfriend, David Crosby. Mitchell soon recorded her first album, *Joni Mitchell*, in the L.A. studio adjacent to where Stephen Stills and Buffalo Springfield were recording theirs. Since Stills was a friend of Crosby's, he was soon asked to play bass guitar on Mitchell's song "Night in the City." Meanwhile, Graham Nash, member of British Invasion band the Hollies, traveled to Laurel Canyon because he'd become close friends with Mamas and the Papas singer Cass Elliot. One night he introduced himself to Mitchell, and less than a year later Nash quit the Hollies, moved in with Mitchell in the Canyon, and started to write and record songs with Crosby and Stills, including two, "You Don't Have to Cry" and "Suite: Judy Blue Eyes," for Judy Collins.[65]

The Laurel Canyon circle did not develop a cohesive Scene-based genre, but their efforts were central to the flowering of several quite distinct musics, including the singer-songwriter style of James Taylor and Joni Mitchell, cosmic country exemplified by the Flying Burrito Brothers, the country rock of the Eagles, and the psychedelic pop of the Mamas and the Papas.[66] In many music communities, the experimental ethos and musical playfulness of performers of the Avant-garde genre form causes some performers and fans to drift toward other styles. The Scene-based genre of these musics includes only those who reach consensus on the emerging musical mode. What makes Laurel Canyon distinctive is that there no single Scene-based style can be argued to have emerged from this community. All of the performers and fans engaged new modes of music, while preserving the history of this generative place and time.

Laurel Canyon is distinctive among Avant-garde genres both for failing to develop into a scene and also for the preservation of its history. These two outcomes are linked: because many of these performers achieved success in other styles, accounts of their Canyon exploits have been preserved. The success of these performers is due, in no small part, to the willingness of record labels to sign artists working outside dominant stylistic conventions—perhaps an Industry-based extension of the period's notable departure from convention. The relatively low overhead cost of record production, in combination with producers' ideologies, resulted in a large number of diverse artists with record company contracts and highly experimental styles. Guitarist Ned Doheny says of the time (and, particularly, of Jackson Browne's experiment with "music ranch" the Paxton Lodge): "In those days you could actually get people to bankroll fantasies and immense fictions."[67] Moreover, the Canyon ethic of collaboration, exploration, and community encouraged performers to jam with one another, and successful performers were able to promote the works of new recruits. For example, David Crosby took an interest in promoting Joni Mitchell to the "Laurel Canyon cognoscenti as aggressively as any agent," inviting them to his house to hear her play; "the upshot was that before her album was completed, Mitchell was the talk of the canyon and, by extension, the record industry."[68]

This isn't to say that the Laurel Canyon years were good to everyone; within a few short years, Jimi Hendrix, Mama Cass Elliot, Jim Morrison, and Janis Joplin would be dead, and many others, like Mamas and the Papas singer John Phillips, had reached the end of their creative peak. Some early members of the circle, like songstress Judee Sill, never earned as much adoration from the public as they had from fellow musicians in the Canyon.

It is hard to imagine that the success of these performers, or the preservation of the Laurel Canyon scene, would have been possible without these unique, historical circumstances, and this may explain why I discovered no other group exactly like it. While Laurel Canyon was uniquely short-lived, it resembles many other musical styles that were absorbed into proximal music communities. For example, outlaw country coalesced in the mid-1970s as a reaction to the growing banality of the Nashville sound, but it represented a long tradition of "hard country music," running from Jimmie Rodgers and Hank Williams to George Jones and Johnny Cash.[69] Led by Waylon Jennings and Willie Nelson, more artists began to flaunt their drug use, write their own songs, chose their record producers, and record with their own road bands away from the large, corporately owned studios. This "outlaw" movement became a genre in 1976 when RCA re-packaged previously released material by Jennings, Nelson, Jessi Colter, and Tompall Glaser as *Wanted: The Outlaws*, which became the first country music album to sell a million copies. Many artists followed in the wake of this success, but the genre has not had a Traditionalist phase. Instead, the outlaw spirit and way of making records animated loosely organized Avant-gardist movements including Texas country, southern rock, alternative country, and hellbilly, among others.[70]

Grunge rock is an example of a musical style that was absorbed into a stream before it developed a Traditionalist genre. Since there is often a gap of five or more years between the collapse of an Industry-based genre and the coalescence of a Traditionalist one, it is possible that such a "revival" may occur in the future. However, community members have put their energies into creating new forms of music, and incorporating grunge into the rock stream. While the exact reasons for this are unclear, it appears that the rapid and sensational popularization of the style, followed by the suicide of guitarist Kurt Cobain, in combination with a shrinking market for rock and recorded music, all contributed to the drift of fans and performers toward stream-related activities or the creation of new Avant-garde forms. This refocusing of energy away from the musical style has resulted in the absence of a Traditionalist genre in grunge.

Grunge is characterized by loud guitar sounds, simple lyrics about pain and alienation, and the lumberjack-inspired costume of its performers and fans.[71] Early performers were said to have been influenced by punk, heavy metal, and an earlier Seattle style called the "Northwest sound," a "protopunk . . . loud, crude, simplistic, and accessible music" that flourished in Seattle from 1958 to 1966.[72] In the Avant-garde period, performers tuned guitars down to play lower notes and performed in the loud, hard style associated with punk music. The lyrical focus on pain, disaffection, and depression is also shared with most punk rock.[73]

The early 1990s have been characterized as "post-grunge" or "post-alternative"[74] owing to the commercial success of bands such as Green Day, grunge "imitators" like Bush, the rise of an alternative rock radio format, and the introduction of the "Best Alternative Performance" category at the Grammy Awards.[75] However, after Kurt Cobain's suicide in 1994, record labels' desire to find the next Nirvana cooled, and rock purchases slowed: the Recording Industry Association of America reported that rock music fell from 32.5 percent of all purchases in 1997 to 25.7 percent in 1998. Within the rock category, alternative rock sales dropped from 11 percent to 9 percent of the U.S. market.

The drying up of resources for grunge and other forms of rock pushed some performers to innovate in different styles and others to devote their energies to the inclusion of grunge within the rock stream.[76] The canonization of music within streams strongly resembles the labor associated with membership in a Traditionalist genre. The goal for Traditionalist genre participants is preserving a musical style's heritage and schooling the rising generation of devotees in the performance techniques, history, and rituals of the genre. Fans and organizations dedicated to perpetuating the style strive to construct its history and canonize performers who exemplify it. This is exactly the work associated with advocating for a style's inclusion in a stream. Thus the history of grunge rock illustrates the shortening of a trajectory owing to the transition of artists into new styles and stream-related activity.

The histories of grunge and Laurel Canyon illustrate the effect that competitive pressures from proximal styles place upon performers. The development of musical trajectories is often inhibited by the seduction of performers, fans, and organizations into peer musics. Several other musical trajectories were affected by the pull of performers toward new styles, including outlaw country, psychedelic rock, and thrash metal. While these musics' trajectories were blocked by the "pull" of other musical styles and streams, some fail to accumulate genre forms because the actions of participants within the circle effectively "push" against the expansion of the community. The persistence of what I call "niche music" is explored in the following section, as the second of three inhibiting factors on the development of musical trajectories.

Niche Music

Among the sixty musical styles examined, eleven evolved lively Scene-based genres, but never became Industry-based genres nor formed a Traditionalist genre. There appear to be two explanations for this. In a few cases, music practitioners place a premium on constant reinvention as a technique to avoid what they see as the corrupting influence of mass markets on musical authenticity. This takes the form of planned obsolescence in dance and electronic musics, and I explore house and techno as examples of this practice. In other cases, the niche community to which the music appeals resists expansion. Death metal is an extreme example. Its often violent, sexist, racist, and homophobic lyrics, as well as the anti-social behavior of devotees, foreclosed the possibility of production and distribution by major music companies.[77] Less extreme examples include free jazz, garage, grindcore, and South Texas polka. I explore South Texas polka as one of several immigrant community musics that fail to morph into hybrid styles with wider appeal, and thus do not develop beyond a Scene-based genre. In both classes, these musical styles remain Scene-based genre forms, and thus both "push" and "pull" factors combine to provide a second cause for deviation from the two musical trajectories.

The electronically based dance musics of house and techno are related in a stream of songs composed with computers and electronic instruments. This stream evolved into a group of at least three hundred styles by 1999 and has since increased in size.[78] The proliferation of styles is a function of the rapidly evolving nature of the music, the marketing strategies of record companies, and the use of substyle names as a gatekeeping device that generates status orders within scenes.[79] The stream is united by the technologies employed in the production of songs, by magazines like *Urb* and *1000 Words* that review multiple styles, and by specialty record stores that sell works across the stream. Advances in technology played a key role: the development of the electronic drum machine, and particularly the modified Roland 303, was crucial in the development of the sounds and techniques associated with these musical styles.[80] The sound layering that characterizes these styles was the result of digital samplers and computer-based sequencers that were developed for sound programming.

House emerged from remnants of the disco scene in black and gay clubs, especially Chicago's Warehouse Club.[81] Resident DJ Frankie Knuckles is credited with shaping its characteristic sound (including the dominant use of electric piano), and the practice of combining pieces of long-playing records into compilations that were pressed into new twelve-inch vinyl records.[82] Chicago's house music was propelled by a metronomic, four-to-the-floor (4/4) beat played between 120 and 140 beats per minute.[83] Rather than reviving disco, Chicago DJs created a new musical form that intensified the attributes critics disliked most about disco: its repetitive sounds, electronic instrumentation, hypersexuality, and drug culture.

While playing at the Warehouse Club, Knuckles transitioned between records in multiple styles, including Philadelphia soul, Euro-disco, and sound effects like running trains.[84] Mixing these elements with rhythm and drum machines, his new compositions were played on a reel-to-reel tape recorder.[85] Knuckles and several other DJs led the scene, offering parties at Chicago clubs including the Warehouse and the Music Box.

The first record, Jesse Saunders and Vince Lawrence's "On and On," was artist-released, and its success resulted in the creation of many "vanity" labels run by local DJs. The musical style attracted a good deal of attention after a group of Chicago DJs performed a set at the New York–based New Music Seminar (NMS) in 1986. The international success of "Love Can't Turn Around" (with Farley "Jackmaster" Funk) brought the music to the attention of British record labels. By the end of the 1980s, house music had been introduced and transformed in Great Britain into a local form called acid house. But in Chicago, house music withered under both endogenous and exogenous pressures. Police began to ban after-hours parties and refused to provide late-night licenses to clubs. Radio station 102.7 WBMX went off the air, sales of house records slowed, and the DJs (who could) left for Europe and New York.[86]

During the mid-1980s, three middle-class black teenagers (Juan Atkins, Derrick May, and Kevin Saunderson) in a Detroit suburb called Belleville created their own form of electronic music, inspired by the electronic sounds in disco, new wave, rap, electro-funk, and, especially, the German group Kraftwerk.[87] Playing in local clubs starting in 1981, the teens crafted the sound of what would later be known as techno. The sound resembled Chicago house, but with a stronger influence of funk and thus more syncopation than the Chicago style. A scene quickly coalesced around the circuit of local parties and the fifty local DJs competing for dominance. Fans were predominantly middle-class, black, and straight. Before long, "ghetto youth from the projects" of Detroit started to attend the parties, and scene members enforced the group's boundaries by posting "the phrase 'no jits' on the flyers—'jit' being short for 'jitterbug,' Detroit slang for gangsta."[88] According to DJ May, "It was the beginning of the end. That's when the guns started popping up at the parties, and fights started happening. By '86, it was over."[89] This was the year that British record label scouts came to Detroit, searching for new talent. The scene migrated to Europe, and many performers found success abroad using a modified musical style: faster in tempo, and increasingly instrumental and synthesized.[90] The U.S.-based techno scene was over.

Dance music, like house, resists expansion into Industry-based genres in part because of the planned obsolescence of the music. The concept of "planned obsolescence" describes a condition in which producers intend that objects will be discarded by users before their life expectancy has been attained. Two products that are often subject to planned obsolescence are fashion and automobiles. We tend to discard clothes and cars before the end of their functional life. Musical styles within the stream of electronic/dance music exemplify this condition. Kembrew McLeod quoted one DJ who quipped, "I sometimes pull out records that are two years old, but not often."[91] This stands in stark opposition to a music like rock where recordings that are two, three, or even four decades old still sell so many copies that they have to be removed from *Billboard* magazine's list of top-selling albums to enable the list to retain its focus on "new music."[92]

The planned obsolescence of musical styles within the electronic/dance stream is partially a function of how the genre ideals of these styles conceptualize authenticity. Within the scene, being a fan of music or wearing clothing styles that have been discovered by mainstream media is "the kiss of death."[93] Being seen as passé and/or receiving accusations of having "sold out" to commercial interests are so universally loathsome that DJs cycle through multiple names and logos over the course of their careers.[94] Strategies of planned obsolescence are also a means by which hard-core scene members retain control over defining and defending the borders of the community. Knowledge of and facility with the variety of musical names and styles is possible only for the most committed members. This specialized knowledge defines the boundary of this social world, just as it has been found to do in other creative fields.[95]

In addition to the planned obsolescence of the music, electronic/dance styles have not progressed into Industry-based genres because the performers are relatively "faceless," and record companies have had difficulty marketing them through the traditional promotional machinery.[96] The depersonalization of the music is an important convention of production: DJs play the music of other artists, and often do so anonymously or under pseudonyms. The few artists who have had chart success within this stream are those who had marketable images, including the Prodigy, an

English group, and Madonna's 1998 collaboration with William Orbit, *Ray of Light*. Most aficionados would argue that these artists worked on the margins of the electronic stream, citing both musical and stylistic reasons for their exclusion.

Electronic/dance communities subsist as Scene-based genres by associating authentic scene membership with attitudes and behaviors that are antithetical to expansion, while other musical styles resist the promotional machinery because they are tightly linked to ethnic or immigrant identity. South Texas polka is one example of the latter.

The polka emerged in eastern Bohemia during the 1820s as a dance form for couples.[97] With its even (2/4) time, it was probably influenced by the Polish musical form *krakowiak*.[98] The central and eastern European styles of polka were brought to America by immigrants and attained Scene-based genres in four locations where these immigrants settled in great numbers: Chicago, Cleveland, Minneapolis, and southern Texas. Each of these four regions developed distinctive artistic communities and styles of polka. The South Texas polka Scene-based genre emerged from German and Bohemian immigrant communities in the late 1880s. By 1900, most social gatherings within these communities featured polkas among other social dances. Not long thereafter, a Texan form of the *nortena* music of northern Mexico merged with older polka styles and a new music called *conjunto* emerged.[99]

In the 1880s and for four decades thereafter, South Texas polka musicians relied upon community organizations to provide space for performances. According to one estimate, eastern European immigrants built as many as one hundred lodges, pavilions, or society halls during this period.[100] Polka musicians scheduled performances on weekend nights in the Czecho-Slovak Benevolent Society (CSPS) or the Slavonic Benevolent Order of the State of Texas (SPJST), and entire families would pay fifty cents to dance until late in the night. The music included polkas as one of many performance styles, including *besedas*, waltzes, and schottisches. There is no consensus about the date when these events began to be staged in dance halls and other commercial establishments, but it appears to have happened during the 1920s or early 1930s. Following a national trend, polka and other ethnic musics were featured at various expositions, including the San Antonio Bicentennial of 1931 and the Texas

Centennial of 1936.[101] During the Depression years, radio stations featured ethnic broadcasts, and "Czech hour" in South Texas often included polka performances. By 1930, as many as one hundred Czech bands were active in the region, including Adolph and the Boys, and the Patek family band from Shiner, Texas.[102]

The music has persisted as a Scene-based genre, played regionally and supported by a small group of dedicated performers. There is a Texas Polka Music Association Hall of Fame, and a Texas Polka Music Association survived for most of the 1990s (1991–98). Both organizations were initiated by the same man, who also maintained the *Texas Polka News*, a newsletter on past and present polka musicians, until his death in 1998. Texas boasts several other organizations, including the Texas Po.L.K. of A. (Polka Lovers Klub of America), which has several score of chapters in Texas, and dance clubs supporting local musicians. There are a number of large festivals where the music is played, although none is solely dedicated to South Texas polka. There is also a stretch of highway I-10 between Houston and San Antonio known as "Polka Road." Although traces of a Traditionalist genre exist, including heritage organizations and festivals, they do not serve the function of supporting large-scale academic research on musical history, nor are these exclusive venues for the music's perpetuation.

South Texas polka demonstrates features found within most immigrant music communities. Many immigrant groups arrive and settle into ethnic neighborhoods.[103] These neighborhoods include musicians trained in popular styles from their native land, community members who share their tastes, and local institutions eager to provide space for events that will maintain cultural traditions. The barriers to expansion of this taste community may be less strong in cases where the immigrant group grows in numbers, or the enclave expands geographically. The German-Bohemian communities in Texas appear to have been particularly slow to expand, and included only twelve thousand people by 1920.[104] Their assimilation was slow as well, a feature attributed to their isolation in rural areas and successful development of self-sustaining communities.[105]

The maturation of immigrant enclaves often brings with it financial success for some occupants, and status mobility can cause the erosion of some traditions and adoption of others. The drift of immigrant groups toward popular styles was recognized decades ago by sociologist Herbert Gans. Of such assimilation pressures he had this to say:

When the immigrants and their children became upwardly mobile and wanted a taste culture of greater sophistication and higher
status, they found it easier to choose from American culture than
to upgrade the immigrant low culture or to import higher status
culture from their country of origin. Some Jewish taste culture was
Americanized, but peasant taste cultures, for example Polish, Italian, [and] Greek, have virtually disappeared except for traditional
foods and religious practices—and a few dances and songs which
are performed at occasional ethnic festivals.[106]

It is by and large the case that the children of immigrants (and, especially, their grandchildren) forsake the language and other cultural habits
of their parents, including musical tastes.[107] Therefore, a combination of
factors explains the failure of South Texas polka to grow beyond a Scene-
based genre: social and musical isolation, local support for immigrant
musical styles, and the failure of inheritors to advance or hybridize the
music during the assimilation process. To the extent that other immigrant
communities face similar circumstances, we might expect polka to function as a model of cultural development.

However, the temptation to generalize the features of South Texas
polka to other immigrant musics should be checked, and two counterex-
amples serve the purpose. As I noted above, South Texas polka mixed with
nortena styles and produced a new music, *conjunto*, by the mid-1920s.[108]
While polka survived as a popular, regional style, *conjunto* captured larger
audiences. Another music, western swing, was hived off from the musical traditions of West Texan, white immigrants. While *conjunto* emerged
from a community-level exchange among Mexican, Mexican American,
and Bohemian musicians, western swing was the product of European
fiddle and guitar music made by the black and Anglo itinerant workers
in Texas.[109]

Both *conjunto* and western swing represent hybridized music, styles
that combine immigrant and host community aesthetics. These hybridized forms had some success outside ethnic enclaves, as one would expect,
given that they emerge from and speak to multiple constituencies. South
Texas polka, on the other hand, remained a local phenomenon, despite its
similarities to polkas produced in Cleveland, Minneapolis, and Chicago.
The social closure of audience communities from the surrounding social

system appears to be a critical factor determining the trajectory of its music. Preliminary evidence suggests that music made in what Mackun described as "fringe" or "transitional" communities[110] (those with fewer than 40 percent of families from an ethnic group) differs from that created in communities with "solid boundaries," including more than 40 percent of families from the same background. In the former case, we would expect a trajectory that is not inhibited from developing an Industry-based genre, just as I have demonstrated was the case with *conjunto* and western swing. In the latter case, of communities with solid boundaries, South Texas polka may be a better guide to predicting the trajectory of the community's music.

Music trajectories stall and fail to produce Industry-based and Traditionalist genre forms if community members engage in strategies to avoid mainstream popularity, or produce music so strongly associated with specific community ideals that it fails to attract outside listeners and performers. Although it may produce the same result, this cause is distinct from situations in which the racist organization of music production prevents music from reaching potential audiences. Racist exclusion is the final cause for the deviation of musical styles from the two trajectories, and I explore it in the following section.

The Racist Organization of Musical Production

In the discussion of grunge rock, I demonstrated that an Industry-based genre does not necessarily terminate in the emergence of a Traditionalist movement. Similarly, Traditionalist genres do not need to depend on an existing Industry-based phase in order to flower. Three musics, delta blues, doo-wop, and New Orleans jazz, developed a Traditionalist genre without ever having become an Industry-based genre. I attribute this to particular features of the racialized system for music distribution in the first half of the twentieth century, a system that limited the accessibility of black music to many Americans. Beginning in the third quarter of the twentieth century both delta blues and New Orleans jazz experienced revivals as Traditionalist genres.[111] In order to understand how racialized production systems block the access of musical communities to widespread distribution, I consider the case of New Orleans jazz. I contrast this with gospel, which relied almost exclusively on black-owned and -operated production and distribution systems, and, as a result, was able to realize an Industry-based genre. In the contrast, we see that it was not the case that mass audiences for black music did not exist in the early twentieth century, but rather that a racist production system prevented them from hearing the music except when it was provided by a parallel production system supported by, and designed for, black Americans. This then leads me to investigate the success of rap music, which had its origins at black-owned independent and small record labels, but came to be embraced (in a limited economic sense) within the mainstream mass media. The history of racial organization of musical production in the United States is, therefore, a series of stages whereby black-owned industries are created and eventually come to facilitate the mainstream popularity of particular music.

The music designated here as "New Orleans jazz" is also known as Dixieland jazz, hot jazz, or early jazz, and emerged in Louisiana during the opening years of the twentieth century. The style reflects the cultural mélange found in the city of New Orleans: a blend of brass band marching songs, French quadrilles, ragtime, and blues. The emphasis on collective, polyphonic improvisation and its definitive sound are created by a front line of trumpet, cornet, trombone, and clarinet and a rhythm section of piano, guitar, banjo, drums, double bass, and tuba. The term "Dixieland" was widely used to describe the form in the wake of the first million-selling hit records by the Original Dixieland Jass Band in 1917, although Louis Armstrong's All-Stars may be more commonly associated with the music. The rise of swing in the 1930s ended the careers of many early jazz players, but the music experienced a revival in the 1940s and 1950s. New Orleans jazz is an early example of racist exclusion from Industry-based genres.

The New Orleans jazz style had coalesced by the time trumpet player Oscar Celestin led the Tuxedo Brass Band, around 1910. Some historians trace the music to 1897 and the cornet playing of professional barber Charles "Buddy" Bolden.[112] By 1901, Bolden was listed in the city directory as a musician, although it appears that most early jazz performers worked manual labor or in the trades in addition to performing music.[113] Early performers, including Bolden, played multiple styles of music including ragtime, quadrilles, waltzes, "sweet music, and . . . nothing but the blues," according to bassist George Foster.[114] Steadily working musicians heard each other's music, drifted in and out of each other's bands, and were linked through kinship and neighborhood ties.[115]

The music is said to have flourished in Storyville, a neighborhood dominated by nightclubs, saloons, brothels, barrelhouses, bistros, and "Negro dance halls," all of which hosted jazz performances. By many accounts, jazz players disliked playing performances in Storyville establishments because the working conditions were miserable and the pay was low, and so they received the news of Storyville's closure in 1917 as a mixed blessing.[116] Artists like Buddy Petit, Kid Rena, and Lee Collins continued to play in roadhouses, in vaudeville shows, on riverboats and lake boats on Lake Pontchartrain, and in little towns in Mississippi, Alabama, Georgia, Florida, and Louisiana.[117] Like scores of other African Americans in the war years, jazz musicians—among them, Jelly Roll Morton, Freddie Keppard and the Creole Band, Sidney Bechet, King Oliver, and Louis Armstrong—migrated out of the South. Although some headed west to Los Angeles or east to New York City, most moved up the Mississippi River, first to Memphis and St. Louis, then to Kansas City and, finally, Chicago.

The combination of wartime migration and the closure of Storyville establishments meant that New Orleans failed to retain those artists who would become the most famous and well-paid early jazz artists. These migrant players developed Scene-based jazz communities in cities up the Mississippi River, and by the 1920s distinctive Chicago and Kansas City styles joined New Orleans in the newly formed jazz stream. Musicians appear to have followed a common migratory pattern: a core group of performers settled in a new location and soon called for their compatriots to join them. The ties born of family and neighborhood connections "as well as their familiarity with each other's playing style, kept the New Orleans musicians close to each other when they began to leave the city to pick up their careers in other places."[118]

It was during this period that the word "jazz" was first used to describe a style of music, although there is considerable confusion about its first use.[119] It appears to have been a derogatory adjective used to describe "negro music" in Chicago, although a white New Orleans band, the Original Dixieland Jass Band, was the first successful group to embrace the term. The first nonderogatory use of the term in the New Orleans press was an April 1933 article in *Louisiana Weekly* titled "Excavating Local Jazz," written by a local, black elementary school teacher who clearly believed its history had already been entombed.[120]

The growth of the music was stunted by the force of a moralizing campaign. White bandleaders, politicians, and music critics argued that jazz was a degenerate form of music, and hazardous, especially to the young. The music was identified as "the direct cause of heart attacks, drunkenness, and neural deterioration, but its effect on morals was most often stressed."[121] In news reports, the music was blamed for "the heart attack of an elderly classical cornetist, an unfavorable trade balance between the United States and Hungary, the waning quality of Italian tenors, the frightening of bears in Siberia, and the decline of modern civilization."[122] Musicians and city officials declared it was both hazardous and unmusical. For example, while explaining his decision on a contract dispute over the copyright to "Livery Stable Blues," Chicago judge George A. Carpenter said, "I venture to say that no living human being could listen to that result on the phonograph and discover anything musical on it."[123] The same moralists supported Prohibition to attack the growing power of new immigrant groups, including urban Catholics and eastern Europeans. They simply extended their campaign to African American migrants in the post–World War I period by denigrating jazz. Antijazz activists pressed to outlaw performances, and statutes prohibiting the public performance of jazz were enacted in some communities, including Cleveland, Detroit, Kansas City, Omaha, Philadelphia, and fifty other cities. This activity sharply contrasted with reporting in the black newspaper the *Chicago Defender*, which championed jazz, a position consistent with their editorial mission of countering antiblack discrimination with praise for the products of African American culture.[124]

Although the Original Dixieland Jass Band had significant success with recordings produced in 1917 and 1918, the music as a whole never entered an Industry-based genre. The racial segregation of record production and distribution is largely to blame. Despite the fact that white and nonwhite bands worked in close proximity in New Orleans, racially mixed ensembles were quite rare, and the groups tended to play different styles, with whites sticking primarily to martial music and waltzes. The segregation of bands in jazz persisted until well into the swing era. While so-called Negro bands did record in the early 1920s, they were confined to "race record" labels, distributed exclusively to black consumers. The advent of radio put competitive pressures on recording companies to expand their audiences, and music created by and for black Americans was produced by the considerable number of small labels that arose in the years of the First World War.[125] Okeh Records was the first to create a race series in 1921, and many labels soon followed suit, including Paramount (1922), Columbia (1923), Vocalion (1926), and Victor (1927).

New Orleans jazz remained a Scene-based genre until a flowering of interest in the late 1930s stimulated the growth of a Traditionalist genre. In May of 1938, Alan Lomax, then director of the Folklore Division of the Library of Congress, initiated a twelve-hour-long recording of Jelly Roll Morton's history of jazz music, including an account of his early years spent in New Orleans. The Second World War interrupted the revival of interest in the music, but in 1945 independent label Circle Records (owned by jazz critic and art historian Rudi Blesh) began to release these recordings. This was followed by new recordings by musicians from the Scene-based period, including Bunk Johnson, George Lewis, and Jim Robinson. According to one eyewitness, the impetus behind these recordings and performances was "to preserve and document a musical style, rather than achieve any kind of economic success."[126] Live performances by these artists generated national press coverage and moved poet William Carlos Williams to describe them in verse.[127] In New Orleans, artists and local entrepreneurs invested in a vacant art gallery on St. Peter Street and called it "Preservation Hall," reflecting its mission as a venue that preserved New Orleans jazz music. This preservationist spirit informed the establishment of the jazz Archive at Tulane University (1958), the Jazz Museum (1961), and the first Jazzfest (1968). As in other Traditionalist genres, music historians, academics, and fans scrambled to collect and preserve memorabilia and stories from the Scene-based New Orleans jazz genre.[128]

Racialized debates around jazz characterized it from the early years of the music, when "Uptown" black and Creole of Color bands vied against "Downtown" white and Creole bands for local renown. The discrimination players experienced in Chicago and other northern cities, compounded by the attention paid to all-white bands, further exemplified these tensions. The Traditionalist genre of New Orleans jazz became a venue for explicit conversations about the power of race and racism within the musical community. An academic account from 1973 captures the way in which Traditionalist genre members grappled with these racial dimensions of the Scene-based genre. Describing the emergence of musicians who could play in Bolden's style, Buerkle and Barker relate that the dissolution of Civil War and Spanish-American War military and naval bands was the key to providing used musical instruments to the "Uptown blacks" of New Orleans:

> The Uptown blacks, fresh off the plantation, gradually gained possession of many of these European instruments. They really didn't have anyone to teach them or, especially to *tell them the official limits of their horns*, so they just blew them their own way. The tonalities linked with their African rhythms, were combined to produce Buddy Bolden's sound. They just played like they felt and sang. (Emphasis in the original)[129]

In this account, the graduated racial differences so characteristic of New Orleans (including quadroons, Creoles, and Creoles of Color) were collapsed into a single category, and blackness was associated with Uptown neighborhoods, pathologized as spaces of sociocultural and racial dysfunction. The "Uptown blacks" are described as instinctual bearers of African rhythms, as if musical rhythm were a genetic trait. Traditionalist academics had difficulty ennobling the genre without invoking essentializing narratives of racial consciousness or musical talent. In making arguments such as this one, scholars understated the importance of European-derived musical elements in early jazz, including their melodic, harmonic, and structural attributes.[130] The romanticization of early jazz emphasized that it should sound like African American church music or field songs.[131] The claims of white performers in the Traditionalist period to have "revived" black jazz were reminiscent of early all-white bands like the Original Dixieland Jass Band or Paul Whiteman, crowned the "King of Jazz" by 1923: "As one would expect there was a great deal of bitterness in the veteran black Jazzmen as they began to notice this new chapter of their 'invisibility' unfolding before them."[132] And, as Grazian[133] found with the blues clubs in Chicago, tourists seeking to hear "authentic" New Orleans jazz, in places like Preservation Hall, expect "to hear jazz played by musicians with a particular racial composition; nobody would expect to find old white men playing at Preservation Hall."[134]

The history of New Orleans jazz demonstrates how important larger social structures are in determining the course of music genre trajectories. In this case, the Traditionalist genre of New Orleans jazz is fueled by racially essentialist claims about early performers. Rather than repeat the earlier claims about African Americans' "natural" savagery, rhythm, and rampant sexuality, the new generation of "enlightened" listeners provided explanations of jazz greatness premised on blacks' unequaled "natural" musical talent, dignity, and authenticity. The later proponents of jazz shared the same essentializing impulse as their earlier counterparts, but cloaked it in the language of tolerance and respect.

While New Orleans jazz failed to achieve an Industry-based genre form, other musical styles were able to do so, as I have noted in the case of gospel. Gospel emerged in the second decade of the twentieth century, in the black neighborhoods of Chicago. Reverend Thomas A. Dorsey is credited with its invention, influenced by earlier praise music composers including C. Albert Tindley. Dorsey worked as a choir director and was a prolific composer, writing several standards of the form including "Precious Lord, Take My Hand," which years later became a million-record seller for Elvis Presley. Although he clashed with the existing choir director and was disdained by members of the highly regarded Senior Choir, Dorsey and his music were successful in drawing into the church Chicago's booming population of recent migrants from the South.[135]

Among the members of the "school" growing around Dorsey, perhaps the most important was a young southern migrant named Sallie Martin.[136] She joined Dorsey's choir in 1932, despite not knowing how to read music, nor being an exceptional singer: "Sallie can't sing a lick," Dorsey once said.[137] Sallie's genius lay both in her unrefined but passionate delivery, and her exceptional business acumen. It was Sallie who helped Dorsey organize choirs to sing his music, and who built his sheet music business into an empire.[138] While the sluggish religious publishing industry relied on sales of hymnals, sheet music was a successful commodity in the popular music industry. Sallie focused on sheet music sales and created what was "for many years the largest African-American-owned gospel publishing company in America."[139]

Dorsey and Martin promoted their music by traveling a "gospel highway" they had created: a network of churches and auditoriums that would host gospel performances. Dorsey and Martin charged a small fee for admission to these events and sold sheet music at the concerts for a nickel a song.[140] Dorsey and his singers traveled the gospel highway without rest from 1932 to 1944; Mahalia Jackson joined them between 1939 and 1944. Within a year of Sallie's debut, "gospel churches especially trained to sing

Dorsey's tunes began sprouting all over Chicago's South Side."[141] Sallie and Dorsey would soon establish gospel choruses in all the major cities of the South and Midwest.

While Jackson remained firmly rooted in the gospel tradition until her death in 1972, Sam Cooke transitioned from the hugely popular gospel group the Soul Stirrers into recording pop music by 1957. His first single, "Lovable" was recorded by Specialty Records and released under the name Dale Cook; since it sold only twenty-five thousand copies, Specialty released Cooke. His producer retained the unreleased material from the recording session and later released "You Send Me," one of the cuts from those early sessions.[142] The song was a hit. The massive popularity of Cooke's music, fueled by his unparalleled productivity, made gospel-inflected R&B attractive to artists who might otherwise have remained within the praise music tradition.

The success of Cooke's recordings drew attention to the music that had been a lightning rod for controversies over "integrated music" since Roosevelt's inaugural gala. As a focal point for the integrationist cause, and with its legitimacy as "godly music," gospel was in a unique position to retain some of its independence from white-owned mass entertainment companies. And because of Sallie Martin's work to create and sustain a sheet music business, Dorsey and his collaborators strategically positioned themselves to generate a parallel, black-owned system of musical production. Jackson attributes this to Dorsey's exposure to the race record industry while he was working as a blues musician.[143] These experiences illuminated the damaging effect that profit motivation can have on community morality: "with the help of Sallie Martin, he turned instead to a different form of commerce—entrepreneurial black capitalism—which he saw as offering the advantages of modest profits and commercial distribution while remaining tied to the values and goals of the communities it served." Dorsey would later use the success of black entrepreneurship in gospel music sales to champion the genre above other African American musical forms: "hear me and hear me well," he said, "gospel singing; gospel songs; gospel song books and gospel stores where they sell gospel songs; has been lucrative and has brought in more money to many more people than the blues."[144]

Seemingly despite its location in the praise music stream, gospel resembles most popular music styles in its progression across genre forms. The trajectory of gospel music should be viewed as both typical and exceptional among twentieth-century American popular musical styles. It is typical of the trajectory followed by most music in that it grew from an Avant-garde genre into a Scene-based, then an Industry-based, and finally a Traditionalist form. On the other hand, gospel is exceptional in that it relied on black-owned and -operated production and distribution systems, and exists within the praise music stream. Only rap music has been comparable in its ability to sustain a viable black-owned market niche within the field of production.[145]

On October 13, 1979, "Rapper's Delight" by the Sugar Hill Gang became the first rap single to enter the *Billboard* R&B Singles chart—it would later peak at number four. Sugarhill Records, the independent label on which the single was recorded, was the leading producer of rap music in the Top 100 charts from 1979 to 1983. Independent labels like Sugarhill owned 84 percent of the charting rap singles over these four years.[146] The initial demand for contracts by rap artists was fielded by Harlem independents whose directors were familiar names from the previous three decades of the city's black music. At New York's rap center were Bobby Robinson (Enjoy Records), Danny Robinson (Holiday Records), Sylvia Robinson (Sugarhill Records),[147] and Paul Winley (Winley Records). The handful of songs owned by major labels in these early years of the musical style were all released on label affiliates reflecting owners' lack of confidence in the sales potential of the new music, and a desire to buffer themselves from the legal and social risks associated with endorsing "black street music." Carmen Ashhurst-Watson, president of Def Jam Records' parent company, Rush Communications, claimed:

> The people who were involved on the business end of early rap music were people who were, in fact, frightening, whether they were just sort-of frightening, or pretty rough-looking guys, or very tough. They [mainstream record company executives] also found the images of the artists frightening. Rappers were not tuxedo-wearing black guys, they dressed like working-class kids—which translated into looking like the black guys you feared would mug you on the street.[148]

Major label entrepreneurs desired to profit from rap, but feared the people involved in making the music and those who would criticize it. It was only after more than thirty independently recorded rap songs charted among *Billboard*'s Top 100 that major firms began to record rap songs—and even then they did so only on affiliated labels.

By 1984, rap was experiencing increasingly broad popularity. The number of independent labels recording rap music more than doubled between 1979 and 1987, but their share of the market decreased from 84 percent to 60 percent of the chart.[149] This was due, in large part, to the increasing interest and success of artists on major-affiliated labels; a full 93 percent of rap singles released by the majors were distributed via an affiliated label.[150] Most of these affiliates were black-run; the big labels hired black executives to run these affiliates and divisions, and sometimes recruited leadership from the rap independents.

A number of black-owned labels (B-Boy, Def Jam, Bust It, Tommy Boy, Luke, and Death Row Records) were established in the 1980s and 1990s for the purpose of recording rap music. The major labels didn't wrest total control from independents; they wisely resisted as "it became apparent that the independent labels had a much greater understanding of the cultural logic of hip hop and rap music."[151] Since the decentralization of the recording industry, major labels had been allowing independent and affiliated labels to do the work of identifying and harvesting new and innovative music (as I noted earlier, this open system of production was believed to sustain musical diversity, and profits). Rap labels were seen as having a familiarity with aesthetic and musical nuances of successful music, as well as having the social networks that support new trends. Perhaps most importantly,

> The existence of local ties also invigorates the claims to authenticity for artists and entrepreneurs. Videos feature rappers against the background of their 'hood, references are made to local cultural landmarks or events, and alongside extras on the video, friends and acquaintances are featured.[152]

The importance of "local" or "street" knowledge was affirmed by marketing campaigns and in the words of rappers. Consider, for example, what rapper and label owner Heavy D said about his intentions: "I'm not going to get rich holding the mike and writing lyrics. I've got to start owning a lot of some of this shit here. That's why I just started my own record label."[153] Heavy D was not alone: rappers Sean "Puffy" Combs, Queen Latifah, Eazy E, and Master P all started their own record labels. The value of authentic, local knowledge (however contrived it actually was) preserved this black-owned niche of the music industry, and rap culture cultivated, celebrated, and supported black entrepreneurialism.

Emphasizing the ability of gospel and rap artists and entrepreneurs to create and sustain black businesses in the entertainment industry should not come at the expense of criticizing a system that has traditionally provided two avenues for success: the commodification of stereotypes for major label profits, and the segregation of black-owned spaces for production, distribution, and reception. The system is fixed such that black artists face a differential opportunity structure, where self-expression can determine their financial, cultural, and social segregation, and commercial success may depend upon self-abnegation. The latter is arguably true for nonblack artists, who certainly account for others' tastes in the creation of their work. But white artists needn't traffic in racial stereotyping in order to do so.

Those musical styles that did not acquire all the genre forms within the AgSIT or IST trajectories share in common at least one of three forces that inhibit, derail, or otherwise modify a musical style's transitions within a trajectory. The objective of this analysis was not to identify necessary and sufficient conditions for inertia within a trajectory, but rather to provide some preliminary hypotheses to guide future research on the topic. I explored three causes for the blocked emergence of genre forms. First, I examined the absorption of performers and fans into proximal styles, including both Laurel Canyon artists and post-grunge musicians, and into streams, as in the case of grunge rock. While these musics were weakened by the "pull" of other styles, some musical styles failed to accumulate genre forms because the community resisted expansion. While death metal's violent, sexist, racist, and homophobic lyrics foreclosed the possibility of major label distribution, some immigrant and dance music styles (including South Texas polka, house, and techno) are simply incompatible with the promotional machinery of the U.S. recording industry. Some participants in Scene-based genres also specifically scorn "popular" music, like the many performers in electronic/dance music (e.g., house and techno) who engaged in practices that ensured the planned obsolescence of the style. Finally, I explored the consequences of racist exclusion for musical trajectories. The reluctance of major labels to produce and release gospel and rap music provided both musical communities the opportunity to create and sustain a black-owned niche within the industry. New Orleans jazz, on the other hand, experienced a much more typical confrontation with racism in music production, weathering the force of a moralizing campaign with explicit racist overtones, only to find that the same essentializing impulse lay behind the music's resurgence as a Traditionalist genre, several decades later.

Conclusion

In this chapter, I began with a review of two trajectories that typify contemporary American popular music. Two-thirds of the sampled musics started in Avant-garde circles; most generated support from local people and institutions, and attracted the attention of mass marketers; and after a period of international visibility many became the domain of those seeking to preserve the traditional genre ideal.[154] A smaller number of musics emerged within scenes, and became Industry-based genres; some of these became Traditionalist genres. Perhaps the greatest surprise was that nine musics emerged within the music industry, as artists, producers, or marketers seized the opportunity to innovate, and several of these later developed Scene-based and Traditionalist forms. Noting that many music communities do not acquire all the genre forms within a trajectory, I next identified three causes for the blocked development of musical styles. These were (1) the absorption of particular styles into proximal styles and streams, (2) aesthetic and social factors that prevent the expansion of the musical scene to new audiences and performers, and (3) racist exclusion. To illustrate each cause, I explored the history of several musical communities, including gospel, tango, Laurel Canyon, grunge, house and techno, South Texas polka, New Orleans jazz, and rap.

I have focused on identifying developmental sequences for musical genres and the illumination of those processes. The causal mechanisms that aid genres as they transition from one genre form to the next were explicitly not my concern.[155] However, the identification of necessary and sufficient conditions for the production of new genre forms will promote rich and interesting questions. Certainly, my discovery of the IST trajectory points to the ability of industrial workers to produce innovative aesthetic material. However, there is a darker side to the impact of multinational corporations on musical innovation, where firms constrain artists to produce only marginally different aesthetic content in order to sustain firm profits.[156] One might join this work with the study of genre formation to examine how the increasing role of multinational corporations in the early stages of musical innovation impacts the incubation of musics in Scene-based genres. It is likely that they may "prematurely" harvest Scene-based genres in order to profit from them as Industrial genres. What, then, are the consequences for the aesthetic content and trajectory of those musical styles?

This leads into a larger set of questions concerning pace and duration of sequential change. In all cases, Avant-garde genres are short-lived, but the other genre forms vary significantly in duration. What are the consequences for a music if it remains in one genre form for an unusually long or short period? One might hypothesize that a long period of isolation in the Scene-based phase can allow members to craft a stronger sense of solidarity—one that they later utilize to sustain control over the genre ideal after large businesses begin to exploit the style. New, complex techniques of analyzing sequences have recently been introduced in the social sciences and may be helpful in the study of music trajectories.[157] For example, common dance traditions among communities of English morris dancers have been identified through the study of the sequences of dance steps.[158] If it were possible to get high-quality data on the pace at which music communities acquired various resources, a very sophisticated model of genre trajectories could be developed. With these sequences, and a careful measurement of contextual influences, we would be able to generate a predictive model of musical development.

Much writing on genre emergence focuses on the ingenuity and creativity of particular artists, but key artists and cultural entrepreneurs are often familiar with the development of earlier musics. These stories are likely to have influenced their actions as they set out to form a new music. The members of some musical circles intend to imitate the choices of their predecessors, emulating the aesthetic achievements of those they respect. In other cases, they seek the critical acclaim other artists attract. In rare but important situations, artistic circles disavow other bands as models, particularly those against whom they position their genre ideal. Rival genres are among the most important elements in a genre's environment, and, as I noted above, contentious battles between rival genres (like that between funk and disco, or disco and rock) often importantly shape Scene-based musics. However, we know very little of the role played by these frictions in the development of genres. It could be that competition over resources produces similarities between musics. Seen in this light, the similarities of trajectories recounted in this chapter may be the product of imitation, whether strategic or unintentional.

The dynamics of opportunity structures seem to dictate that when a dominant genre in a field is aging, only one of the contending new genres will be able to take its place. Is this process inevitable, and what happens to the other contestants? Do they get absorbed by the winning genre, do they simply wither, or do they consolidate their strengths as Scene-based or Traditionalist genres and survive on the margins of commercial music?

Research by a number of authors shows that discrimination against marginalized elements of our society has had a complex influence on genre formation and trajectories.[159] Most U.S. musics have emerged seemingly despite ethnoracial discrimination against their practitioners. Most of the remaining genres have come out of the problems and aspirations of marginal elements of our society, most prominently youth, immigrants, women, and those from impoverished areas including regions of the South and urban slums. By way of contrast, the lifestyle and complaints of wealthy white men have not been the inspiration for the development of any of my sample of commercial genres. There are also a great number of minority groups that haven't contributed to our mainstream musical culture, in spite of their size or richness. These include Jewish music, Nordic music, and Romany music. The fetishization of African American expressive culture, dominant but marginalized before the civil rights movement, has now been made explicit, and is acknowledged by critics and academics as the source for the development of so many musics. Contrasting this history with the similar discrimination against, but lack of musical interest in, other minority groups (e.g., Jews, Latinos), I note that racial dynamics focus and constrain musical genre formation.

The viability of the two types of trajectories deserves comment. Genres within the IST trajectory that emerged out of the interaction of creative artists and sympathetic industry officials occurred in companies including Sun Records, Atlantic, Stax, Motown, and Chess that, at the time, were independent companies and not divisions of a multinational corporation. Is their organizational freedom and intimate contact with the relevant market necessary for the generation of genres in an industrial context? If so, the increasing consolidation of the industry does not bode well for genre formation in the IST trajectory. Likewise, with the amount of detailed market research on active music fans and the rapidity with which new trends are incorporated into the mix of music they offer, will it become more difficult for genres to incubate as we have described they do in the AgSIT trajectory?

Evidence of impediments to genre formation indicates the important role that shifting social, political, economic, legal, and cultural factors play in conditioning the actions of genre stakeholders. Prosperity, war, depression, ethnic rivalries, gender relations, demographic shifts, and culture wars shape the course of genre histories. Macrosocial factors may be responsible for the remarkable creativity and productivity of musicians in the postwar United States. The country emerged from the Second World War with its industrial infrastructure intact. Most of the key inventions in radio, television, and record making (and the electric guitar), were made in the United States. The newfound wealth of teenagers in the 1950s fueled the explosive growth of the market for commercial music, and the growing worldwide comprehension of the English language made U.S. commercial music popular and emulated elsewhere. Finally, the growing popularity around the world of the music's three-minute song format, working within the confines of an eight-note scale, disciplined the freer sonorities and meter of folk musics around the world. The newfound ease of musical creation, distribution, and consumption made possible by digitalization and the new media has fueled the development of diverse genres.

Will genre-making dynamics in commercial music continue, given the rapidly changing social, technological, and legal environment of the twenty-first century? If the production of genres continues, it may be attributed to the socialization of artists and audiences into discourses of innovation, and the ongoing need for professionals to occupy themselves with craftwork. Additionally, the advance of flexible production and niche marketing may generate felt aesthetic needs among artists and fans for many years to come. The increasing tolerance of pop charts for hybrid and varied content may encourage the collapse of genres into marketing categories and business strategies. With the amount of detailed market research on active music fans, and the rapidity with which new trends are incorporated into the mix of music they offer, will it become more difficult for genres to incubate?

There is more work that needs to be done if we are to understand the transformation of musical styles into streams. What predicts the interest of community members in canonizing their style within a stream of music? What factors influence their ability to do so? I would hazard a guess that style-to-stream transitions are less a function of attributes of the musical community, and more dependent on extramusical factors, including the stream's profitability, its size and diversity, the state of the market for entertainment, and the pacing of a music's transition across genre forms. My sense is that musical styles that transition into the Industry-based genre form more quickly than others are more likely to experience absorption into the relevant stream, and that the appeal of such canonization draws the attention of participants away from stylistically specific activities.

The processes by which musical styles are added to streams are relatively opaque. In some cases, like gospel, award ceremonies are moments in which these inclusionary practices take place. In studies of both the Booker Prize and the Grammys, we find that such periodic events attended by powerful actors play a critical role in definitions of status, rank, reputation, and fame, but also define and affirm the "central tokens of value in the society in question."[160] Can we analyze the inclusion of styles in award categories and the celebration of stylistic leaders at ceremonies as examples of such tournament rituals?

The institutions we rely on to cultivate artistic tastes and preserve our cultural heritage (schools and museums, in the main) have ignored or excluded most of the musical styles that have been my focal concern. So what are the links between popular and "legitimate" art?[161] While some differences are immediately and undeniably clear (e.g., for-profit vs. non-profit organizations, large vs. small audiences), the recent legitimation of jazz as art music blurs the line between the two. For jazz, artistic legitimation may function as a fifth genre type, and the legitimating ideology that helped promote it to artistic status would then be seen an important resource for that genre form.

The legitimation of music-as-art is the second of two "legitimation moments" in the life of a musical community.[162] In the first, music transitions from obscurity to craft status—that is, the activity one is engaged in transforms from something that is unmarked or described in vague terms ("tinkering," "talking," "fooling around," "playing") into *musical* activity. This takes place whenever a community transforms from an Avant-garde into a Scene-based genre. Both the move from obscurity to craft, and that from craft to art, require that some group of people agree to view the work in a new and different way, and, in these cases, to view it more favorably. Groups need only reach some degree of relative consensus that playing has become music, or craft has become art—absolute consensus is rarely possible in social life. In both cases, this consensus builds first among small communities of artistic practitioners (what Crane calls "independent reward systems") and later acquires generalized social acceptance ("heterocultural reward systems").[163]

This discussion of consensus building leads me to consider the resources, or genre attributes, that might be found to characterize a fifth genre form called "legitimate art." One important resource is the consecrated authorities who must redefine craftwork as artwork. Art genres require the labor of critics, publishers, and scholars, each of them experts with credentials within the relevant field. Studies of visual art, dance, and even styles of music have revealed the importance of these experts in the legitimation of art. For example, museum and gallery workers played a key role in legitimating African tribal and religious artifacts, the art of the insane, and pop art, each of which is now treated as art.[164] Universities also play a critical role in this process. Once music becomes art, universities can create centers of study and even entire departments dedicated to scholarship on that style, and this has aided in the legitimation of both modern dance and jazz as art.[165] These experts must cultivate and deploy a particular justification for viewing a craft form as art.[166] These justifications, or "legitimating ideologies," provide an explanation for a style *as art*.[167] For example, the artistic ideology applied to jazz performance emphasized the music's complexity, traditions, and emotional resonance, effectively analogizing it to other serious art forms.[168] Art genres must also obtain patrons, and, historically, audiences for newly legitimate art include those who have themselves recently accomplished some degree of upward social mobility. For example, the dramatic increase in the number of Americans with postsecondary educations provided some of the starting conditions for the legitimation of film as art.[169] Similarly, the rise of the eighteenth-century novel to artistic status was a function of the expansion of the reading public.[170]

Unlike the focal music in this text, the "classical" genres of opera and orchestral music exist within a nonprofit organizational ecosystem. However, some of the newer forms of art music evince characteristics of the genre forms I discovered in commercial music. For example, noted American classical music composer John Adams worked with a circle of performers and composers in Boston during his undergraduate and graduate schooldays, and later with a group of northern California composers and students centered in San Francisco.[171] Just as in popular genres, these composers, students, critics, and audience members interacted and collaborated to shape the direction of musical innovation and social life within the community. When an art genre gathers a knowledgeable audience, critics and impresarios acquire characteristics that resemble those of their Scene-based counterparts. There the paths clearly diverge, because, in the fine arts, the next phase depends not on mass-market success but on mobilizing the resources and prestige to create a fully institutionalized art world—a world where the elite elements shape the canon, allocate the resources, define works and workers of quality, and distribute the rewards, and they do this well into the canonization stage.[172]

Powerful, high-status individuals and organizations are critical to the legitimation of craft as art. Without critics, academics, and other professionals lending credibility to the view that a craft has now become an art, it stands little chance of being viewed as such. These credentialed experts are fitting new styles within the existing hierarchical classification system for music. The rank order that places craft above art is presented to us as if it were natural and inevitable. The consequences of this social construction will be explored further in chapter 5.

The valorization of a musical style as "art" may be a process comparable to the absorption of musical styles into streams. If art genres are conceptualized as a fifth genre form, they may constitute an additional step in the AgSIT trajectory; alternatively, their incorporation may cause the split of musics with art genres from those without them into two distinct trajectories. The evidence from jazz suggests that musical communities form streams and then art genres, and the seeds for these two stages are sown in the Industry-based period.[173] In any case, we have much more to learn about why blues and rock have failed to be valorized as art despite concerted efforts by powerful agents.

It may also be helpful to reconceptualize streams as a genre form, or to distinguish genres that produce smaller-scale innovations from those that are "germinal." In the course of this work, it became abundantly clear that genres do not all have the same influence in altering the field of commercial music. We might distinguish between genres that are only marginally different and those that are germinal, that is, those that represent a significant departure from how earlier judgments about music were made. Germinal genres tend to spawn a number of genres that are only marginally different from one another. Such germinal musics include bebop, rock 'n' roll, and old school rap, whose progeny include hard bop and cool jazz, psychedelic and glam rock, gangsta and booty rap. If the distinction proves useful, it would be important to understand when and why germinal genres emerge when and where they do.

One possible explanation can be found in the genre ideals of streams, if such a thing can be said to exist. When streams highly value innovation over tradition, they appear to be the most likely to generate new stylistic distinctions. If you compare pre-1970s jazz with blues or electronic/dance music with country, this distinction appears to hold. It may also be the case that streams with high product start-up costs tend to evolve gradually but without the need for genre distinctions. Broadway musical theater is an excellent case in point, as is the variety show that began in minstrelsy, became vaudeville, and transferred to radio and TV variety shows. In any case, if the distinction between germinal and nongerminal musics proves useful, we may be able to further refine the types and trajectories of music genres.

In order to limit the number of variable impacts on genre forms and trajectories, I initially limited my focus to popular musics created in the twentieth-century United States. I eventually expanded the focus to include music produced in other countries. Although a preliminary survey reveals that the four genre forms do exist, to greater or lesser degree, across the globe, there proved to be another widely distributed form not discovered in the United States. This *Government-purposed* genre will be the focus of the following chapter.

Chapter 4

The Government-purposed Genre

Thus far, I have focused on documenting musical genre forms in the United States. In this chapter, I expand our view to include music produced in other countries. A preliminary survey of the popular music of countries with widely differing political economies, music cultures, and levels of development revealed that the four genre forms (Avant-garde, Scene-based, Industry-based, and Traditionalist) do exist to greater or lesser degrees across the globe, but there proved to be another widely distributed form that I did not find when I initially examined twentieth-century U.S. musical styles.

In a number of countries, popular genres receive substantial financial support from the government or oppositional groups with a direct interest in the ideological content of popular music. Sheltered from the exigencies of the market, these popular genres owe their existence to the changing ideological interests of political actors, ranging from governments to oppositional social movements. These are Government-purposed genres. All countries have laws, regulations, and subventions that advantage some music genres over others, but what is distinctive about Government-purposed genres is that they are created and supported to further particular government or partisan-group politicocultural objectives. Government-purposed genres are forms of popular music that engage in state-based politics and are most often found within states with controlled or regulated markets.

Government-purposed music genres were not found among my sample of U.S. music because I restricted myself to market-based or commercial genres. There is, however, ample evidence of Government-purposed influences on genres in the United States. Government statutes have been used to advantage some musics over others. Most consequentially, art-music advocates have been successful in gaining official consecration by the federal government and the subvention of funds for various sorts of music identified as "art," from opera to jazz and folk music.[1] From the early part of the twentieth century until the late 1940s, copyright laws were used to exclude most African American, Latin, and country music from network radio—then one of the most important mediums for exposing new music.[2] In addition, social movements have used music ranging from jazz, gospel, and folk to rock and disco, among others, to advance their goals, and diverse groups have tried to censor or suppress the musical expressions of African Americans, teenagers, leftists, and others considered dangerous.[3]

Government-purposed genres are hardly new. The Nazi Party and, subsequently, the Nazi government of Germany, for example, shaped music genres to fit their political agendas, and at the same time the Nazis moved to co-opt, censor, or suppress genres deemed subversive.[4] A similar pattern of facilitating some music genres while suppressing others characterized government policy in Soviet Russia.[5] Suppression and facilitation are commonly linked in the development of Government-purposed genres. The viability of Government-purposed genres depends more on the perception of their political utility, while the four forms identified in the previous two chapters depend more on the genre's popularity and commercial viability.

Outside the United States, I find two major types of Government-purposed genres: those sponsored by governments that benefit from national distribution and legal protection, and an antistate type supported by an opposition party or constituency that shares its critique of the existing sociopolitical and economic order. In order to better understand the dynamic role of governments and partisan interest groups in facilitating Government-purposed genres, I selected for examination four countries in which political interests have clearly been very important. The cases are not intended to be representative of a broader universe. Nevertheless, they were deliberately drawn from dispersed regions, having divergent musical traditions and exhibiting different political dynamics. Specifically, these cases have been drawn from East Asia (the People's Republic of China), South America (Chile), southeastern Europe (Serbia), and Africa (Nigeria). Western Europe is defocalized in the analysis because its musics are better known, relatively well researched, and perhaps not as strongly contrasting, in relevant respects, with those of the United States.

Attributes of Government-purposed Genres

Government-purposed genres do not share the same set of attributes found in the U.S. data. What is more, all Government-purposed genres do not share a single pattern of attributes. Patterns did begin to appear, however, when the examples were divided into two groups based on a criterion important in the political system: whether the sponsoring political entity was the government in power or was an "antistate" opposition party or constituency. Table 4.1 represents schematically the two kinds of Government-purposed genres and their distinguishing attributes. Not all of the dimensions were found in each of the genres examined, but table 4.1 represents what was found across the four country cases discussed below.

Five main dimensions differentiate the two types of Government-purposed genres. First, state-sponsored genres depend upon a bureaucratic organizational form, while antistate genres variously depend upon social movement organizations or communal scenes. The latter resemble, in large part, the Scene-based organization in American music styles. That is, they may be based in particular neighborhoods and receive only intermittent press coverage, and members may be focused on codifying technical innovations and developing consensus on style, particularly in order to differentiate their approach from rival, local groups. In contrast, government officials may define each of these genre attributes within state-sponsored genres. By definition, state-sponsored music genres have a national scope. While antistate genres primarily address local or national political issues in their lyrics and public personas, it is not uncommon for members to link such issues to larger social structures

Table 4.1. Distinguishing Attributes of Government-purposed Genres

	Government-purposed Genres	
Dimension	State-sponsored	Antistate
Organizational form	Bureaucratic	Social movement / communal scene
Scope of activity	National	Local / national / international
Goals	Further regime objectives	Deride regime / offer alternatives
Financing	Government	Social movement / party out of power / foreign governments / NGOs
Legality of performance	Legal	Always subject to repression

including colonialism, the intrusion of foreign capital in local industry, and the impact of multinational music corporations on performers' authenticity and freedom of expression. Correspondingly, the genres differ with respect to the goals of their community, with state-sponsored music oriented toward furthering regime objectives, and antistate musicians oriented primarily toward a critique of the regime and support for alternative political objectives. Government entities formally and informally finance state-sponsored genres, and a wide variety of sources of support are available to the antistate genre. These include relevant local, national, and international social movements, insurgent political parties, foreign governments sympathetic to minority interests, and nongovernmental organizations not included in the other categories. Finally, while Government-purposed genres are protected by the national and local legal system in state-sponsored genres, antistate music often operates beyond the pale of legal protections and is always vulnerable to repression.

Thus these five characteristics (organizational form, scope of activity, goals, financing, and legality of performance) differentiate the music styles considered here into two types: state-sponsored and antistate Government-purposed genres. In the concluding section of this chapter, I consider additional dimensions that may be discovered upon further investigation. First, I consider these five characteristics in four country cases.

China

Several Chinese musics typify the state-sponsored Government-purposed genre. The first of these was commissioned by the Chinese government following the 1949 Communist revolution led by Mao Zedong. After the nationalization of the culture industries, the state-owned China Record Company (Zhongguo changpian gongsi) was asked to create a new form of music that combined Chinese opera (*xiqu*), folk songs, and revolutionary art songs in order to displace Euro-American popular music.[6] The company's monopoly of production, in combination with censorship efforts directed at imported music, led to the wild success of this new musical style. Musicians, like other cultural workers, were encouraged to labor among workers and peasants so that their art would be informed by socialist experience, and factory workers, peasants, soldiers, and students were encouraged to write music.[7] In addition, revolutionary songs were imported from Russia and translated into Chinese.

During the Cultural Revolution (1966–76), the government again mandated the creation of a new music—a form of revolutionary "model opera" (*yangbanxi*), which formed the core of what might be called "revolutionary mass culture."[8] The government-owned popular music industry was directed to "serve the people" (*wei renmin fuwu*) by producing *tongsu yinyue*, music for the masses, including praise songs to socialism.[9] These songs had relatively plain-sounding, folk-influenced melodies supported by Western-style accompaniment and a token few Chinese instruments to give the music a form of cultural credibility.[10] The irony was that Chinese leaders commissioned a revolutionary musical style that had such strong Western influence, in its instrumentation, harmonic structure, and technique.[11] Broadcast over large, public speakers and over the radio, these songs were an inescapable part of daily life in the 1970s.

A loosening of restrictions in the wake of the Cultural Revolution, the increasing availability of cassette tape technology, and the creation of institutions to train musicians in popular styles affected Government-purposed genres in China.[12] The government mandate was changed from "serve the people" (*wei renmin fuwu*) to "serve the people's money" (*wei renminbi fuwu*), as exemplified by *gangtaiyue*, a Western-style genre incorporating a smooth melodic shape, simple harmonies, and electronic sounds. The lyrics tended to be mildly plaintive love poems.[13] The flowering of domestic pop and rock musicians was highlighted by a series of large, public concerts signaling the official acceptance of Euro-American–style popular music in China.[14] Many of these events were sponsored by nongovernmental organizations and were broadcast on local or national television.

In sum, the first thirty-odd years of the People's Republic of China were marked by the implementation of three Government-purposed musics, all with features of a state-sponsored genre. In each case, the government mandated the invention of the music, and supported it financially and through the bureaucratic infrastructure of state-run cultural organizations. Production was focused to domestic distribution, and the sounds and lyrics reflected regime objectives, even as those changed in the face of increased intolerance, and then increased liberalization.

China also produced at least one Government-purposed music genre of the antistate type in the aftermath of the Cultural Revolution. Western-influenced Chinese rock music (*yaogun yinyue*) was an integral part of the student democracy movement of the late 1980s. It was influenced by the presence of a large diplomatic community in Beijing and a sudden influx of American foreign exchange students.[15] North American visiting student David Hoffman is said to have established China's first rock band, Dadi (Mother Earth) during the early 1980s. Soon thereafter, exclusively Chinese bands formed, including Qiheban (Seven-Tier Boards) and Bai-touweng (Bald Eagle). Early rock artists subsisted off the income from performances at underground clubs, parties, and foreign-run restaurants, where there was a sense of "extra-territoriality."[16] The single most influential means of publicity for early rock performances was a calendar of events printed in a biweekly English-language newsletter, distributed for free to hotels, restaurants, and schools in Beijing.[17]

The so-called Western influences on Chinese rock deserve special mention, because they have been used to justify the government crackdown on the music, and they have also constrained artists who seek to express their Chinese identity through song. Take, for example, the group Tang Dynasty, formed by Kaiser Kuo and Ding Wu in late 1988. The group's very name represents a commentary on Western cultural imperialism; the promotional material for the album explains: "While Western Europe struggled through the hardships of the middle ages, Chinese culture flourished during the Tang Dynasty as the center of world trade and the highest point of world civilization." Reenvisioning "civilization" is of a piece with the band's appropriation of a Western genre: "The most important thing is, here you will hear the self-confidence of the Chinese, because they have done what you thought only Westerners could have done."[18] The album jacket features several references to Chinese history, including the use of calligraphy, and the music employs sonic hints of Beijing opera and Xinjiangese folk, while employing traditional Chinese instruments. Although aspects of the group's iconography and rhetoric clearly appear to critique the government's celebration of modernization and economic growth in China, some rock artists employ references to traditional Chinese culture as a means of demarcating a unique aesthetic space, and sometimes both are at work.[19] For example, Zu Zhou, singer of the band NO, plays his *gu zheng* (a stringed instrument) with a pair of scissors; he says, "I am most interested in using Chinese instruments as well as revolutionary songs . . . But I would definitely refuse to make them sound beautiful, I would try to make them sound uncomfortable. I like uncomfortable things."[20] Cui Jian is also credited with displacing the West in his appropriations of Western rock by reinventing folk songs, using traditional Chinese instruments and singing styles and famously telling an audience in 1989, "If Western rock is like a flood, then Chinese rock is like a knife."[21] On the other hand, some Chinese rockers were influenced by Western clothing styles associated with the rock stream and used English band names. They also described events as "parties" (in English), and developed an aesthetic and subcultural argot that bore resemblance to that used by Western rock bands.[22] From this, we can see that Chinese rock artists have a complicated, oppositional stance against both Western and Chinese culture.

Mainstream Chinese audiences were first introduced to domestic rock when singer Cui Jian performed his song "I Have Nothing" at the annual "One Hundred Pop Stars" (Baiming gexing) concert at Beijing's Worker's Stadium.[23] The band is credited with introducing postrevolutionary China to Western rock culture, and its "ethos [which] combined individualism, nonconformism, personal freedom, authenticity, direct and bold expression, and protest and rebellion."[24] Within weeks of the concert, bootleg recordings of the performance had spread across the country. Jian later released China's first rock album, *Rock and Roll of the New Long March* (1989). On it, his lyrics allude to Mao Zedong and his comrades, not to venerate them, but to challenge them.[25] Chinese rock was really an eclectic mix of punk music, traditional Chinese instruments, synthesizer dance music, and jazz improvisation.[26] The lyrics, at least in the late 1980s, emphasized the illusory nature of China's idealist nationalism, and a search for sincerity, purity, and authenticity. Jian's vocal style is pinched and rough, and his lyrics are often unintelligible; his rhythmic accompaniment borrows heavily from Western rock, while the melody is often compared to Northern Folksong styles (although Jian denies the association), and instruments often include those in the Chinese repertoire, including the *suona* (a reed instrument), and the *dizi* (a transverse flute made of bamboo).[27]

The relationship between the democracy movement and Chinese rockers is an extremely important and complicated one. First, rock music provided a soundtrack for protest; Jian's satirical "I Have Nothing" was heralded as the generational anthem of college-age Chinese.[28] He wrote songs in praise of the movement, including "Opportunists" ("Touji fenzi"), which he performed for hunger strikers in Tiananmen Square. The lyrics include the following passage:

> We don't have an experience at all
> And we don't like the past
> But our hearts understand how to keep going
> So there will definitely be some new results
> We don't know if life requires techniques
> Or if we should just get busy and work hard
> Anyway, things have already started so we can't be afraid of chaos
>
> Oh, when we get an opportunity we have to express our desire
> Oh, when we get an opportunity we have to express our strength[29]

This is one of the few songs in which an emphasis on individuality is commuted in favor of identifying a collectivity with shared complaints against the status quo. It also is among the most direct statements of self-empowerment and political challenge.[30] Perhaps this was Jian's way of identifying the sympathies between rock musicians and student activists. Both student leaders and rock musicians emerged from the demonstrations: China's Central Television reporter Wei Hua was fired after she burst into tears while reporting the June 4 massacre; she soon became the first notable Chinese, female rock singer. Performers and fans alike had faith in the transformative power of the music; writer Wang Shuo claimed, "What didn't happen through June 4th will happen through rock."[31] Second, the visibility of the protests and of rock music in China drew foreign investors to the music. EMI Records, through their Hong Kong and Taiwanese affiliates, released the album on which Jian's song appeared. Their distribution chains made it possible for the world outside China to hear this new style of rock, and for Chinese artists in all styles to launch an international recording career from inside the country. Third, the number and aesthetic diversity of bands increased dramatically, and included folk-influenced styles and those closer to heavy metal. Finally, that same visibility drew increased surveillance and restrictions on rock musicians from the CCP. The government regulations over employment meant that most rock musicians in China remained technically "unemployed"; activities associated with composition and performance were not recognized by the government. In failing to be registered in a nationalized work unit, rock artists were forced to forsake job security ("the iron rice bowl") and the subventions that ease the extraordinary expense of song recording.

While surveillance of rock artists had begun in the crackdown after the student protests, factionalism within the party permitted enough freedom for rockers to perform for several years. For a moment in time, it seemed as if rock's progressive and popular sounds would be tolerated by the CCP as long as the party benefited financially from the music. Seizing the opportunity to profit from government tolerance, Cui Jian embarked on an unauthorized concert tour in March 1990 and offered to donate concert proceeds toward the debt China had incurred by hosting the Asian Games in Beijing in 1989. Ten concerts into the tour, fans had become so numerous and energized that government leaders felt threatened. The crowds were riled up by Jian's habit of blindfolding himself with a red cloth, an unmistakable symbol of the CCP.[32] Audiences were rowdy, and the authorities clearly worried they'd lose control of the crowds, so they canceled the remainder of the tour and prevented additional rock tours.[33] Concerts were banned from broadcast on state television, and public concerts were mainly confined to rural or regional centers beyond the scrutiny of the central government. Still, the CCP sought to utilize Jian, perhaps to capture the hearts of young Chinese, or as a symbol of China's progression toward a tolerant, market-driven state. Jian was invited by the Ministry of Culture to perform at an antipiracy concert in October 2000, and rock band Hei Bao performed in Tibet in 1995. Also, a rock music school has been permitted to operate in Beijing.[34] In part, this is the result of a progressive faction within the CCP that seeks to use popular culture to assert hegemonic control, as they seek both cultural and ideological legitimacy and funds to support their modernization and surveillance projects.[35] Chinese rock clearly operated at the boundary of legitimate, state-sanctioned culture, but it isn't unequivocally counterhegemonic, particularly once the CCP sought ways to accommodate the music by diffusing its antistate sentiment.[36]

Over time, the surveillance of the rock scene and persecution of its performers had three consequences: the development of an independent distribution system, the increased use of ambiguity to avoid censure, and the evolution of a nonpolitical avant-garde. While early rockers like Cui Jian were forced to sign contracts with foreign labels (in Hong Kong, Taiwan, and Germany), a newer generation tended to dispense with heavy ideological content and instead focused on building a sustainable production network for domestic music.[37] Rock artists and supporters began to innovate means to distribute music beyond the view of censors. Many start-up newspapers and small magazines use the quasi-legal strategy of manipulating official license procedures to produce and distribute rock. Modern Sky, for example, produces a magazine using a music publishing license; because the CD is vital to the magazine, the label does not need to negotiate for publishing approval with the State Press and Publishing Administration. The workplace and focus of the company remain underground, but the magazine and music it creates are commercially available and successful.[38]

Second, the most successful artists, Jian among them, sought to modify their lyrics and cooperate with authorities in order to ensure the wide distribution of their music. Following the Tiananmen Square massacre of pro-democracy activists, political crackdowns on rock music led to the near-total elimination of antigovernment rhetoric. Some artists like Cui Jian have continued to be popular because they bury their critique in ambiguous lyrics and sounds, as when Jian appropriated an old socialist anthem in the song "He zi" in order to call for resistance to Chinese socialist ideals.[39] Many music producers disguise a potentially offensive lyric by substituting an inoffensive homophone when they submit the album to government examination committees.[40] Other rockers simply stopped performing, including Gao Feng, who said: "Rock had no future. It reached a dead end and it wasn't going to develop anywhere. I needed to survive, and I also wanted to become a star, so there was no other choice but to change direction."[41]

Finally, as a result of increased surveillance and censure of the two generations of artists that make up Chinese rock's "first ten years," in addition to shifts in tastes, bands in the late 1990s largely de-emphasized political critique and heavy metal and hard rock sounds. Instead, they represented a modern, urban, international youth sentiment, and were more influenced by punk and electronic music. This has led the rock old guard to disparage contemporary young rockers as superficial; Cui Jian calls them "a generation of charlatans without culture," characterized into subgroups by style rather than substance.[42] Members of this generation are not loath to describe themselves in such terms; drummer He Li said: "Today's young people are different from Cui Jian and those guys; we could care less about politics and society and all that. We don't have any tragic qualities; all our anguish is fake."[43] For many, this transition in values is linked with the increasingly liberal Chinese market. While Cui Jian has stated this in negative terms—"The younger generation . . . they don't care about anyone else . . . they just want to have fun, to be cool, to enjoy a good fuck, earn money"—others view it positively.[44] For example, rock critic Zhao Ke feels that older rock music "is . . . outdated. This era does not belong to those who gather together to scream in one voice. What we need now is individuality, our individual voice."[45]

Chinese rock from the 1980s and early 1990s manifested attributes associated with antistate Government-purposed genres. Support for the music grew out of the student democracy movement. Capitalizing upon the presence of foreign diplomats, a communal scene grew to nurture the music and its supporters. The music's lyrics often critiqued the Chinese government, directly and indirectly, which led to constant government surveillance. As the music's complaints became more pointed, and the music internationally visible, government authorities forced it back underground, although some argue there is a new form of Chinese rock that is state-sponsored.[46] These rock musicians both reject the "revolutionary" roots of the music and express highly xenophobic sentiments. In their critique of Western culture, these Chinese rockers combine a fidelity to national speech codes with an antagonism generated from conventional wisdom about Chinese artists' exploitation at the hands of foreign record companies. Scholars argue that Chinese authorities have rebranded the Maoist revolutionary leaders as pop culture icons, creating a "consumerist and mythic equivalency between Mao and Madonna and Cui Jian" by employing R&B and reggae rhythms to infuse classic Maoist revolutionary songs with new vitality.[47]

In China, a highly centralized and ideologically unified government used music as part of its cultural strategy aimed at unifying a fractionated imperial territory. This deployment of music takes two forms. First, the central government has infused collectivist ideology into the old forms of Chinese court art music, making it both revolutionary and traditional. Second, it made every effort to co-opt elements of Western pop music through the control of TV, radio, record making, vocational training, the direct employment of all musicians, mass public spectacles, and a wide array of awards. These actions were then supplemented with a systematic censorship of all expressions not deemed ideologically correct, and there was systematic screening of imported material.

Chile

Nueva canción, a musical style popularized in Chile in the middle of the twentieth century, is a Latin American form of antistate, Government-purposed music. The music's birth mother is Violeta Parra, who formed the first group, Cuncumen, in 1955, to collect, interpret, and record Chilean folk music.[48] A decade later, Parra established a center for popular art in a suburban neighborhood in Santiago, called La Carpa de La Reina, and her two daughters opened a coffee shop called Peña de los Parra, in Santiago. It was there that neo-folklore transformed into *nueva canción*.[49] The community of sympathizers and fans included students, professionals, and marginalized populations, among them a small group of politically active Quechua, Aymara, and Mapuche Indians. The music was governed by communist ideology. For example, consider the lyrics of Violeta Parra's famous composition "La carta" ("The Letter"):

> They sent me a letter
> In the early mail
> In the letter they tell me
> They took my brother to jail.
>
> I am so far away
> Waiting for news,
> A letter comes to tell me
> There is no justice in my country.
> The hungry people ask for bread
> The militia gives them lead, yes.
>
> Luckily I have a guitar
> With which to lament my pain.
> I also have nine brothers
> Besides the one they locked up.

The nine are communists
By the grace of God, yes.[50]

After the 1970 election of Salvador Allende, a reformer and Marxist, Victor Jara's group, Quilapayun, formulated the political content of the nascent genre, functioning as official cultural ambassadors for the Allende government.[51] Musicians Claudio Iturra and Sergio Ortega wrote Allende's campaign song, "We Will Triumph":

From the depths of our country
The cry of the people rises up
Now the new dawn is announced
All of Chile begins to sing.

We will triumph, we will triumph
A thousand chains will have to be broken
We will triumph, we will triumph
We will know how to conquer misery.
We will sow the fields of glory
Socialism will be the future
Together we will make history
Carry on, carry on, carry on.[52]

In its combination of folk, popular, and commercial music from Amerindian, Euro-Hispanic, and African traditions, this music symbolizes an ideological stance in opposition to the homogenizing tendencies of transnational media and an effort to create (or re-create) a popular culture around the values of communitarism, tradition, and agrarian ways of life.[53] The movement functioned as a rejection of both the imperialism of U.S. popular culture and the Latin American elite's dismissal of indigenous culture.[54] The songs were vehicles used by performers to engage in political criticism and social commentary, and specifically included "telling histories, denouncing opponents, extolling democratic alternatives, and relating specific incidents."[55] Musician Victor Jara explained that "our duty is to give our people weapons to fight against this (the North American commercial monopoly in music); to give our people its own identity with a Folklore which is, after all, the most authentic language a country has, to make our people understand their reality through the protest song."[56] For example, in Jara's song "Preguntas por Puerto Montt" (1968),

he relates the recent military attack on ninety-one farm families who oc-
cupied a plot of land near the southern city of Puerto Montt, denouncing
the Chilean minister of the interior, who ordered the attack:

> You ought to tell us,
> Mister Pérez Zujovic,
> Why the defenseless people
> Were met with rifles.
> Mister Pérez, your conscience
> You have buried in a coffin
> And you cannot wash your hands
> With all the rains that fall in southern Chile.[57]

Musicians and researchers in the group traveled the length of Chile,
finding indigenous songs, stories, and dances to form the basis for popular and original compositions. Violeta Parra, Víctor Jara, and Inti-Illimani
all experimented with the indigenous *cueca* rhythm pattern, and incorporated native instrumentation into their music, especially the panpipes,
charango, and *quenas*. They also wrote songs addressing injustices and
relating the experience of rural, poor, and Amerindian populations. Take,
for example, Violeta Parra's song "Levántate, Huenchullán," in which she
describes injustices against the Mapuche people:

> Araucanians have a deep pain
> That cannot be silenced.
> It is centuries of injustices
> That they have all witnessed.
> . . . Stand up, Huenchullan.[58]

These challenges were addressed to populist movements across Latin
America, as in Inti-Illimani's song "La segunda independencia." The
objective of *nueva canción* musicians is not to emulate folk music, but
rather to transform elements of folk music into a new, popular, political music genre, and to better incorporate the poor and dispossessed
into politics and the economy.[59] The music thus represents a desire to
"bring about political change through a recuperation of national identity
through populist music,"[60] very much as other Americans (e.g., Puerto
Ricans) use music as an ideological foundation for ethnic identity and
self-determination.[61]

Following General Augusto Pinochet's military coup in 1973, the music was outlawed, banned from the airwaves, albums were confiscated and burned during house-to-house searches, and Victor Jara was executed. Pinochet's repressive dictatorship became the prime target of the music's critique, now launched from exiled groups like Inti-Illimani. Like early rock in China, this music was distributed clandestinely in Chile via pirated cassette tapes. The crackdown resulted in the global spread of the music and its cause, and "this internationalizing of *La Nueva Canción* is certainly one of the more ironic accomplishments of the military coup."[62] The music became the voice of *bolivariana*, or Latin American unity[63] and soon spread throughout the region, spawning hybrid styles. Within Chile, the musical style dubbed *canto nuevo* was its successor, although it was forced to employ carefully coded metaphors to critique the Pinochet government.[64]

Chile's *nueva canción* was supported by a communal scene rooted in a club in central Santiago, and later grew into a social movement organized in opposition to a political dictatorship. This included support from folklore associations, worker and farmer syndicates and unions, and eventually radio and television programs, brochure publishing, records, educational programs, festivals, tours, and a coffeehouse.[65] Initially concerned with the reclamation of a regional identity, the music came to be an international force, denouncing a regime and a system of global politics that supported it. It is a Government-purposed genre of the antistate type.

In recent years, these musicians have faced a new criticism from otherwise sympathetic, left-leaning musicologists. The critique focuses on three issues: first, with the exception of Jara, most *nueva canción* performers came from middle- or upper-class backgrounds, and have little ancestral connection to the Amerindian people. Their work to preserve the culture of marginalized Chileans looks to some like a form of appropriation and paternalism, not unlike earlier forms of colonization by European and Chilean whites. Second, in utilizing indigenous instruments, like the *quena* and the panpipes, *nueva canción* performers contributed to their popularization, one consequence of which is that they are no longer considered the exclusive cultural property of the Quechua and Aymara peoples. Some critics feel that exclusivity (of culture) is linked with cultural survival as a distinct people; the fewer identifying characteristics, the more difficult it will be for indigenous peoples to fight the disorganizing influence of the modern state.[66] Finally, although *nueva canción* can now be performed in Chile, it and its successor, *canto nuevo,* draw small crowds because while they conjure positive connotations (of democracy and community), they are also viewed as nostalgia, and as politically impotent.[67]

Nigeria

The period before and after Nigeria's independence from the United Kingdom was one of incredible musical fecundity. Popular musical styles included highlife, palm-wine music, apala, fuji, juju, and yo-pop, and local musicians created local varieties of world pop music, including both American rap and reggae. Despite the massive popularity in the 1950s–1970s of both U.S. and European pop music, and Nigerian popular styles like yo-pop and reggae, tribal music remained widespread and popular. Nigeria's long and storied history of musical production, its large domestic and international market, and modern production facilities led to its designation as the "heart of African music."[68] Perhaps the most internationally popular of these musics has been Nigerian Afrobeat, which emerged in the early 1960s.

Afrobeat employs American funk music and blends it with elements of many West African musics, including highlife and jazz. Fela Anikulapo Kuti, Afrobeat's leading practitioner, began performing in 1961 and continued until his death from AIDS in 1997. Son of a Protestant minister father and a mother who was president of the Nigerian Women's Union, grandson of a well-known Christian Yoruba hymn-writer, Fela hailed from a middle-class, relatively famous family line.[69] He started his musical career in his teens as a highlife musician, working in a variety of bands. He traveled to Trinity College London in 1958 to study music, and returned to Nigeria in 1963 intent on deriving his own sound combining highlife and jazz. His initial failure to inspire fans left him dispirited, and Fela traveled again, this time to the United States in 1969. Fela described the effect of this visit, and his exposure to the Black Panther Party, on his music:

> You see at the beginning, my musical appreciation was very limited, but later I got opened to many black artists. And I saw that in Africa we were not open, as at that time they only let us hear what they

wanted us to hear. When you played the radio, it was controlled by the government and the white man played us what he wants. So we didn't know anything about black music. In England I was exposed to all these things, but in Africa they cut us off. It was after I was exposed that I started using jazz as a stepping-stone to African music. Later, when I got to America, I was exposed to African history which I was not even exposed to here. It was then that I really began to see that I had not played African music. I had been using jazz to play African music, when really I should be using African music to play jazz. So it was America that brought me back to myself.[70]

The distinctive Afrobeat style with which Fela is associated emerged during recording sessions at the famous Abbey Road Studios in London, with a newly formed band called Africa '70, led by drummer Tony Allen. It is marked by extremely long, partially improvised songs that Fela once compared to "movements": "It's like a symphony but in the African sense."[71] His bands employed a range of acoustic and electrified instruments, including guitars, bass guitars, keyboards, a large brass section, various African percussion instruments, and the saxophone (which Fela played). He began to work out of his house in Lagos and renamed it the "Kalakura Republic," or "Rascal's Republic." He explained that the name had come from graffiti on the wall of a prison cell, and defended the term as a point of pride: "if rascality is going to get us what we want we will use that name, because we are dealing with corrupt people so we have to deal rascally with them."[72] Fela ruled the house more as a kingdom than a republic, setting up his own courts, a prison, and a clinic. He lived in the compound with his twenty-seven wives and three children, his brother, his mother, the musicians and dancers in his band, and an array of household pets including a donkey, a baboon, and an Alsatian dog. Fela owned and headlined at a club across the street, called the Africa Shrine (originally, Afro-spot), which became massively successful and hosted visits from Paul McCartney and other international pop stars.

With Africa '70, Fela recorded a string of hits, and earned the enmity of the Nigerian government by tackling issues of poverty, skin bleaching ("Shakara," "Yellow Fever," and "Gentleman"), automobile traffic, and government abuses of the public trust. For example, in a song titled "Teacher, Don't Teach Me Nonsense," he sings, "Who is the Government's teacher?

Corruption and tradition." While his lyrics addressed many local problems, Fela linked these with the relationships Nigeria and other African nations have with European countries and capitalism, making for a truly international critique.[73] The lyrics of "No Bread," for instance, identify postcolonial trade patterns as exploitative:

> For Africa here, him to be home
> Land boku [plenty] from north to south,
> Food boku from top to down,
> Gold de underground like sand,
> Oil de flow underground like river,
> [But] everthin go for overseas
> Na from here it de come?[74]

Although his critiques often reached a global scope, many were focused on the complicity of his own government in the despoiling of Nigeria's culture and environment. In "Government of Crooks," Fela notes the Nigerian government's collusion with foreign oil companies to ruin southeastern Ogoniland, which culminated in the state execution of playwright and activist Ken Saro-Wiwa:

> All of us know our country
> There is plenty oil
> Plenty resources in Africa
> Petroleum is one of them
> All the places where oil lies
> Are spoiled with pollution
> The farms are soaked by oil leaks
> The villages are rife with disease
> Money has ruined the oil areas
> But some people in government
> Have become billionaires
> From oil wealth
> And underhanded crookedness.[75]

Fela's lyrics reflected his belief that Nigeria had transformed from a revolutionary postcolonial republic into a corrupt state in an undeclared war against its own people.[76] To add to his musical critique, Fela formed a political organization, Young African Pioneers (YAP), which circulated

pamphlets criticizing the government and NGOs. He also created a political party, Movement of the People, which contested the presidential
election of 1979.

Fela suffered years of police surveillance and harassment. In 1974 his
household was raided, and he spent two weeks in jail. Later, police at-
tacked his music club with tear gas and axes, and he was left with a broken
arm.[77] In 1977, an army attack on his household by one thousand federal troops caused massive damage: the compound was looted, women
were raped, Fela's mother was defenestrated and later died from her in-
juries, and the only audio track for Fela's movie *The Black President* was
destroyed.[78] He included a montage of newspaper clippings of the police
attack on his home inside the cover of his album *Coffin for Head of State*
(Kalakuta Records, 1981). In 1985, Fela, charged with illegally exporting
fifteen hundred British pounds, was given a five-year jail sentence, but he
was released after serving less than two, following a military coup, international protest, and massive Nigerian marches and outcry.[79] This made
him, by some accounts, Africa's second most famous political prisoner
after Nelson Mandela.[80] Fela would later form a political party and run
for the presidency, only to have his bid ended by the Federal Electoral
Commission.[81] Significantly, Fela's criticisms of the Nigerian government
and civil sphere reflect the traditional role accorded to performers, who
address and redress social dysfunction by drawing the attention of the
community.[82]

In Nigeria we see evidence of a form of a Government-purposed genre
that is antistate. The music grew from a communal scene around a single,
charismatic performer and his collaborators. Fela's output was substantial,
including more than eighty albums (containing 150 songs) and a great
deal of unrecorded or unreleased material.[83] It focused critique on issues
of local and national concern, but also focused on international problems,
just as we saw in Chile. One author argues that Fela and other Nigerian
artists are "political artists [who] launch their campaigns of decoloniza-
tion, announcing their distinctiveness from Western-derived notions of
Nigerianess."[84] Financing of the music seems to have come from local
sources until Fela ventured abroad, at which point African outposts of the
global media manufactured and distributed Afrobeat to its global consumer base. The repression of these musicians was quite severe and lasted
until Fela died in 1997.

Serbia

Socialist Yugoslavia was conceived in 1945 as a multiethnic federation of partially self-governing republics, including Slovenia, Croatia, Serbia (with two autonomous provinces: Kosovo and Vojvodina), Montenegro, Macedonia, and Bosnia-Herzegovina. After the death of Yugoslavian president Josip Broz Tito, a deepening economic crisis and the collapse of Communist states across Eastern Europe led Yugoslavia into a series of civil wars during the 1990s. Ethnic cleansing, NATO air strikes, and political violence resulted in thousands of casualties and more than 2.5 million refugees. Although the region is still volatile, each republic remains relatively diverse, politically and ethnically. Nationalist groups and entrepreneurs, often working with tacit government approval, have been the prime creators of Government-purposed genres.

The patterning of Government-purposed music in the postsocialist era is complex because of Yugoslavia's devolution into seven distinct and contending republics, each with its own complex history and diverging agenda. A further vexing complication is that most of the meager research available in English is written from an ethnically partisan perspective. In particular, the ethnic roots of turbo-folk are contested, with experts variously claiming that its roots and features are Serbian, Yugoslav, Balkan, or Croatian.[85] The music clearly has extremely strong links to Serbian nationalist movements, and particularly to a highly militarized nationalism of the sort that fueled ethnic cleansing in the region.[86] Its sound fuses the earlier form of "New Folk Music" (*novokomponovana narodna muzika*, influenced by traditional Serbian folk melodies, popular and traditional music from Greece and Turkey, rock, disco, and Western pop) with rap, hip-hop, and dance, especially house and techno music.[87] The compound genre name is drawn from turbine-enhanced cars and folk music: "Figuratively, 'turbo' referred to a challenge, speed, fearlessness and participation in the upcoming, fashionable trends, ascribed to turbo-folk artists and audience, while 'folk' signified that 'turbo-folk' represents one of the genres of Serbian popular, folk music."[88] The music was developed and popularized during a period of pathological ethnocentrism in the region, so the transformation and fusion of mythological material and politics follows a trend noted in other places and times, including fascist Europe.[89]

It is clear that forms of turbo-folk can be found across the republics, but that the Serbian state fostered the development of a nationalistic brand of the music. Serbian leaders sponsored the turbo-folk performers and not *rokeri* (local rock performers, who emerged during the last years of the Yugoslav Republic) because the latter were mostly educated urbanites from Zagreb, Sarajevo, and Belgrade—and mostly anti-Milošević.[90] Turbo-folk promoted a system of values that "encouraged the war-orientated, retrograde patriarchy and the prostitution and commodification of women, while accepting the iconography of Western mass culture, the values of the 'American dream,' 'body culture,' culture of leisure and consumption" that were enjoyed by the new Serbian ruling class.[91] The folk elements, in combination with images of Western mass culture, nationalism, and patriarchy, appealed to the power base for this elite, peasants and recent migrants in Belgrade, arriving from rural areas.

Turbo-folk songs were played twenty-four hours a day on the station Ponos Radio (Radio Pride), TV station TV Palma, TV Pink, and Radio Pink. The latter two monopolized the media space, profiting from the political and financial patronage of Milošević's wife and her party, JUL (Yugoslavian Left). TV Pink put out music through its own production company, City Records. Its political perspective was not clearly defined, described as more chaotic than coherent, but nevertheless it was a style that glamorized and promoted the Serbian political elite.[92] Music videos used professional production techniques, including dynamic editing, story-driven visuals, combinations of color and black-and-white film, and rock iconography: violence, sports cars, black leather, and motorcycles. "Folk-divas" wore contemporary, glamorous fashion and were filmed with soft-focused camera lenses. The "happy narcissism" of techno (a scene supported in Belgrade by progressive, peace-making urban teens) was recycled into Serbian turbo-folk as one of several efforts to absorb or eliminate other urban cultural styles, particularly those that could be viewed as antistate propaganda.[93]

Performances were held at election rallies and mixed with populist political propaganda. So important was this music to cultural politics that the wedding video of paramilitary commander Željko Ražnatović Arkan to turbo-folk star Svetlana "Ceca" Veličković was played outdoors for days at top volume by Bosnian residents of Mostar to antagonize their Croatian neighbors.[94] Now, the music's political edge is less obvious: one turbo-folk guitarist recently claimed, "When it appeared in the 1990s, maybe it was political. . . . Now it's more a way of dressing."[95] According to the Belgrade-based playwright Biljana Srbljanović,

> The singers, mostly women who usually wear as little as is decently possible, work hard to evoke the whirling atmosphere of a roadside haunt of long-distance lorry drivers. This type of woman, predominantly a bleached blonde, her lips and breasts swollen with silicone injections, is being deliberately built up as an ideal to be emulated.[96]

This description fits singers like Lepa Brena and Vesna Zmijanac. Female lead singers, like Ceca, "the Queen of Turbo-folk," would appear on the front lines in the battles against Croatia, wearing battle fatigues to raise morale among troops.[97] Ceca also performed a concert to protest the NATO bombing of Yugoslavia in the spring of 1999.

The states of the former Yugoslavia still use music as a mechanism of government ideology but now emphasize the legitimacy of their culturally diverse constituencies. Rock competitions and pop song contests are sponsored by the state and by NGOs, and designed to provide representation to each republic.[98] The most important multiminority festival is Manifestacija, held in Zagreb since 1998, and sponsored by the Council for National Minorities, responsible for the protection and freedom of minorities.[99] Each minority community is represented by one ensemble, and all are given the same amount of time to perform. Tickets are not sold but are instead distributed to minority organizations. Although these festivals do not produce a single genre, we can still consider them to be manifestations of an infrastructure designed for Government-purposed genres.

Thus, until the early years of this century, turbo-folk was a clear example of state-sponsored Government-purposed music. Not only did government authorities encourage and commission works in this genre; they also supported its production and dissemination. The substance of the music is so instrumental to regime objectives that it was used as a form of propaganda by the state. With the prosecution of military and civilian personnel by international war crimes tribunals, and changes wrought by the expansion of EU membership, turbo-folk has muted its nationalistic and ethnic themes and transformed into a sort of Balkan pop music.

Conclusion

In each of the four countries explored here we have found music genres that have developed primarily in a political rather than a market context. In China, we witness an evolving history of central government action, where active promotion of music is temporarily challenged by the anti-state power of rock, only to be co-opted by the machine of nationalization and repression. Chile's *nueva canción* is a Government-purposed genre developed by extragovernmental actors and used to fight a repressive dictatorship, and to critique Western culture and global media. Nigeria's rich musical heritage gave birth to Afrobeat in the mid-1960s, a globally popular, antigovernment genre, whose charismatic leader was subjected to repressive surveillance and violence by the state. Like *nueva canción*, this music was also employed to critique global media as modern imperialist powers. Finally, in the former Yugoslav republic of Serbia, ethnic nationalist groups and entrepreneurs created turbo-folk, but the music has since transformed into a multicultural pop phenomenon.

I stated at the beginning of the chapter that many musics created outside the United States manifested features of the four genre types: Avantgarde, Scene-based, Industry-based, and Traditionalist. Among the musical communities considered for this chapter, those genre types were not found when centralized state systems regulated musical production and markets. Government regulation can impose restrictions on most of the twelve dimensions of genre forms. Prohibitions on assembly (like that found in present-day Myanmar) may delimit the organizational form and scale, and will push the locus of activity into underground, or hidden, spaces. Mechanisms of surveillance and media regulation may prevent musical styles from gaining domestic press coverage, and this may make it difficult for artists to engage in boundary work, to dress and speak as they would like, or even to generate a genre name since identification with a prohibited group may draw censure, imprisonment, or death. Any market regulations will inevitably compress the audience for Government-purposed music, but may facilitate the growth of a black market and the survival of cassette technology even when formats with higher sound fidelity are available. Government-purposed genres are often part of "cassette culture," which sustains the production of music in most of the developing world.[100] Cassettes are less expensive and more durable than vinyl records, enabling consumption by lower-income and rural groups, and production by small-scale producers around the world. Consequently, multinational and national oligopolies have been displaced by (more) decentralized and democratic systems of musical production and distribution.[101] However, when governments regulate the price and profit of recordings, as they do in China, and black market profits do not filter back to artists, artists must rely on nongenre income, even if their work is massively popular. Owing to the fact that Government-purposed genres are forms of popular music that engage in state-based politics and are found within states with controlled or regulated markets, they do not attain the same genre forms as were found in American popular music. Rather, we find novel combinations of genre dimensions: Chinese rockers are constrained to perform in Scene-based clubs although the black market for cassettes and foreign producers distributes their music to millions. The genre ideal of turbo-folk performers combined global pop's focus on conspicuous consumption with parochial concerns of building a national ethnic identity. Rather than simply representing deviations from the genre forms discovered in the United States, Government-purposed genres demonstrate new and consistent constellations of genre dimensions.

The set of attributes displayed in table 4.1 is necessarily incomplete because it is based on just the four country case studies. For example, the table omits a description of the nature of press reporting on Government-purposed musics. Some evidence from Chile and China suggests that state-sponsored genres receive extensive and entirely positive coverage in the national press, while antistate genres receive minimal or negative coverage in the domestic press but periodically receive positive coverage in the foreign press. However, other cases may reveal that less repressive regimes provide more equitable coverage of antistate music genres, or that underground or gray economies support publications that provide favorable coverage, even at the national level.

Second, considerable evidence from Serbia and China suggests that those who create Government-purposed genres also try to minimize the influence of music genres that they think are contrary to the goals that they espouse. While the agents of state-sponsored genres commonly use tools of the state to repress or censor, the adherents of antistate genres may publicly deride or work to shield their followers from music they feel is antithetical to movement interests. In addition, the proponents of both kinds of Government-purposed genres commonly co-opt and ideologically sanitize elements of genres attractive to ethnic minorities or youth that are thought to be opposed to their interests, as I especially noted in the case of Serbian turbo-folk. The question of how closely these patterns resemble the American case, where commercial genres vie for market space, remains to be seen.

Third, I stop shy of concrete hypotheses concerning the relationship between the structure of the political system and the kinds of Government-purposed genres that develop. I can speculate that the development of state-sponsored Government-purposed genres is dependent both on an elaborate, centralized government bureaucracy and on the willingness of the political elites to use terror to shape culture. However, political factionalism may be sufficient to foment state-sponsored music, and certainly some governments use market instruments in ways likely to produce ideologically sonorous music.

Fourth, there appears to be a relationship between a country's degree of linkage into the global capitalist system and the prevalence and forms of Government-purposed genres in the country. Moreover, the Nigerian and Chilean cases reveal that a government's dependence upon trade and industrial production by nonnatives may influence the object of critique for antistate musicians.

And finally, it is possible that the division of Government-purposed genres into two types will be inadequate to the purpose of sorting all such music in the world, and over time. From the cases reviewed, the antistate form seems to be less coherent and may, with more complete information from diverse countries, best be seen as several distinct types of Government-purposed genres.

In the search for attributes that differentiate state-sponsored genres from antistate ones, I examined the musical sources used to craft the genres under consideration. Many are adapted from indigenous folk music or traditional, domestic fine art music, and are intended to displace Western pop music and build an indigenous musical form. This appears to be the case in several postcolonial nations, where evolving notions of nationalism evoke connections to folk music and dance, costume, and oral literature.[102] Many others are designed to attract young listeners by adapting genres popular in the world media system such as rock, punk, and rap. The first kind could be called *customary* and the second, *appropriated*. This distinction should perhaps be added to the set of attributes, but I am unable to do so because both the government and antistate factions selectively sponsor customary and appropriated genres. Furthermore, since folk forms are increasingly played with nonindigenous instruments, and the lyrical themes of appropriated genres are adapted to reflect local concerns and perspectives, the relationship between customary and appropriated genres might best be seen as a continuum rather than as a dichotomy.

One of the most interesting findings in the previous chapter was the discovery of two distinct genre trajectories. But no comparable pattern was clear among Government-purposed genres. This may be so because the trajectories of Government-purposed genres are determined by the exigencies of political needs rather than by developments in the fields of music and commerce. There is a suggestion in the data, however, that if the political field remains stable over a considerable period of time, state-sponsored genres tend to lose their hard ideological edge, and, as is seen in China, new genres are mandated to fit the ideological needs of the regime. There is also a suggestion in the data from Serbia and Nigeria that long-lasting antistate genres follow a pattern like that found among market-based genres developed in scenes. In both cases, the music became the symbolic heart of an emerging generation in revolt against their elders. In time, each genre became an ideologically vacuous product merchandised to a mass market: each experienced a "revolt into style."[103]

In the previous chapter, I noted that musical trajectories are influenced by various features of the surrounding social system, including market structures, racialized production systems, and political and social integration of ideological communities that promote musical forms. Beyond the obvious and direct impact of industrial and political cultures on shaping the life histories of Government-purposed genres, international circuits of social movements clearly influence the spread and adaptation of Government-purposed musical forms. *Nueva canción* provides the clearest case in point. The "new song movement" spread throughout Latin America (including Cuba and Brazil) and to Latino audiences across the globe. The musical threads that unite this community are thin: in some cases, groups employ the folk music of rural regions of their own nations for inspiration; in others, the musicians are influenced by urban sounds and musical styles in contemporary Latin America. What unites musical styles into a movement is a desire to use populist music to foment a national identity that will facilitate political change.[104]

In several cases, most notably Chile under Allende, and Cuba after the revolution, this antistate music transforms into state-sponsored music because the revolutionary movement of which it is a part seizes political control. In Cuba, the official support given by revolutionary governments was signaled in the First Protest Song Meeting, held in 1967. Latin American revolutionary consciousness and mass movements were felt to have been stimulated by the use of mass media, particularly in Cuba, where pro-Castro factions used Radio Rebelde before and after the successful revolution. This demonstrates the close relationship between the role of the mass media and cultural policy.[105] We see here an example of a mass-mediated form of popular entertainment that serves to promote solidarity and community, a combination that North American audiences may feel is in contradiction.[106]

The four nations studied here were chosen because they are relatively well researched and they show clear evidence of hosting Government-purposed genres. There are, however, many countries in which both market and Government-purposed influences are present, and it will be fascinating to learn how music genres develop when market-driven and Government-purposed influences are more or less evenly balanced. In addition, there are music genres in folk communities where tradition is stronger than either market or political forces. In such instances individuals, clans, occupational groups, and other collectivities often have the exclusive right to perform particular songs or genres of music.[107] While such musics are commonly overwhelmed by market and political forces, there is evidence that such communally exclusive forms may flourish under some conditions.[108]

Of course, all reports are at best partial and incomplete because of the authors' particular research focus, and some are blatantly partisan because of the researcher's political proclivities or dismissive evaluation of the music under review. Unfortunately, some of the most compelling cases of Government-purposed music are least completely researched. For example, in the Republic of Turkmenistan the trajectory of Government-purposed genres seems to resemble that of those in China: the introduction of Soviet cultural policy in 1924 apparently sparked the transition from folk instruments and compositional styles to Western instruments, rhythms, and compositional styles. More recently, pop music has been produced secretively or under the supervision of government censors.[109] We know even less about the distinctive Cambodian pop music made by musicians including Sinn Sisamouth and Pan Ron who performed before the civil war that led to the Khmer Rouge's reign of terror. Most of these performers are assumed to have died in the Killing Fields, and little of their music survives. To more completely understand the character and dynamics of Government-purposed genres, we will need a large number of studies with differing research goals that are written from divergent perspectives.

In this chapter, I have focused on genres created by political actors who wanted a music that could further their particular values and goals. I found that such Government-purposed genres of music are rarely examined and are poorly understood. I hope that the observations and categorizations I have made here will encourage others to join in exploring this fertile ground for further research.

Chapter 5

On Classification Systems

Writing in *Harper's Magazine* in 1941, Irving Kolodin reported the maturation of "big band" jazz ensembles into an Industry-based genre form:

> Those with a finger on the pulse of this capricious industry have an amazing instinct for estimating the moment when a band is truly 'hot,' in a sense unrelated to the kind of music it plays. It is at such a moment, when sales of records suddenly swing upward, and a fan club is started in Baton Rouge, and another leader tries to buy off the hitherto obscure arranger who has given the band its distinctive personality, and radio agents file requests for the band to audition, and even [critic Walter] Winchell recommends the performance, then a shrewd booker realizes that the time is at hand to tour the band on as long a series of one-nighters as the men can endure.

Uncovering the social processes that disguise themselves as sudden and capricious changes in fortune has been my goal. Those with "a finger on the pulse" of music understand some fraction of the genre attributes, forms, and trajectories revealed here. Only through a global view, sorting through the hundreds of accounts of individual music communities, are we able to build a thick history of musical change. I have left to the side the question of exploitation within the process of genre development, only so that I can reveal the sociological characteristics of that process. But there should be no doubt that the categories we use in describing the world of music have consequences. In this chapter, I explore those consequences through a consideration of various classification systems used in music and related fields of culture production. This opens a larger discussion of classification systems and their links to legitimacy, power, identity, and social stratification.

Classification in Music

Four chapters ago I used my students' statements about the origins of rap to illuminate how music histories have taught us to think about the meaning of these categories. From what source do these histories derive these categories and the logic of their organization?

The majority of musical histories faithfully represent these industry genre categories. Books and articles focus on the history of rock 'n' roll, or jazz, or rap. The flowcharts and time lines included in these texts document successions of charismatic leaders and serendipitous events to order the history of the style. These provide consumers with evidence that stylistic boundaries are natural and inevitable—that they reflect something real. Such representations collapse a complex, shifting social world full of debate and disagreement into an inevitable chain of events leading to the present, during which necessary transformations take place. They reflect and reinforce industry categories and the boundaries of acceptable performance.

Industry-based genres rarely produce such disputes because the system of categorization generated and maintained by global music corporations is employed at all stages of the music production process. Record companies are organized into specialty divisions denoted by style (e.g., the rock division, the classical division), and hiring, promotion, and work tasks are organized with respect to these styles. Music industry workers are hired as experts within a style, given specialized work tasks that employ that expertise, and promoted or fired on this basis. Specialization within an industrial category guides contact men and women (especially talent scouts, or "A&R reps") toward new music that reflects the modal aesthetics of their specialty style. Once new acts are signed, artist development practices are devoted to producing music that can be easily promoted within an existing category. Once a single or album is completed, marketing and promotions personnel identify distribution channels (e.g., radio stations) that specialize in that style. The product is physically tagged so that points of sale physically (or digitally) place it within a particular space, marked by style. There is, finally, an enormous periphery of magazines, Web sites, and fan organizations that affirm the value of these categories as meaningful divisions of music.

In short, industry organizations act as "classifying agents," organizing a messy field into simple categories that are then employed across a range of organizations. The power of industrial firms to set these categories is so great that they can change how works are classified more or less by fiat.[1] For example, R&B was a sales category applied to what had been known as "race music" (which was itself a term invented by record executives); the Seattle sound was renamed grunge rock, black rock became funk, and soul was reclassified within R&B. Perhaps the most familiar example is the minting of a new style called "world music," in order to help folk music from outside the United States find a larger audience.

When classifying agents employ categories, such as style, to assist in the comparison of artists and art works, they engage in what is termed commensuration. Commensuration is the act of transforming "qualities into quantities that share a metric."[2] The commodification of goods is the quintessential moment of commensuration: commodities are goods to which prices are assigned *in order that* they can be exchanged in the marketplace for other goods. It is the act of pricing, assigning a currency value, that transforms the qualities of these goods into quantities that have a shared metric. Many objects undergo commensuration, including law schools during the ranking process, and intelligence, through the application of standardized tests and scores. By quantifying and then translating objects into a common metric, commensuration creates relations among entities, but also obscures other relationships, rendering potentially large amounts of information irrelevant. And there is enormous attention and emphasis placed on commensurating artists, works, and styles within Industry-based genres.

One important commensuration instrument is the various "market information regimes": formats that provide regularly updated information about market activity supplied by an independent retailer, presented in a predictable format with consistent frequency, and available to all interested parties at a nominal cost.[3] Market information regimes for cultural objects include Nielsen ratings, best-seller lists, and consumer preference reports. Within a field, the existence of a particular market information regime conveys the impression that the information is valid and vitally important, and its availability creates demand for its use in interpreting that environment. These instruments thus function as and reflect existing classification systems, ordering products into categories, and linking these categories with consumer groups. The *Billboard* chart, which provides a weekly ranking of music according to sales and airplay reports, is the music industry's most important market information regime. Since the first chart was produced in 1958 ("Hot 100 Singles"), the world of recorded music has been divided into charts marked by format (single vs. album) and style (pop, rock, dance). Then songs and albums are ranked within styles, based on sales and airplay rates collected from a sample of points of sale and radio stations. *Billboard* has insisted that it uses the most statistically sound method of computing chart position, even publishing its weighting formula. These weekly performance charts influence management decisions within labels, and function as important reputation signals among performers and firms. The charts commensurate songs and albums by determining their comparison group (allocating each song and album to one or more of the charts that exist at any point in time), and by commensurating sales and airplay counts into a rank order. On any given week, the difference between the number one- and number two–ranked song may be hundreds, or thousands, of sales. Thus the charts obscure some information (differences in sales counts) in order to highlight other information (performance relative to one's contemporaries).

The subjective character of this ostensibly "statistically sound" measure of performance was dramatically revealed in 1991 after *Billboard* began to use digital point-of-sale information (provided by market entrant Sound-Scan) instead of store surveys. Within one week, the top of the charts transformed; country albums and songs took spots away from pop music, and rap music became the fastest-growing popular style. Moreover, a greater total number of albums reached the number one position in that and successive years, and did so more quickly. Finally, there was a decrease in the number of independent labels and new artists appearing in the chart. As the industry's primary market information regime, the *Billboard* charts offer a highly subjective system of classifying music, even as they purport to provide objective market information.

The selectivity of the larger system of genre classification (of which *Billboard* charts are but one manifestation) has also been challenged as a racist structure, which obscures the contributions of black performers. Critics of the system provide an alternative classification system for music that locates each style's origins in a black progenitor.[4] This was a direct criticism of, and response to, the evaluative discourse that existed in American musicology before the 1970s. Until that time, the history of American music was often told as the story of white performers' "elevation" of primitive, emotional black music. In such accounts, music innovated by black Americans had to be "refined" or "improved" by white bands before it was released to the public.[5] These white inheritors then claimed credit for its invention, a practice I noted in chapter 3 in my description of the (white) Dixieland Jass Band, self-proclaimed "inventors" of New Orleans jazz. In an essay from 1955, Langston Hughes added other white "innovators" to the list: "Paul Whiteman took unto himself the title of 'The King of Jazz' and gave the first jazz concert in Aeolian Hall. George Gershwin wrote the first jazz concerto, also the first blues opera—and made himself not only famous, but rich." Hughes concluded, "Almost as fast as the Negro originates something new in the world of music, the whites take it and go, sometimes even claiming it as their own creation."[6] The co-optation of black music comes with an additional cost: the "watering down" of the music. In his 1963 book *Blues People*, author and cultural critic LeRoi Jones (Amiri Baraka) makes this charge against blues musicians, and Nelson George[7] has claimed that R&B experienced a similar transformation in the 1970s.

When African Americans were credited with musical innovation, their creativity was attributed to racial intelligence, intuition, or accident. Commentators described African Americans' innate sensitivity to rhythm, wild and irresponsible expressions of identity, masculinity, force and power, and their closeness to nature, particularly as expressed in irrepressible, wanton sexuality. (I noted this tendency in my discussion of early New Orleans jazz players, in chapter 3.) Thus blacks were credited only with unlearned musical innovation: breaking rules without knowing they exist. These racialized notions of innovation and musical ability were in wide circulation, and their pervasive, embedded character provided media corporations with economic incentives to recycle them.[8] As music critic Jon Pareles noted in a 1987 *New York Times* article:

> Like the movie business . . . the major-label record business generally offers black performers a choice of stereotypes: nice pop band (Kool & the Gang), slick pop crooner (Luther Vandross), or nasty funk band (Cameo). These stereotypes are self-perpetuating across the music business.[9]

In many cases, the consequence of such displays is that notions of black "nature" and musical talent are viewed as genetic, rather than being seen as "the result of sustained learning, practice, discipline, and, most importantly *intelligence*."[10]

Music made by black Americans was also treated as a vector of infection, passing these "black" traits to the audience, a contagion effect that resulted in moral panics around white teens' exposure. In the jazz age, hot rhythm bands were believed to "get into the blood of some of our young folks, and I might add older folks, too."[11] Thirty years later, rock 'n' roll received the same treatment. A psychologist described rock 'n' roll as a "communicable disease" and a "cannibalistic and tribalistic" form of music, and in 1956 *Time magazine* reported one psychologist's belief that the effects of rock 'n' roll on teenagers "bear passing resemblance to Hitler mass meetings."[12]

In short, popular music has virtually always included a notion that African American influences must be safely incorporated into European stylistic patterns. During the rock era, African American cultural sensibilities were foremost in popular culture, but the presence of black artists on the charts was meager at best. The crossover of black dance music in the 1970s finally put black influence at the forefront, and black artists on the charts, but they still needed "white interpreters."[13]

Critics of the prejudice woven into the industry classification system proffered an alternative, built from a revisionist history in which the African American influence on American music organized the field. Their alternative classification system rests on the distinction between blues-based, and therefore African American–derived, music and all other styles. The *blues system,* which includes aspects of mode, rhythm, form, harmony, and pitch, is found in diverse styles, including blues, jazz, rock 'n' roll, gospel, country, and R&B.[14] Generally speaking, scholars identify a handful of attributes associated with the blues approach including a tendency to produce a "swinging" rhythm, or a metrical contrast like what we find in cool jazz, boogie-woogie, and funk. This is linked to an emphasis on physical motion as an integral part of both musical composition and appreciation. Music of this sort tends to include a high density of music within a frame—it "fills the space"—a feature performers often accomplish by using all the instruments in a percussive manner.[15] Finally, many American musical styles use antiphony, or a call-and-response musical structure, which emphasizes audience participation. This includes the punctuation of religious music with shouts of "Hallelujah!" and rap

DJs exhorting "all the ladies in the house" to say "ho!" The blues system is found in several streams, including blues, jazz, R&B, and rap.

A classification system built on a distinction between blues-based and other music involves a moral reversal of the elements associated with black performance. What was once seen as "intuitive," emerging from an embodied, experiential intelligence, is now seen to issue from the intellect and to require a complex, cognitive synthesis of musical traditions.

While revisionist scholars offered an account of blues-based music to address racially essentialist conceptions of innovation, a separate critique took shape that focused on the oligarchic control of music corporations in the United States. This classification system invokes a gross distinction between "independent" and nonindependent music, and has been a particularly popular way to classify music since the 1980s.[16] In earlier periods, the term "independent" was used to describe companies and artists that produced music without the assistance of the four or five major record labels. But in the wake of the so-called Harvard Report (prepared for CBS Records), major labels set up semiautonomous label groups to align with independent labels.[17] Independent labels were attracted to these contracts because they promised autonomy (since they typically stipulated that majors would exert control only over the budget), combined with the production and distribution muscle of the majors. These changes effectively resulted in a new kind of label, neither independent of major label control nor under its direct oversight. Many such "subcontracted" labels touted their independence from the majors, including Creation Records in Britain, which came to play an important role in the widespread success of so-called Britpop, the music associated with groups like Blur, Suede, Elastica, and Oasis.[18] By this point, "'independence' as a mode of musical production and 'indie' as a stylistic subcategory" had been totally confounded, and "'independence' came to denote a set of values and practices that many invested with considerable moral, ethical, and political weight."[19] The new style of indie music was politically, morally, and ethically united without any accompanying musical similarities. That "indie" now refers to a set of values rather than to a mode of musical production makes it both ambiguous and contested. Its power as a marketing category led to its adoption by labels, musicians, and fans in multiple streams, but particularly within the musical styles found in rock and rap.

A large minority of consumers identify themselves as fans of independent rap. They conflate authenticity and independence, reflecting their belief that major label artists operate under market imperatives and are consequently unable to compose sincere or authentic lyrics. There is some empirical evidence for their sense that the assertion of a major label oligarchy changed what lyrical style was popular. The four (then, three) major labels did assert an oligopoly sometime during 1988. However, they did so using the open system of production, whereby independent rap labels like Def Jam were offered pressing and distribution deals by major labels. The smaller labels' existing management largely remained in place and continued to market themselves as indie. In doing so, they retained their indie-oriented fans, while gaining access to more money for production and distribution and, therefore, a larger opportunity space within the marketplace. The post-1988 period was marked by the flowering of ten novel subgenre styles (including West Coast and jazz rap), despite fears that a major label oligopoly would trounce innovative rap music. However, while these styles were musically distinct, there was a dramatic uptick in the number of songs with violent and sexually explicit lyrics. Between 1988 and 1995, major labels charted up to five and a half more songs with these puerile lyrics than all their independent competitors combined. Looking at this rise in "hard-core" rap lyrics, we see evidence that oligarchic control transformed lyrical content. But it isn't clear that this came at the cost of artists' freedom of expression or authenticity. A close study reveals that post-1988 hard-core rap lyrics employed a "hustler" protagonist, and this character appeared to resolve the conflict between major label control and authenticity. The hustler "is . . . an outsider, but one with a comfortable relationship to commercial culture and material success." By using a hustler protagonist in hard-core songs, major label artists (particularly, formerly indie ones) were able to blend "street" credibility—authenticity—with commercial success.[20] Hard-core lyrics reveal not a lack of control or authenticity, but rather the adaptation of artists to the open system of production.[21] This new production system makes attributions of "indie" status extraordinarily complex and frustrates easy use of this classification system. Just sorting out the ownership structure of a label, or estimating the degrees of control artists exert over their creative process, can be a lifelong project, as production of culture scholars will tell you.

Fights over the classification of work or artists as indie, like debates over the authenticity of performances (see chapter 2), have the potential to disrupt the legitimacy of genre classification systems. By drawing attention to the difficulty of sorting works into categories, or to the various interpretations audience members have of these categories, such disruptions can call the categories into question. Likewise, novel items can cause disorder within classification systems. When Miles Davis released a rap album (*The Doo-Bop Song*), it sparked disputes about its place within the music classification system: is it rap or jazz? Or is there a new category of jazz rap, and this is the first you're hearing of it? What *is it*? In that this album (or others like it) is not obviously located within one or another position in the classification system, sociologists will refer to it as a "boundary object."

Boundary objects are those things that "inhabit several intersecting social worlds . . . *and* satisfy the informational requirements of each of them."[22] Boundary objects can produce "noise" or disturbance within classification systems. For example, boundary objects within the marketplace cannot be easily evaluated by means of legitimate categories (e.g., musical styles); that is, they are objects that defy the "categorical imperative."[23] Thus boundary objects often face depressed demand because critics within the field are confused about the product's identity, and don't review it, and its resulting illegitimacy reduces its appeal to consumers.[24] When objects are incomparable to others, they face social penalties, including near invisibility to (potential) consumers.[25] Musicians like Sigur Rós, Philip Glass, Bright Eyes, and the Carpenters have all been described as "unclassifiable" in the music system, although each has been successful at attracting fans. Songs face the same fate: lacking a melody, rhythm, or original music or lyrics, the Beatles song "Revolution 9" may defy categorization both as rock and as "Beatles-style music." A similar case is that of one-off stylistic departures (Neil Young's album of doo-wop, *Everybody's Rockin'*), and collaborations of stylistically different peers (e.g., Joni Mitchell's jazz collaboration with Charles Mingus).[26] Albums, songs, and performers that fit into more than one category can be rendered irrelevant but also produce opportunities for new identities.

The study of music genre forms reveals that there are stages during which multiple legitimate categorization systems exist for the same music. In these moments, boundary objects are produced, and interest groups

can employ them to articulate their differences from others, spark-
ing innovation with the classification system. This occurs in two stages:
Scene-based and Traditionalist genres. In both genres, there are at least
two groups of music community members with different definitions of
legitimate music.[27] In Scene-based genres, members fight over definitions
of the genre ideal, the codification of performance styles, and the uses
of technology. For example, Scene-based rap musicians engaged in bitter
battles over the legitimacy of the Sugar Hill Gang, a manufactured group
that borrowed lyrics from scene members to use in the first broadcast recording of the style, "Rapper's Delight." Questions were raised about both
the legitimacy of recording DJ/MC performances and property rights
over lyrics.[28] In Traditionalist genres, a fracture develops between those
who seek to maintain the spirit of the Scene-based phase, and those who
seek to maintain its music.[29] They are engaging in what economic sociologists call "mutual monitoring": paying attention to fellow producers,
rather than attending to the desires of consumers for their music.[30] It is
typically the case that these groups dispute the categorization of performers, not songs. Traditionalists argue in defense of their older music, while
avant-gardists defend the value of new compositions. Such debates have
swirled around many superstar performers, including James Brown (after
his turn to soul, and then to disco), Miles Davis (with the album *Bitches
Brew* and again in his "rap phase"), John Lennon and Paul McCartney
(in their post-Beatles projects), and, perhaps most famously, Bob Dylan
during and after the 1965 Newport Folk Festival when he "went electric."
These examples illustrate the power of boundary objects: groups that generate consensus about how a work or artist is categorized win legitimacy
for the group and its mastery of the system of classification. Identities are
constituted by these narratives.[31]

One of the more provocative ways to identify boundary objects in music is using the algorithms of the Music Genome Project, now a technology employed by Pandora on their music players. Founders Will Glaser
and Tim Westergren decided to identify all the relevant characteristics of
music at what they conceived of as the genomic level. Over 400 attributes
are used to identify songs, including the gender of the performer and the
level of distortion of the guitar. Songs in the jazz stream employ approximately 400 genes, rock and pop have 150, and rap uses 350. In any song,
the relevant attributes are identified and then their presence is scored in

half integer increments between 1 and 5. Once each song has been coded by a musician, a process that can take a half hour, a selection of songs are then recoded to ensure reliability. After all the songs are entered into an algorithm, a distance function is used to identify similarities and differences between all pairs of songs.[32] While a person with access to the data could theoretically choose any selection of characteristics and identify groups of songs that have the most distal scores on those dimensions, it isn't clear that this would help most listeners. After all, most of us can't (or wouldn't) say whether we enjoy a "dry recording sound" more than a "wet" one, or whether we prefer a dry recording sound coded at 3 to one coded at 4.5 of 5 possible units. Instead, Pandora invites listeners to name songs they enjoy and let the algorithm pick new songs; listeners can then give a "thumbs up" to those they enjoy. Over time, the algorithm learns to make more sophisticated predictions based on the taste of the user. In the context of the Music Genome Project we can think of boundary objects in two ways: as those works that have the greatest distance from all other works based on their objective characteristics (from the initial coding), or as works that listeners cannot decide whether they like. (If we are not ambivalent, this means the work *is* classifiable, into groups of works we like or don't.)

In its way, the global coding of music genes poses a problem for the existing style-based classification of music. Our common sense has been manufactured on the basis of industry categories but this may not always lead us toward the same conclusions as does the Pandora algorithm. For example, Pandora founder Tim Westergren told the *New York Times* that a user wrote to complain about a suggestion made for his Sarah McLaughlin station:

> "I wrote back and said, 'Was the music just wrong?' Because we sometimes have data errors," he recounts. "He said, 'Well, no, it was the right sort of thing — but it was Celine Dion.' I said, 'Well, was it the set, did it not flow in the set?' He said, 'No, it kind of worked — but it's Celine Dion.' We had a couple more back-and-forths, and finally his last e-mail to me was: 'Oh, my God, *I like Celine Dion*.'"[33]

In this anecdote, the algorithm offers a user the "right" music for his station, but the wrong music for his own sense of taste. Indeed, our taste is a function of our common sense, but this common sense is not ours, but rather how we have been fitted into a classification system for people, according to taste.

As I have described above, two challenges have been made to the industry classification of music: a blues-based division and one based on the centralization of control in the music industry. *Banding Together* presents a third. My method of sorting music communities into genre stages based on their possession of resources is a less subjective method of classifying music than the others. I have argued that understanding the attributes of music genre communities *in general* provides us with a social grammar we can use to understand the cultural language of popular music. I never intend that readers "value" one community relative to another, nor do I make any arguments about the quality of the music they produce. That said, this classification schema is built from subjective accounts of music communities—the music histories that functioned as data for this project.

The ability to transform subjects' observations and opinions into objective or measurable facts is, as every sociologist knows, a function of methodological quality. The quality of this translation is dependent upon the number of distinct points of view included in the analysis. That is, it depends upon the construction of what I referred to in chapter 1 as a "thick" history. A good scholar must search for different points of view on events, seek out disconfirming evidence, and accumulate as many accounts as possible. This is as true in ethnographic work as it is in quantitative, cultural studies of the sort I have presented. In the next section, I address more directly the importance of differentiating objective and subjective classification systems, looking outside of music.

Toward a Model of Classification Systems

A key element in the design of a classification system is the degree to which one seeks to employ endogenous criteria or objective ones. You can imagine that all classification systems can be arrayed on a spectrum from those that are objectively verifiable (e.g., counts of things) to those that rely on subjective estimations of qualities (e.g., opinions of things). Arraying classification systems on this spectrum is an easy way to illuminate the extent to which they are appropriate to particular tasks. Insofar as science seeks to organize all the members of a population, and these populations are either nonsentient or otherwise unable to provide accounts of how they would organize themselves, we require an objective sorting mechanism. However, there are circumstances—particularly in the human sciences—in which we seek to represent how the members of a group organize their *own* social world. In cases where we are interested in these representations, a subjective sorting mechanism is best suited to the task. But classification systems fail to achieve scientific goals insofar as they represent subjective orders as objective ones.

Let us begin with one of the most commonly used, and ostensibly objective, classification systems: that which assigns every living being into relationships with one another according to biological attributes. Biologists currently rely on a system of phylogenic classification, through which organisms are linked to one another by virtue of descent from ancestor species, reflecting the role of evolution in species formation. This represents a more objectively verifiable system of classification than the earlier Linnaean taxonomy of organisms (*Systema Naturae*, 1735), which divided life into three kingdoms, then classes, orders, genera, and species. The Linnaean system for classifying plants relied on the salience of characteristics (like the number of stamen) *to scientists* as a sorting characteristic. Thus the plant kingdom (for example) reflected a subjective classification system deployed by scientists, rather than an order of nature.

Our contemporary classification system for race shares many characteristics with the Linnaean system. We typically classify individuals into racial categories on the basis of salient characteristics including skin color, nose shape, and hair texture. However, differences in the number and composition of these categories, both over time and across contexts, illuminate their social construction. These categories are a function of social, not natural, categorization. So-called racial scientists of the nineteenth century sought support for their racial classification system using measurements of body parts, arguing that any correlation found would support their claims to objectivity and scientific veracity.[34] Similarly, defenders of both intelligence tests and entrance exams (e.g., the SAT, the GRE) have argued that correlations with outcome variables (like course grades) demonstrate the objectively verifiable character of these classification systems. However, critics argue that exam performance, IQ, and course grades are all predicted by qualities like parental education and race. When the effects of these attributes are controlled for, the relationship between performance and outcomes disappears, and such measures are revealed as social constructions (not empirically verifiable, generalizable measures). These two contested bodies of research came together in the 1994 publication of Herrnstein and Murray's *The Bell Curve*, which purported to provide scientific evidence of the relationship between race and intelligence (e.g., stipulating that ceteris paribus whites are more intelligent than blacks).[35] Stephen Jay Gould and others successfully refuted this argument, pointing to a variety of errors in conception, measurement, analysis, and generalizability of results. It is now commonly accepted within social science fields that racial categories and IQ scores are subjectively constituted systems.

A second classification system that has attracted criticism of late, and with which the readers of this text are likely to be familiar, comprises the variety of instruments that purport to rank institutions of higher education, or departments within them. The recently released 2010 National Research Council (NRC) report on U.S. doctorate-granting institutions utilized, for the first time ever, two ranking orders: one based on reputation and an "objective" one based on resources. The former was designed to reflect the subjective rank ordering of departments by a sample of faculty, and the latter includes measures like the research productivity of faculty and the GRE scores of admitted students. As with the IQ test, the instrumentation of the objective resource count has been challenged. Among the many complaints, critics claim the research productivity measure (essentially, a count of publications, divided by the number of faculty) has been distorted by the categorical omission of books and the inflation of faculty numbers by departmental reporters. The GRE has its own internal and external validity problems (as I began to describe, above); moreover, it appears that the NRC rankings weighed the quantitative score heavily, thereby privileging the departments that select students based on this characteristic and arbitrarily underranking departments that specialize in qualitative research. In short, critics claim that the NRC rankings offer no reliable, objectively verifiable classification of departments. This, despite the fact that such a ranking would be valuable to administrators who seek to improve their departments, and students and faculty seeking to choose the institution best suited to their needs. Moreover, departments that have lost or added resources may not suffer reputational consequences for years, a fact that drove the interest in using a resource-based measure.

One of the more interesting things we've learned about ranking systems within and outside the academy is that they have a tendency to be reactive. That is, in response to being evaluated, observed, or measured, individuals alter their behavior. Social scientists observe reactivity (also known as observer effects, or the Hawthorne effect) when the information provided by respondents differs depending on whether or not researchers are present, as in Becker, Geer, Hughes, and Strauss's 1961 study of medical school students.[36] Respondents who gain status or satisfaction from participation in the study may selectively share information they believe the researcher seeks to hear; this is commonly referred to as "expectancy effects."[37] The concern is that undetected observer effects will produce results that speak to how respondents perceive their relationship with the observer, rather than revealing the social phenomena of interest.[38] But individuals react to scientific or professional *instruments* just as they react to the presence of scientists. Research on the insurance industry demonstrates that buying insurance (and rates are based on quantitative assessments of risk) increases our risk avoidance behavior, rendering our insurance less valuable.[39] In fact, the general observation has been made that knowledge of theories of economic behavior shapes how individuals behave economically, a characteristic Callon calls "performativity."[40] As it turns out, measures of law school quality (quite like the NRC rankings, in spirit) are also highly reactive measures.[41] In particular, the publication of the *U.S. News and World Report*'s ranking of schools resulted in the redistribution of resources to favor increases in a school's rank. This was done despite the felt importance of other factors, like the school's commitment to distribute resources in accordance with a mission statement. It also encouraged career placement officers to install graduates into *any* job (so that placement statistics will be high) rather than incentivizing them to help students find the *right* job for them. Finally, the existence of a ranking system encouraged law schools to misrepresent their program's resources, to enroll low LSAT entrants in summer programs so they were not averaged into the rankings, and pressured faculty into spring semester leaves of absence after the faculty count was completed.

Reactivity not only poses a threat to the valid collection of information but also, as this example illustrates, can actually change behaviors by bringing them into alignment with the expectations of the instrument. Reactive measures can produce new classes, impact the priority of measures within the system, and—at an extreme—force the replacement of one classification system with another, all while purporting to be inert attempts to measure qualities that are objectively interesting and important.

The classification system for genre presented here is objectively verifiable, or has that potential, once more research is underway to operationalize the genre dimensions presented in chapter 1. My focus has been on data that reflect actions and resources, not perceptions and opinions. Nevertheless, the classification system for genre that resulted may share with subjective, reputational rank orderings the quality of reactivity. There are anecdotal data that music genre members are aware of how other genre communities have fared when faced with particular challenges and opportunities for growth. Insofar as this research systematically presents these circumstances, and relates various outcomes, it may influence the choices musicians make in the future. For example, armed with the knowledge that sympathetic local press coverage may singly be responsible for catapulting scenes into Industry-based genres, local musicians may more earnestly court journalists. The awareness that Traditionalist genres tend to focus on rehashing the accomplishments, and replaying the music, of a Scene-based phase, may encourage entrepreneurs to put more emphasis on innovation. This would increase the likelihood that new, Avant-garde genres would form. While neither of these outcomes appears to be particularly hazardous, it is nevertheless important to identify the potential outcomes of the creation of classification systems, particularly when the subjects being arrayed are sentient and able to engage in reactive behavior.

On Science, Markets, and Memory

I sought to identify a general theory of sociocultural classification that would help us to see and understand shared elements, not only among musical communities, but among other symbol-producing fields as well. For example, innovative movements in science operate in ways that are much like those I have described in music genre formation. The goal for both scientists and artists is the production of culture; innovative ideas and procedures on the one hand and art on the other. The cabals that are at the heart of field changes in science have been called "scientific and intellectual movements" (SIMs) in honor of their social movement–like characteristics.[42] The primary differences between scientists and commercial artists lie in the institutional framework in which they function. SIMs are born in the academy, with its highly particularistic norms, codified rules of method, and standards of scholarly quality. The institutional framework of SIMs (in the natural sciences) is a narrow world of acknowledged experts in university, corporate, and government laboratories underwritten largely by a set of money-granting agencies. The fine arts similarly operate within a nonprofit organizational context, while I have noted that sometimes commercial music transitions across such contexts, after artistic legitimation processes are set in motion. But in the world of music, these conventions are not so neatly articulated, nor are the structures that reproduce them so rigid. Moreover, the adjudicating audience can be quite large and more diverse, and the rules for success are both less formal and more fluid.

Contemporary science operates in a context of well-defined method, established rules of evidence, accumulated knowledge, and general agreement about the problems of contemporary interest. Just as genres emerge out of creative circles where potential innovators interact in face-to-face settings, so do the "invisible colleges" of scholars.[43] These groups form around the dissatisfactions of faculty and students with the dominant practices in a given discipline. Some of these factions are able to gather sufficient resources to produce and convey knowledge.[44] Thus the growth of academic disciplines resembles musical styles in the AgSIT trajectory. New knowledge that affects the scientific field is announced at conferences and published in journals. Money and publication are controlled by the processes of peer review; that is to say, petitions are vetted by acknowledged experts in the particular scientific subdiscipline. Movements in science operate in a world where the definition of how to do "good science" is clearly codified as "the scientific method." What is more, the definition of "good science" is in the hands of the academy, not in those of the public at large, or political authorities, or a clerical hierarchy, though all of these have been vital to shaping science in other societies, past and present. Thus SIMs operate in a tough but highly specified small world of gatekeepers. This is in sharp contrast with the market-based institutional world of genres, where a number of distinct stakeholders have an important part in determining what fits within genre bounds. These include musicians, elements of the music industry, critics, and fans. The support of any one of these is not sufficient for genre growth, but support from all of these is necessary.[45] In those cases where there is an academy that has a major say in what is acceptable music, such as was true in art music in the early twentieth century, genre builders operate much more like science workers.[46] The bitter antagonism between new genre proponents and defenders of the status quo resembles the intense rivalries between schools of thought in academia.[47] Is there any equivalent of a Traditionalist period in science? Much like the "bandwagon effect" found in the study of cancer genetics, the Traditionalist genre form is marked by contests over authenticity between new recruits mobilized by the excitement of the scene and long-standing members' deeper understanding of the meaning of the movement.[48] Movements to change science are terminated when the distinctive ideas of the genrelike entities get incorporated into the general corpus of science.[49] Perhaps this offers a model for how to conceptualize the folding of musical styles into streams.

I take the development of scientific subfields as a case study of the theory of symbolic classification suggested here. In principle, I could select for this purpose any community in which boundaries are drawn between groups. A rich application may be found in organizations and markets, and the field of their study is already populated with works that seek to illuminate categories, classification schemes, and identities. In strong resemblance to my rejection of "thin" music histories, the leaders of this approach take as a core principle that "an actor's position in the market and the rewards associated with it cannot be reduced to individual attributes or performances."[50] To understand the market for new products, for example, one must understand the process by which they are either classified within legitimate categories or able to produce new ones. To the extent that innovations cannot be made to conform to existing types, they meet with one of two results: utter failure, or massive success.[51] This is the categorical imperative that arguably reproduces existing market structures.[52] Under particular market conditions, a focused, legitimate identity facilitates entry into the field, but its value declines over time. Once established in such a field, an actor may benefit from the perception that she has a complex, multivalent identity.[53] If the field of popular culture, or the genre community, resembles the feature film labor market, there may be a rich reward to combining these studies of internal labor markets with the examination of genre trajectories. If it were possible to simultaneously model the transit of individual performers across the shifting sands of music genres, we would emerge with a much more complete understanding of strategic action within this arena.

It is perhaps also possible to use this model of classification to understand stages in the development of collective memory, including perceptions of the famous or infamous, or what we conventionally refer to as reputations.[54] As shared, established images of social actors, reputations emerge from a social process by which information and events are filtered through a selective lens.[55] Certain details acquire relevance and gravity, while others are disregarded or censored out of the stories that concatenate into reputations. This process may occur in stages that resemble genre forms. First, small groups of personal intimates collaborate to construct reputations for one another that are quickly and rather reliably constrained by observed behavior. After all, these reputations are shaped through direct interaction. Most of what we know about this process comes from small group research, like studies of adolescent groups and psychosocial development.[56] Over time, the small group shares reputation-constituting stories with friends outside the immediate circle. Members of this secondary group have no personal interaction with the object of the reputation, and so they have little evidence or reason that would lead them to reject its features. At this stage, reputations are "local": relevant to and consumed by a bounded group, who, by virtue of sharing social space, produce reputations that have fidelity to the self-perception of the individual involved.[57] In some cases, these reputations spread beyond the local scene and enter into the public, media discourse. A menu of media frames predate the entrance of any particular reputation into its purview, so this transition is marked by the translation of the existing local reputation into something that matches, even if it extends, media frames. Media studies scholars have offered a great number of case studies of celebrity, media frames, and scandals that illuminate the dynamics of mass reputations.[58] These studies document the existence of standard frames into which events and social objects are placed during the construction of "stories," but also the need for reputations to fit into accepted genres or styles.[59] Finally, most reputations drop out of mainstream circulation at some point, and historians and dedicated fans are ceded responsibility for carrying on the memory of the individuals and constructing the dimensions of their reputations. The study of artists and politicians provides insights on what resources reputations need in order to survive. To secure a reputation, artists must dedicate some effort to protect their legacy, including the preservation of extensive documentation of their life and work. Artists and politicians must have "reputational entrepreneurs," or supporters with some (financial, social, or personal) stake in their reputation.[60] Artists or their promoters must develop links to cultural archives (like museums) and frequently benefit from later cultural or political identities that promote their "rediscovery."[61]

The development of reputations thus resembles the characteristics of an AgSIT trajectory in music: initiation in a small group of colocated intimates, expansion into a Scene-based local community, an explosion into mass culture, and eventual retreat into a small group of dedicated preservationists. Each stage of the process is marked by changes in the locus of control, as rising levels of interest on the part of increasingly diverse publics results in the loss of control of intimates (and their complaints about the increasing inauthenticity of reputational claims), and the assimilation of reputations into industrial categories.

Defining music genre sociologically as a creative group process rather than as a discourse about taxonomy or a market category facilitates understanding of the processes of classification and systematic change. It may shed light on processes of classification and change in other creative domains in sociology, the arts, management, and the sciences. More broadly, this inductive schema illustrates the relevance of sociology to the study of culture, and the centrality of the study of culture to the problems of contemporary sociology.

The Future of Music

The great majority of musical styles in the United States were created in the second half of the twentieth century. To what should we attribute this difference? It could be that history has erased or blurred distinctions that were important in earlier days, or that technologies were not sufficient to capture them. Alternatively, it could be that there are forces in place that increase the rate of genre formation. Features of U.S. culture, political economy, and technology may have promoted and sustained unique levels of innovation in the postwar period. Having survived the Second World War with its industrial infrastructure intact, the United States played host to the mass production of music for teenagers. Increasing English-language fluency around the globe fueled the popularity of American commercial music and its three-minute song format. Later in the century, the invention of digital technologies for the production and distribution of music fueled the development of diverse styles. Will these new virtual environments for music scenes become the major seedbed for genre development in the twenty-first century?

If musical innovation survives in the new millennium, it may be that the most dynamic new trends are the result of the flow of genres across national boundaries. Genres such as bebop jazz, punk, rap, and post-disco dance music have reached audiences outside the United States and taken root in communities, inspiring both satellite music communities and new hybrid forms. Do Avant-garde or Scene-based genres emerge around exported U.S. music, and if so, to what extent do they resemble the ones examined here? Similarly, how do U.S. musicians form communities around the appreciation and production of Westernized versions of so-called world music, and how do these differ from indigenous forms?[62] Given the importance of this trend, and the book's focus on U.S. music to the relative exclusion of the vibrant creativity occurring elsewhere, I turn now to an extended discussion of the dynamic flows of music across national boundaries.

Some of these U.S.-based styles that have been exported are being re-imported to the United States and the United Kingdom along with Westernized versions of diverse indigenous genres. As most commentators are at pains to point out, this is not an exchange among equals. Global flows of music are conditioned by the control and domination accomplished by the consolidation of worldwide production and distribution in the hands of three Western companies.[63] This puts American and Western artists in a privileged position within production and distribution chains, one denied to most musicians in Africa and Oceania. This neocolonial system of control and domination has been in place since at least the introduction of the syncopated brass music of West Indian regimental bands stationed in West Africa during the mid-nineteenth century. In Central Africa, locals were introduced to the rumba in the interwar period, and African American dance music impacted East Africa after World War II.[64]

Why have U.S. commercial music genres had such an important influence on the commercial music of most parts of the world? Surely, the economic dominance of the United States through the second half of the twentieth century is a factor, but it can't be all-important because the global popularity of Japanese and Chinese commercial music has not risen commensurate with their growing influence in the global economy. We must look elsewhere. Here are several clusters of macro factors that may be of importance, although their statement here may be overdetermined.

As I noted above, the United States emerged from the Second World War with its industrial infrastructure intact, and a flowering of musical innovations resulted. The Armed Forces Radio Service disseminated the latest U.S. commercial music to people in most parts of the world. Voice of America (VOA) and shortwave radio broadcasts, immigrants, military personnel, and merchant seamen have all been vectors of musical diffusion, spreading musical styles to nonnative contexts. For example, sailors served as a vital link in the diffusion of Cuban, Puerto Rican, and salsa recordings to Colombia for twenty years in the mid-twentieth century, before formal networks of record distribution had reached these locales.[65] Similarly, Latin American migration to the United Kingdom spread salsa to that country in the 1980s, before entertainment corporations consolidated their control over music channels to reach this growing market.[66]

The U.S. legal environment must also have been important in the country's comparative advantage. U.S. laws and regulations in force in the third quarter of the twentieth century made for highly competitive radio and record industries, while radio and TV in many other countries were provided by their governments, and were programmed with material that the elite thought the public should consume. This gave very little scope for freedom of expression and stifled the development of new genres in these countries. At the same time, while U.S. laws concerning public morality, and alcohol and drug use, were relatively strict, their enforcement was spotty, so many genres were supported by club owners and other entrepreneurs who championed the latest innovations in order to dispense alcohol, drugs, and sexual services. By the end of the century, the laws that protected media competition had been gutted, while the laws of intellectual property had been extended. Given the experience of earlier decades, these actions should make it more difficult for new genres to flourish within the old media. At the same time, the newfound ease of musical creation, distribution, and consumption made possible by digitalization and the new media has fueled the development of diverse genres.

Scholars have argued about how to view these exchanges. On the one hand, many emphasize the hegemonic control of Western music companies and consumers over the material made available elsewhere. On the other hand, many American composers have been influenced by African music, and many composers working in the jazz and blues idioms have visited Africa—among them, Jimmy Cliff, Bob Marley, James Brown, Tina Turner, Max Roach, and Gilberto Gil. The influence of American composers, working in idioms with clear African musical roots, had "encouraged the exploration of local roots by contemporary African musicians" and fueled the rise of Afrobeat, Senegalese *mbalax* music, and blends with Caribbean styles (e.g., the Zairean *rumba congolaise*).[67] The argument for such influence is provided by the fact that interacting cultures with similarities have a familiarity or shared context that fosters what scholars have called "co-orientation," "cultural triangulation," or "'cultural analogues' that enhance acculturation."[68] For example, the influence of African American styles in West Africa and the Congo was "no mystery," since "Cuban music was returning with interest something that had largely come from there anyway, so there was a most natural affinity."[69] Arjun Appadurai has suggested that we understand the new global economy as a "complex, overlapping, disjunctive order, which cannot any longer be understood in terms of existing center-periphery models (even those that might account for multiple centers and peripheries)."[70] This has led scholars to address the "transversality," "polylateral" or "multilateral" flows, of contemporary popular music. This complex process of appropriation and hybridization may pose problems for any simple argument about the importation of Scene-based musics in the United States or any other country.

Moreover, the production of music in nonnative contexts can provide some unexpected benefits to music communities. For example, prior to 1989, the most successful East German rock bands had recording contracts with West German firms.[71] Although copyright and royalty regulations in the GDR sent 75 percent of revenue from sales of these records back to the state, artists faced no restrictions on the content of their music. This production system opened possibilities for critique: "As soon as the musicians realized their own power, they started to include critical songs in the versions of their albums produced in West Germany," and the GDR risked being seen as censors (and losing a stream of hard currency) if they attempted to control the albums' introduction across the border.[72] Consequently, rock music was able to play a critical, if poorly reported, role in setting in motion the destruction of the Berlin Wall and the end of the GDR.

In Closing

As I noted at the start of this chapter, we have been encouraged to deploy our tastes to categorize music rather than to understand how categories come to define our tastes. Our tastes are more than personal dispositions, idiosyncratic orientations toward the world and its importance to us. They are also not inert social constructions. Our tastes are instruments of power. There are three important components to this instrument.

First, tastes encode the power of your origins. When it comes to taste, the socialization process—specifically, the process of acquiring a "habitus"— plays a central role in shaping our desires, aspirations, and choices. The concept of a habitus reflects a broad notion of taste, one that captures our ways of understanding, manners, possessions, and how all these inform the limits and possibilities of future expectations and actions.[73] Inculcated through primary socialization, tastes tend to be shared by parents and children, and, similarly, by coethnics and by groups with common membership in a nation-state or a socioeconomic class. Consequently, we must reject the notion that tastes are somehow natural or innate, and instead acknowledge that they are learned and then internalized.[74]

This is thus somewhat contrary to our commonsense understandings— most of us tend to view our tastes as idiosyncratic, unique, and deeply personal. In fact, it is the commonsensical nature of our view of taste that allows tastes to operate as a mechanism of social reproduction. To the extent that we treat them as natural and inevitable, we refuse to critique our tastes. In refusing to critique them, we ignore one of the means by which our social structure is reproduced. The fact that our tastes draw us into relations with others who share our origins also sends the signal that they are "natural." The famous "boy's club" of corporate America has sustained itself in the wake of fair labor laws because group affiliation is founded on the unity of group members' interests (e.g., going to a strip club, or sailing). These cultural activities function to solidify bonds between socially equivalent individuals and increase their distance from others. Lacking knowledge of and taste for cultural forms impedes our developing certain relationships just as illiteracy prevents us from reading. In fact, consecrated art forms, like opera and classical music, were defined in order to construct a boundary around elites—and defined the group as one populated by those who had access to and consumed the most cultivated art.[75]

Second, this socialization process teaches us not only what tastes are appropriate to our life circumstances, but also how to make meaning from the consumption process. Meaning making, then, is a continual process of drawing social boundaries between those who are "like us" and those who are not.[76] We are socialized into a certain set of tastes, but also into a certain set of interpretative frameworks that we use to make meaning from cultural experiences.[77] For example, elites appear to consume popular culture products, like television sitcoms and fast food, with an "ironical stance."[78] Elites also tend to consume culture using a "critical" rather than a "referential" frame.[79] In a comparison of how upper-class and working-class Brazilian viewers reacted to a soap opera, working-class audiences used a "realistic" frame in critiquing the narrative: they interpreted the show as if it were real, describing the plot using the names of characters (and not the actors' names), and evaluated the likelihood of events that transpired on the show.[80] Elite viewers, on the other hand, approached the text with a "critical lens": they distanced themselves from the events portrayed by referring to production processes, used the names of actors and not characters, and maintained an ironical stance in justifying the pleasure they took in watching the show.[81] Group boundaries are maintained based not "on *what* is consumed, but on *the way in which items of consumption are understood.*"[82] Thus it is not only what you like, but also how you interpret the meaning of culture that wields power.

Taste is used to exert and reveal power in subtle ways. After all, class is more than just an attribute. More than simply a function of one's income, wealth, or a combination of these factors with education, family background, or occupational aspirations, class is also a performance. As a performance, class works like a script, foretelling our use of language, mannerisms, and dress, and our taste preferences.[83] Even though many of us consume the same popular culture, we can draw very different meanings from our consumption experience. Our basis for interpretation is constrained by the social groups to which we belong.

This offers an alternative vision of the book's purpose. This book is an instrument that can reveal what taste would obscure: that music communities share a basic grammar, and a set of attributes that emerge and fade. As a complement to existing sociological studies of taste, *Banding Together* offers an illustration of how categories of style themselves change. Work on artistic styles typically takes individual and group tastes as a starting point, leaving aside the question of how taste categories transform over time. Finally, rather than treating tastes as if they cohere only to styles (that is, assigning individuals a taste for jazz, or rap), my approach allows us to consider that audiences may have a taste for the avant-garde or the popular, in whatever style is available. We are now able to think about this behavior as a social preference for one kind of music community over another.

This final point leads me back to where I began: with my students' assessments of the "legitimate" lyrical content of rap music. As educationally advantaged, young adults, my students have a taste for progressive, politically and socially relevant music, just as their middlebrow brothers and sisters tend to prefer Industry-based genres, regardless of style. Like all of us, they assign positive value to their own tastes, and these tastes reflect their origins and community values. The history of rap music they produce is thus a partial history, assembled from details that support the value of *their* tastes. Thus the study of classification systems reveals the link between our values and how we assign value, as a function of our participation in (musical) communities.

Notes

Chapter 1
Music Genres

1. My students are not alone in framing rap's significance into these two positions. Academic and musicological texts on rap music tend to adopt one or the
other position. Take, for example, the following excerpt from an essay titled
"Marooned in America: Black Urban Youth Culture and Social Pathology": "As
inhabitants of extreme-poverty neighborhoods, many rap artists and their audiences are entrenched in a street life filled with crime, drugs, and violence. Being
criminal-minded and having street values are much more suitable for living in
their environment." In this excerpt, Lott (1992, 71, 72) describes rap as a cultural
expression of the poor and dispossessed, and as a form of social documentation and critique. Later in the article, he also addresses the criticism raised my
students, arguing that "at its worst, this [street] knowledge is manifested through
egotistical sexual boasting" but rappers' driving objective "is to be politically as-
tute, that is, to have a full understanding of the conditions under which black
urban youth must survive." The description of rap as political music, for better or
worse, is the dominant professional understanding of the genre, despite evidence
that alternative readings of its history are available.
2. Marshall 2007.
3. We inevitably begin researching history in the present and work our way back-
ward. However, when we record historical accounts to share them with others,
we start with origins and proceed forward to the present. What is produced in
this process is a path-dependent historical process that denies history. History
is not a record of the events that lead to some preconceived end but an account
of the processes of institutionalization by which events become embedded in
chains of significance.
4. Bearman, Faris, and Moody 1999, 508.
5. Of course, the more ancient the event, the less likely it is that its meaning will
change. For this reason, Sewell (1996, 878) argues: "One may state as a rule of

thumb that how an analyst should delimit an event will depend on the structural transformation to be explained. . . . Such decisions must be made post hoc: with some confidence when dealing with an event that occurred two-hundred years ago and whose consequences have generally been fixed for some time, more tentatively when the consequences of a rupture have only recently begun to appear and when additional, perhaps surprising, consequences may yet emerge." For example, the causes and consequences of the American Revolution, or the drafting of Magna Carta, are relatively unlikely to change. Bearman, Faris, and Moody argue (1999, 505–6), "We cannot affix (forever) a single meaning to events embedded within sequences, or event sequences embedded in populations of other event sequences. We can nonetheless try to assess what kinds of events, event sequences, and sets of interrelated event sequences are likely to be conditioned by future events. In simple terms, some events, event sequences, and cases are dead. Some events and event sequences are subject to radical revision. We can confidently talk about the meaning of dead events." Taking up this line of inquiry, I argue here that music histories are not dead events but are, rather, constantly in play, being reinterpreted and relearned by successive generations of artists and fans. Consequently, their meaning should be viewed as contingent, and subject to revision. However, the structure of music communities appears relatively fixed, and so this is a classification system—a historical event—in which we can have greater confidence.

6. Schematic representations of music illustrate the "thin" characteristics of histories most clearly. Flowcharts and time lines document successions of charismatic leaders and serendipitous events in order to represent the history of the field. For example, one "complete headbanger's history" of heavy metal styles lists album releases, the founding of organizations, and famous controversies like Ozzy Ozbourne's decapitation of a bat during a 1982 concert performance (Christie 2004). The succession of such events indicates the meaning of the style: it is traced back to certain innovators, then changes course with influential events, and typically reaches its end with the contributions of a crossover act that attracts mainstream audiences. Thin histories are also found in more musicologically focused texts, where the succession of ideological or aesthetic changes that represent "discoveries" or "advances" are credited to performance groups. For example, Gribin and Schiff (1992) present a table reporting five stages of doo-wop music, including developments in the use of nonsense syllables, falsetto singing, and seven other attributes of performance.

7. Becker 1982.

8. Historical accounts tend to emphasize idiosyncratic reasons for innovation or musical decline. These include the loss of musicians to drugs or suicide, the steering power of opportunistic promoters, and the failure of audiences to recognize talent.

9. The link between a group's size and its characteristic features is not new to sociology. In his "Sociology of Pure Numbers," Georg Simmel noted that while coop-

eration and trust characterized groups of two, a set of divisive behaviors emerged only once the group grew to include three individuals (Wolff 1950, 145).

10. For the general claim that there is no theory of dynamic change in classificatory schemes, see DiMaggio 1987. For efforts within the domain of nation building, see Anderson 1983; in social movements, see Traugott 1995; with respect to name-giving practices, see Lieberson 2000; and in French cuisine, consult Ferguson 2004.

11. Scholars have examined the impact of Internet technology (Kibby 2000; Lee and Peterson 2004; P. Williams 2006), regulation and deregulation of industries (Chevigny 1991; Adams 1994), the impact of firm and market structure on innovation (Peterson and Berger 1975; Lopes 1992; Dowd 2000, 2004; Lena 2006), the distribution of musical tastes over time (Peterson and Simkus 1992; Peterson and Kern 1996; Watson and Anand 2006; Peterson and Rossman 2008), the relationship between music and identity (Brace and Friedlander 1992; Hudson 1997; Glynn 2000; Krims 2000; DeNora 2000), the histories of performers and fields (Liang and Stobbe 1993; Kennedy 1994; King 2002; Jackson 2004), censorship and surveillance (Rossman 2004; Tepper 2010), and the social construction of authenticity (Peterson 1997; Jensen 1998; Lena 2003; Grazian 2004; Urquía 2004).

12. This definition of genre is indebted to the one in Neale 1980, 19.

13. In contrast, scholars of the humanities employ the idea of genre to focus attention on the "text" of the cultural object, which is abstracted from the context in which it is made or consumed (Fowler 1982; Swales 1990; Hyon 1996; Devitt 2004; Apperley 2006; Frow 2006; C. Williams 2006). This textual approach to genre is found in the work of most musicologists, who identify genre as a set of pieces of music that share a distinctive musical language (Merwe 1989). In general, genre is used to designate a mode of production (e.g., concerto), and style is used to refer to the means of producing those genres (e.g., baroque concerto). Some sociologists carry forward the idea of genre-as-text, but they are careful to show how genre is influenced by the context in which it is made and consumed. Dowd (1992) shows the societal influences on the musicological structure of popular music, and Cerulo (1995) shows how national anthems mirror the societal context within which they are created. Other lines of work use genre without problematizing its content or development (Bourdieu 1984; Peterson and Kern 1996). Among the sociological approaches that focus on participants involved in a collective project, readers may refer to Peterson's (1997) study on the creation of country music, DeVeaux (1997) on bebop jazz, Garland (1970) on soul, Bennett (2004) on the Canterbury sound, Cantwell (1984) on bluegrass, and Kahn-Harris (2007) on the European varieties of heavy metal rock. Also, sociologists have used cognate terms, analogous with the meaning of genre employed here, including subculture (Thornton 1996), scene (Bennett 1997), and neo-tribe (Maffesoli 1996).

14. Negus 1999, 29–30.
15. Kadushin 1976; Williams 1981; Becker 1982.
16. Albrecht 1970, 7–8; Crane 1992, 112.
17. Lamont and Molnár 2002.
18. Waksman 2009, 8. Relatedly, Jason Toynbee (2000) has argued that genre is a system that regulates the exchange between repetition and difference, similarity and variation.
19. Becker 1982. "Free music" is an interesting limiting case because, as Toynbee (2000) notes, although its practitioners say that what they play is guided by the dictates of the musical sounds of the moment, and not by the expectations of other players, audiences, and critics, they nonetheless play within conventions well understood by progressive jazz musicians (see also Attali 1985; Lewis 1996).
20. Walser 1993, 4.
21. Hamm 1995; Fornäs 1995.
22. McLeod 2001, 60.
23. Brewster and Broughton 2000.
24. Gendron 2002.
25. Ennis 1992.
26. I believe that Ennis is borrowing his usage from disc jockey, television personality, and payola profiteer Alan Freed, who said in the 1956 film *Rock, Rock, Rock* (in which he played himself), "'Rock and roll' is a river of music that has absorbed many streams: rhythm and blues, jazz, rag time, cowboy songs, country songs, folk songs. All have contributed to the big beat."
27. Ennis 1992.
28. Goosman 2005, 83.
29. Waksman 2009, 242.
30. On the cuchifrito circuit, see Leymarie 2002, 267–68.
31. Fabbri 2001, cited in Waksman 2009, 57.
32. Tsitsos 1999, 407.
33. Christie 2004, 242.
34. On political economy, see Attali 1985. On urban social dynamics, see Lloyd 2005. On cultural production, see Becker 1982.
35. Eliot 1989; Dannen 1990; Simmons 2001.
36. Goosman 2005, 103.
37. Goosman 2005, 83.
38. As I noted earlier in the paragraph, there has been unfortunately little systematic research on the kind and amount of funding artists receive during their careers. As I write, scholars at Indiana and Vanderbilt Universities have designed an innovative survey initiative to examine patterns in the financial support of artists working across fields, including music. Once launched, the Strategic National

Arts Alumni project (SNAAP) will gather data on the artistic lives and careers of alumni who trained as visual, performing, or literary artists in secondary and postsecondary institutions. These data will allow scholars to gain a better understanding of the systemic factors that helped or hindered the career paths of alumni, including the financial resources of artists at various career stages. Ultimately, scholars and granting agencies may be able to use this information to provide more effective financial interventions in order to assist in the diversification and advancement of the arts. In music communities, we may discover that bartering arrangements among constituencies in Scene-based genres are the best means by which to develop capacity and expertise, while government subventions are ideal to support the expansion of niche musics into Industry-based genres.

39. Talley 2005, 234.
40. Bauck 1997, 234.
41. Thornton 1996; Binder 1993.
42. Pruter 1996, 256.
43. McCarthy and Zald 1977, 1220. However, I employ a weak definition of grievances in that I do not postulate that these are sufficient for mobilization (contra Smelser 1963) and I seek to examine the ways in which these grievances are framed by issue entrepreneurs and organizations.
44. Rochon 1998, 21.
45. Lovesey 2004, 346.
46. Bourdieu 2003, 101.
47. Pruter 1996, 256.
48. Quoted in Stokes 1991, 205.
49. Frith 1983.
50. Frith 1996.
51. Rubinstein 1995.
52. Hebdige 1979.
53. Schilt 2004; P. Williams 2006.
54. Quoted in Jones 1992, 119.
55. Goosman 2005, 5.
56. Moore 2005, 238.
57. Moore 2005, 239.
58. Quoted in Moore 2005, 239.
59. According to Gribin and Schiff (1992, 23), "When Alan Freed coined the phrase 'rock 'n' roll' in 1952, he was referring to rhythm and blues and group 'street corner' music, or doo-wop (which had just come into existence). It was not until 1955 that 'rockabilly,' a combination of country rhythm and blues and country and western music, blossomed and was added under the rock 'n' roll umbrella.

From that point on, rock 'n' roll comprised a combination of three separate musics—rhythm and blues, rockabilly and doo-wop."

60. Waxer 2002, 4.
61. Quoted in Hosokawa 2002, 289.
62. Ripani 2006, 5.
63. Biddle and Knights 2007; Negus 1999; Inglis and Robertson 2005.
64. Garofalo 1994.
65. Hamm 1983, 290.
66. Weisbard 2008.
67. Anand and Peterson 2000.
68. Nidel 2005, 2.
69. Negus 1999, 164, 165.
70. Negus 1999, 163.
71. Collins 2009, 62.
72. On the lack of distinctive stylistic or idiomatic features, see Biddle and Knights 1997, 219. On the perception of an underdeveloped market potential for folk music from outside the United States, see Inglis and Robertson 2005, 161.
73. Caves 2000.
74. Arian 1971. Musical production in the United States is split among for-profit and nonprofit organizations. Scholars working to understand nonprofit organizations, and the art music they produce, focus on how such organizations function to produce genre boundaries and canons (DiMaggio 1982; Dowd et al. 2002), identities and roles for performers and organizational functionaries (Glynn 2000), and their declining significance in the taste profiles of Americans (Peterson and Kern 1996; van Eijck 2000; Bennett 2006; Bukodi 2007; Peterson and Rossman 2008). On the other hand, the study of for-profit musical organizations focuses on decision making in uncertain markets (Hirsch 1972; Anand and Peterson 2000; Ahlkvist 2001; Ahlkvist and Faulkner 2002), career trajectories for artists (Faulkner and Anderson 1987; Dowd and Blyler 2002; Faulkner 2003), and the diversity of genres, performers, and songs (Peterson and Berger 1975; Lopes 1992; Dowd 2004; Lena 2006; Watson and Anand 2006).
75. For a range of examples, see Glynn 2000; Krims 2000; DeNora 2000; Salganik, Dodds, and Watts 2006.
76. Bourdieu 1993.

Chapter 2
Three Musics, Four Genres: Rap, Bluegrass, and Bebop Jazz

1. Price 1975, 55–56.
2. Rose 1994a.

3. I borrow the concept of "stream" from Ennis (1992), who argued that there are families of music that retain their coherence through shared institutions, aesthetics, and audiences.

4. Malone 1968; Rosenberg 1985.

5. DeVeaux 1997; Shipton 2001; Becker 2006.

6. Lieberson 2000.

7. Becker 1982; Alexander 2003.

8. McNeil and McCain 1996; Kahn-Harris 2007.

9. McNeil and McCain 1996, 41.

10. Peterson and Ryan 2003.

11. Seabrook 2010, 26.

12. Ellison 1966, 199–200.

13. Quoted in Fricke and Ahearn 2002, 26.

14. Rose 1994a; Fricke and Ahearn 2002; Chang 2005.

15. Rose 1994a.

16. Peterson 1997.

17. Rosenberg 1985; Peterson 1997.

18. Pearson 1987.

19. Gitler 1986.

20. DeVeaux 1997.

21. Paniccioli 2004.

22. Quoted in McNeil and McCain 1996, 3.

23. Notable examples include Shank 1994 on rock and country in Austin, Texas; Cohen 1991 on the Liverpool scene; Becker 2004 on jazz in Kansas City; Grazian 2003, 2004 on blues in Chicago; and Urquía 2004 on salsa in London.

24. On virtual scenes, see Kibby 2000; Bennett 2004; Bennett and Peterson 2004; Lee and Peterson 2004. See Kahn-Harris 2007, 81 on distros.

25. On the Chicago blues scene, see Grazian 2004. On newer scenes, see Cohen 1991.

26. Feather 1949; Gitler 1986.

27. Price 1975, 32–33.

28. Rosenberg 1985, 55.

29. Fricke and Ahearn 2002; Lena 2003; Chang 2005.

30. Rosenberg 1985.

31. Price 1975, 35.

32. Cantwell 1984.

33. Thornton 1996.

34. Florida 2002; Lloyd 2006.

35. Gaines 1994; Thornton 1996; Urquía 2004; Walker 2006.

36. Escott 1991; Hesmondhalgh 1998; Kruse 2003.

37. Bauck 1997, 233; George 1998, 57.

38. On bop, see DeVeaux 1997. On rap, see Fricke and Ahearn 2002.
39. Shank 1994.
40. George 1998; Ford 2004, 46–47.
41. Smitherman 1997, 4; Krims 2000; Lena 2003.
42. On mods and rockers, see Cohen 2002 [1972]. On the disco demolition derby, see Jones and Kantonen 2000; Lawrence 2003. On the debates between heavy metal and punk rockers, see Waksman 2009.
43. Chadbourne 1997; Spring 2004. On many occasions, such "moral regulation" is designed to systematically persecute populations marked by race, class, or gender differences. New York City's infamous "cabaret laws" systematically targeted African American performers in the 1920s by restricting the types of nightclubs where jazz could be performed, what areas of the city could host such establishments, and who could perform within them (Chevigny 1991; see also Adams 1994 on the regulation of spaces of leisure in Toronto).
44. Tepper 2009, 289.
45. Attali 1985; Thornton 1996; Martinez 1997; Olson 1999; Redhead 1999.
46. Laing 1985.
47. Rose 1994a; Chang 2005.
48. Martinez 1997; Lena 2006.
49. Kofsky 1970.
50. Cantwell 1984.
51. Mann 2008, 87.
52. The "adopted pose of rustics" from Mann 2008, 87. On being "exiles," see Stewart 1988, 235.
53. Lopes 2002.
54. DeVeaux 1997.
55. Rosenthal 1992.
56. Fricke and Ahearn 2002; Chang 2005.
57. Rose 1994a, 196 n.78.
58. Shusterman 1991, 616.
59. Rosenberg 1985.
60. Peterson and Beal 2001; Lee and Peterson 2004.
61. Studies of the market-based popular music field include Peterson and Berger 1975; Lopes 1992; Frith 1996; Negus 1999; and Dowd 2004.
62. Peterson 1990, 101.
63. Hirsch 1972.
64. Anand and Peterson 2000.
65. Peterson 1990; Anand and Watson 2004.
66. Lena 2004, 2006.
67. Rosenberg 1985, 169.

68. Whitburn 1996, 119.
69. Anand and Watson 2004.
70. Krasilovsky and Schemel 2000.
71. Krasilovsky and Schemel 2000.
72. Peterson 1997.
73. The claim that bluegrass was a term first used in print in 1957 comes from Neil Rosenberg, personal communication, July 7, 2006. Lomax's description is found in the October 1959 issue of *Esquire Magazine*. Refer to Cantwell 1984 and Rosenberg 1985 for a description of how bluegrass came to be bracketed with country music.
74. Some attention has been paid to the dynamic relationship between rap music and branding, in part because rap artists seem to have systematically adopted the practice of mentioning brand names within their lyrics. Seeking to capitalize on this predilection, brand managers quickly moved to find ways to commission such mentions from artists, and dedicated services like Lyrics Marketing opened shop. The difficulty, as the business press and artists are at pains to emphasize, is that paid mentions of brands may be viewed as scripted, inauthentic, and insincere, conclusions that would hurt both the artist and the brand. For press on the topic, see Kiley 2005.
75. Gillett 1974; Laing 1985.
76. Thornton 1996.
77. Lopes 2002.
78. Binder 1993; Thornton 1996.
79. Santelli 1980.
80. Lopes 2002.
81. Chang 2005.
82. Cocks, Stengel, and Worrell 1985; Laing 1985; Thornton 1996.
83. May 1985.
84. May 1985.
85. Barol 1986, 85.
86. Quoted in Cocks, Stengel, and Worrell 1985, 70.
87. Bork 1996, 125, 133.
88. Quoted in Fernando 1994, 169.
89. Price 1975, 38.
90. Peterson 1997; Grazian 2004.
91. Cantwell 1984; Eyerman and Jamison 1998; Lopes 2002.
92. This occurred in rap (Salaam 1995; Krims 2000), bop (Peterson 1972; DeVeaux 1997), and bluegrass (Cantwell 1984; Rosenberg 1985).
93. Peterson 1972; Lopes 2002.
94. Goldsmith 2004, 6.
95. Rosenberg 1985, 352.

96. Nusbaum 1993.
97. Quoted in Goldsmith 2004, 5–6.
98. Inter alia Abrahms 1970; Wepman, Newman, and Binderman 1976; Crowley 1977; Levine 1977; Smitherman 1977; Dundes 1981; Gates 1988; Baker 1990 [1972].
99. See Powell 1991; Shusterman 1991; Chambers and Morgan 1992; Bernard-Donals 1994; Salaam 1995; Martinez 1997; Smitherman 1997; Cheney 1999; Ogbar 1999; Parker 1999; Pinn 1999; Wahl 1999; Marable 2002.
100. On the "features of ghetto life," see Shusterman 1991, 619. For Chuck D's description of rap, see Chambers and Morgan 1992, 83.
101. For a discussion of the religious sentiments in rap music, see Cheney 1999. For an examination of Black Nationalist sentiment in rap, see Decker 1993; Henderson 1996.
102. Bennett 2004.
103. Rosenberg 1985.
104. Rosenberg 1985, 372.
105. Artis 1975.
106. Grazian 2003, 13.
107. Kelley 2004, 140.
108. On bluegrass, see Rosenberg 1985. On punk, see Laing 1985. On salsa, see Urquía 2004.
109. Kelley 2004.
110. Grazian 2003, 13.
111. Kelley 2004.
112. Examples of such case studies include DeVeaux 1997 on the formation of bebop jazz; Ginell 1994 on the rise of western swing; Pruter 1996 on doo-wop; Brewster and Broughton 2000 on the creation of contemporary dance music; Cohen 1991 on rock 'n' roll culture in Liverpool; Chang 2005 on the evolution of rap; Laing 1985 on early punk rock; DeNora 1995 on the construction of Beethoven as a genius; Hoskyns 2006 on the 1960s–70s psychedelic California singer-songwriters of Laurel Canyon; and Marshall 2006 on the rise of reggaeton beginning in the 1990s.
113. Frith 1996; Regev 1994, 2002; Lopes 2002.
114. Salaam 1995; Krims 2000.
115. Quoted in Potter 1989, 1.
116. Quoted in Potter 1989, 1.
117. For good histories of gangsta rap, see George 1998; Rose 1994a; Lena 2003, 2004; Chang 2005.
118. Krims 2000; Lena 2003, 2004.
119. Lena 2006.

120. Perkins 1996; Krims 2000; Osumare 2001; Olavarria 2002.

121. Cantwell 1984, 172.

122. Rosenberg 1985, 359.

123. The most notable examples of social psychological research on nascent state phenomena follows in the tradition of Francesco Alberoni (1984).

124. Modleski 1982; Alexander 1992.

125. Negus 1999.

126. On unconscious planning, see Gustafson and Cooper 1979; Gustafson et al. 1981. On reflexive monitoring, see Giddens 1979, 56; Edwards 1998. On practical consciousness, see Nonaka and Toyama 2003. On leadership and domination, see Weber 1978 [1924]; Johnson, Dowd, and Ridgeway 2006.

127. Lawrence 2003, 185.

128. Heritage and Greatbatch 1991; Drew and Heritage 1992; Gibson 2008, 366.

129. Tilly 1997.

130. On youth cultures, see Hebdige 1979. On Scene-based musical communities, see Reynolds 1998; Bennett 1999; Haenfler 2006; Kahn-Harris 2007. On fashion, see Davis 2006.

131. See Crane's 1999 discussion of these phases in haute couture.

132. On local leaders, see Bikhchandani, Hirshleifer, and Welch 1992.

133. DiMaggio and Powell 1983.

134. Hesmondhalgh 1998.

135. Mohr and Guerra-Pearson 2010.

136. Shank 1994; Forman 2002.

137. Waksman 2009, 5.

138. Dubrow 1992, 116.

139. Lawrence 2003, 134.

140. Vaccaro and Cohn 2004; Lorenzen and Frederiksen 2005.

141. Garofalo 2003, 39.

142. Peterson 1973; Santelli 1980.

143. Fischer 2003, 227.

144. Cloonan 2003, 18.

145. Bastian and Laing 2003.

146. Interested readers should begin their consideration of censorship and art with Cloonan and Garofalo 2003 and Tepper 2010.

147. Goldsmith 2004, 12.

148. Goldsmith 2004, 7.

Chapter 3
Music Trajectories

1. Aminzade 1992, 459.
2. Christie 2004.
3. Vincent 1996.
4. Gribin and Schiff 1992.
5. Aminzade 1992, 462. When sociologists examine variations upon trajectories, they often rely upon "path dependency theories," theories assuming that past choices and temporally remote events can help explain how particular decisions delimit future options (Mahoney 2000). Aminzade (1992, 463) argues that path dependent analyses should meet four conditions: (1) they should explore the causes of key choices that were decisive in future opportunities; (2) they should identify key points in a sequence where alternative paths were not taken (often using counterfactual analysis); (3) they should identify mechanisms of inertia; and (4) they should be launched by contingent events where "individual actors often exercise substantial power to channel the direction of subsequent events along a particular path." While I seek to identify the conditions that prevented many musical forms from acquiring all the genre forms within their trajectory, my reliance on case studies completed with other objectives in mind prevents me from meeting Aminzade's conditions. Instead, I focus on identifying mechanisms of inertia that cause musical communities to deviate from one of the two trajectories found in musical histories.
6. I am grateful to Bill Roy for making this observation.
7. Dorsey began his musical career at an early age, playing jazz piano behind Bessie Smith and Ma Rainey. Inspired by composer C. Albert Tindley, who wrote now-classic gospel songs like "I'll Overcome" (later changed to "We Shall Overcome") and "Stand by Me" in the early 1900s, Dorsey began to write praise music (Cusic 2001, 53).
8. Darden 2004, 167.
9. He borrowed five dollars and mailed five hundred copies to black churches across the country; in an interview he explained: "It was three years before I got a single order. I felt like going back to the jazz field of music." It wasn't until Dorsey was invited to perform and sell sheet music at the 1930 National Baptist Convention that he gained confidence in the music's selling power (Heilbut 1997, 27). He would sell four thousand copies of the sheet music at the convention (Darden 2004, 169).
10. Darden 2004, 170.
11. Heilbut 1997, xxvi.
12. Heilbut 1997; Darden 2004.

13. Heilbut 1997, xxix.

14. Heilbut 1997, xxvi.

15. The dozens of gospel hits were "heard everywhere in black neighborhoods, on street corners, through open windows, down alleys, in bars and restaurants" (Heilbut 1997, xxix).

16. Cusic 2001, 55.

17. Although some viewed the bookings as ignoble, the Ward Singers performed at Disneyland in the early 1960s, at the New Frontier and Caesar's Palace in Las Vegas, and at the Monterey Jazz Festival, and they even headlined a USO tour of Vietnam in 1966. In his later years, James Cleveland worked with popular music artists like Elton John and Liza Minnelli, and on films including *Roots* and *Porgy and Bess*, advocated on behalf of gospel music (putting pressure on the Grammy Awards to increase the number of gospel categories), and became the first gospel singer to receive a star on the Hollywood Walk of Fame (Darden 2004, 272–73).

18. Warrick, Hillsman, and Manno 1977, 32.

19. The Dorsey style influenced male quartets and small groups, including the Dixie Hummingbirds, Pilgrim Travelers, the Soul Stirrers, and the Golden Gate Quartet. The Golden Gate Quartet is worthy of special mention both because they were imitated by other quartet groups and because they play an important role in national history. The group recorded an album with the Library of Congress to mark the anniversary of the Thirteenth Amendment to the Constitution. This brought the Golden Gates to the attention of Eleanor Roosevelt, who requested that they perform at her husband's inaugural gala. Joining actors, singers, and the National Symphony Orchestra, the Golden Gates performed in January 1941 at Constitutional Hall, operated by the Daughters of the American Revolution (DAR). The DAR had four years earlier blocked African American opera star Marian Anderson from performing there. Anderson's exclusion from the venue led to her famous performance on the steps of the Lincoln Memorial, on Easter of 1939 (Darden 2004, 186–87). The Gates' performance marked an important symbolic step forward in the integration of musical performance spaces.

20. Cusic 2001, 60.

21. Roberts 1979, 16.

22. Roberts 1979, 15.

23. Irene Castle may also be memorialized as the first woman in New York to bob her hair (Roberts 1979, 45).

24. Roberts 1979, 45.

25. Roberts 1979, 46.

26. Roberts 1979, viii. The form of jazz called swing is the only one of these Scene-originating musics to acquire a Traditionalist genre form. Swing grew out of the late 1920s efforts of sweet dance bands to incorporate into their music elements

of what was called at the time "hot jazz." Composers and arrangers found ways of orchestrating hot jazz improvisation over written dance band parts, satisfying the interests of both dancers and jazz fans. In the hands of Duke Ellington, Glenn Miller, Count Basie, Benny Goodman, and the like, swing became the dominant form of industrial pop music by the late 1930s. Its Industry-based form withered in the late 1940s, and, beginning a decade later, a vigorous swing Traditionalist genre was established (Shipton 2001; Magee 2005).

27. Peterson and Berger 1975.

28. Independent labels have lower overhead costs, a smaller administrative staff, and fewer artists to nurture; all these elements allow small labels to focus on serving a local or particular public to which they feel they have access. They are able "to produce records for a far smaller audience than the big companies, and in this way they are able to quickly latch onto new trends in music, to nurture local traditions and to produce music for minorities" (Gronow and Saunio 1988, 143). Independent labels are ideally suited to tap small markets.

29. Dowd 2004, 1417.

30. Hirsch 1972, 644. This industry structure was seen to attenuate the negative effect of an oligopolistic marketplace on artistic creativity because the technical subsystem resembled a "craft administration of production" (Stinchcombe 1959; Hirsch 1972). Stinchcombe (1959) argues that this craft mode of production is a function of the uncertainty of consumer demand and the use of "cheap" technology. See Hirsch (1972) for an explication of the craft mode of production in three cultural industries: publishing, movies, and record production.

31. Dowd 2000; Dowd and Blyler 2002.

32. Open system theorists argue that the effect of market concentration is mitigated by the structure of production, so product homogeneity in the 1940s and early 1950s should be attributed to centralized production (i.e., a closed system) and not major labels' oligopolistic control of production (Frith 1987, 1988; Burnett and Weber 1989; Lopes 1992; Burnett 1995; Dowd 2000, 2004; Dowd and Blyler 2002).

33. Dowd 2004; Lena 2006.

34. Teddy Riley, producer and former president of Uptown Records, is credited with the invention of new jack swing, a style of music within the rap stream that emerged in mid-1980s New York City. "New jack" (in addition to being a nickname for the city of its birth) was late eighties slang for the "extra fly" gold-name-plate-wearing, high-top, fade haircut urban kids. The "swing" in the appellation derives from the intense syncopation and laid-back up-tempo beat of Riley's percussion. The music relied heavily on a ballad form, and most artists combined up-tempo dance songs with slower music on their albums. Over the next decade, Riley worked with MCs like Heavy D and Kool Moe Dee, vocalists like Keith Sweat and Bobby Brown, and superstar producers like Jimmy "Jam" Harris, Kenny "Babyface" Edmonds,

Antonio "L.A." Reid, Jermaine Dupri, Prince, and even Michael Jackson. New jack swing's pop ascendancy from 1987 to 1989 is undeniable: Uptown recorded six acts that released platinum or multiplatinum albums, including Al B. Sure!'s debut album *In Effect Mode* and Bobby Brown's hit single "My Prerogative." In 1992, Uptown founder Andre Harrell signed a multimedia deal with Universal/MCA (valued at $50 million), created the television show *New York Undercover*, and signed future superstar Mary J. Blige. Harrell's habit of allowing his exacting standards and the high cost of recording to push his projects over budget culminated in the shuttering of Uptown's doors in 1997.

35. Soul is a good example of the pattern. African American religious singers had long borrowed from black secular music and rhythms to give their sacred songs intensity and popular appeal. Following World War II, singers raised in the church reversed this process, bringing elements of energized gospel music into the presentation of their secular songs. These ranged widely from the rocking songs of Little Richard and the shouts of James Brown to the ballads of numerous R&B quartets. These efforts coalesced as a coherent style in the hands of Ray Charles and his Atlantic Records owner-producer, Ahmet Ertegun. Charles had some success with secular reworkings of gospel songs, but in 1954 he had a huge hit with the transformation of the well-known gospel anthem "My Jesus Means the World to Me" into "I Got a Woman (way over town that's good to me)." The blend of music struck Ertegun as a smash: "the record blended elements like a hybrid flower. It had a dancing beat like a Jump blues, but it was built on gospel's 'rise to glory' chords, and the cheerful lyric, infectiously delivered by Ray, gave that mix a pop music gloss" (Lydon 2004, 114). The first January issue of *Billboard* magazine pronounced the single "One of the most infectious blues sides to come out on any label since the summer . . . a driving beat and a sensational vocal" (Lydon 2004, 117). It rose on the regional charts and peaked on the R&B chart at position number two; Alan Freed started to play it on his nationally syndicated rock show at 1010 WINS. Elvis Presley immediately added it to his act. Over the next ten years many artists followed his lead, including Solomon Burke, Otis Redding, Aretha Franklin, Sam Cooke, Jackie Wilson, and Wilson Pickett (Garland 1970; Gillett 1974; Guralnick 1999). In the 1960s Motown Records became very successful by crafting a line of "softer," "safer" soul songs.

36. Vincent 1996.

37. Vincent 1996, 55.

38. For example, Maurice White (of Earth, Wind & Fire) said: "We'd have skeletons of songs, but there was a lot of improvisation in the studio. We were very free, very spontaneous." Drummer Clyde Stubblefield said of James Brown's funk band, "Nobody in the studio knew what was going on except the horn players" (both quoted in Vincent 1996, 18).

39. Quoted in Vincent 1996, 13.

40. Clinton quoted in Bolden 2008, 15.

41. For a time, in the early years, the negative connotations of the word "funk" (an unpleasant odor, a synonym for "fuck") prevented its promotion on the radio (Danielsen 2006, 7), and formed a barrier to older, black fans, many of whom associated the term "with the most degrading and dehumanizing racial stereotypes associated with blacks, including sexual profligacy, promiscuity, laxness, lewdness, and looseness" (Bolden 2008, 15).

42. Lornell and Stephenson 2001, 21.

43. Neal 2008, 4.

44. Vincent 1996, 92.

45. According to Vincent (1996, 93): "The album seemed to encompass the entire landscape of the black experience. It was broad in scope, yet intimate. It was joyous, but it had a dead-serious sensibility to it. It was too hot and too black to be rock, too positive to be blues, and too wild to be soul."

46. Funkadelic members abandoned the buttoned-down look of doo-wop and dressed in an eclectic style that resembled that of Detroit rock groups of the time, including the MC5 and Iggy Pop and the Stooges. These rockers' influence was also felt on the music, when, after Funkadelic's equipment was delayed en route to a gig at the Sacred Heart College, they borrowed white rock group Vanilla Fudge's Marshall amps, triple-stack S.V.T.'s, and the drummer's fiberglass drums (Wright 2008, 36). According to bandleader Billy "Bass" Nelson, this moment was when "we really changed from rhythm and blues, Motown wannabes into what we evolved into: the real Funkadelic" (quoted in Wright 2008, 36).

47. Quoted in Wright 2008, 41.

48. Wright 2008, 41–42.

49. "Review" 1979, 30.

50. Ellis 2008, 99–100.

51. Danielsen 2006, 7.

52. West 1988, 182.

53. Clinton intended a sociopolitical critique and offered an escapist mode of transcendence—an outer world in which we could find ourselves "one nation under a groove." This transcendence took the form not of an elimination of boundaries, but of their inversion, with "black" as "the primary position, the positive, the first, the normal" (Danielsen 2006, 136). Paul Gilroy suggests that the album and cover work express "a utopian desire to escape from the order of racial oppression, as well as cosmic pessimism that despairs over the possibility of actual flight. In Clinton's hands, the hi-tech imagery of interplanetary travel is tamed by its association with the ancient wisdom of African civilizations. Clinton's image has been superimposed on his ghetto environment—the organic link" (1994, 254).

54. Vincent 1996, 271.

55. Brown 2008.

56. Lena 2003. Southern gospel came about in quite another way. The genre is highly inflected with black influences, but the designation is used to clearly distinguish its predominantly white close-harmony style from related trends in gospel. Southern gospel owes its institutional foundations to several shape note publishing companies, including the James D. Vaughan Publishing Company, the A. J. Showalter Company, and the Stamps-Baxter Music and Printing Company. Southern gospel was the unintended by-product of marketing efforts begun in 1910 by the Vaughn Music Publishing Company to sell their new line of religious songbooks featuring four-part harmonies. The company hired a male quartet to perform works from the songbooks in churches across the South and Midwest. The four-part quartet had not been a popular aggregation before, but it was the most cost-efficient way to promote songbooks.

    Touring quartets rapidly became popular, and enterprising singers formed publishing companies and sent out singing quartets of their own. This created a great demand for new songs well suited to four-part harmonies. V.O. (Virgil Oliver) Stamps was among the most successful of these singers; in 1925, while working as a singing field representative for Vaughn, Stamps founded the Stamps-Baxter Publishing Company in Dallas, Texas. By 1940, over one hundred touring southern gospel groups used "Stamps" in their names, in exchange for exclusive rights to buy and resell Stamps-Baxter music books. Several quartets recorded for RCA in the 1920s and were played on regional radio stations. It wasn't until the 1960s that groups again obtained contracts with major labels, and television programs featured the genre. Over time, the genre began to suffer from poor sales and the release of groups from their recording contracts, a phenomenon artists blamed on poor promotion by record companies. In their southern gospel period, the Oak Ridge Boys were signed to ABC-MCA but left because they felt the record company was not promoting their music. The group found they made greater profit from selling their own records at concerts and at Christian bookstores (personal observation, Richard A. Peterson).

    By the 1980s the old circuit was no longer drawing young fans, but the form has experienced a revival as a Traditionalist genre since the 1990s (Goff 2002; Murray 2006). The Southern Gospel Music Association formed in 1994; in April 1999 it founded its own Southern Gospel Museum and Hall of Fame, which is located within the Dollywood Theme Park in Pigeon Forge, Tennessee. The museum is charged with the historic preservation of "our music, its people and its ministry" (http://www.sgma.org).

57. Peterson and Berger 1975; Lopes 1992; Dowd 2004; Weisbard 2008.

58. Negus 1999.

59. In several cases, most conspicuously alternative country, disco, gangsta rap, and psychedelic rock, the creative energies that might have gone into tradition building went instead into building new genres, including Americana; the newer forms of dance music: techno, house, and jungle; Top-40 rap; and glam rock (Curtis 1987; Brewster and Broughton 2000; Lee and Peterson 2004; Chang 2005; Lena 2006).

60. Walker 2006.

61. Holzman and Daws 1998, 224.

62. The connection to "tribal life" is from Holzman and Daws 1998, 224. The comparison to Vienna is found in Weller 2008, 277. "There was a freedom" from Hoskyns 2006, 45.

63. Walker 2006, 114.

64. Quoted in Holzman and Daws 1998, 227.

65. See Holzman and Daws 1998; Hoskyns 2006; Weller 2008.

66. Holzman and Daws 1998; Hoskyns 2006; Walker 2006; Weller 2008.

67. Hoskyns 2006, 27.

68. Walker 2006, 109.

69. Malone 2002. The Nashville sound was also an unintended by-product of music industry actors, but in this case it was the work of major music corporation producers who were also accomplished musicians, most notably Owen Bradley and Chet Atkins. Working in the late 1950s, they established an assembly-line system of production because they wanted to create a standard, high-quality country music at a low cost. Songs provided by professional songwriters were given to artists matched to the songs, and a set of professional "session" musicians created arrangements in the studio. What began as a system of production soon developed distinct musical qualities that collectively became known as the Nashville sound. The genre flourished in the 1960s and was supplanted in the 1970s, but to date it has not had a Traditionalist form (Malone 1968; Jensen 1998). Like the Nashville sound, cowboy music was the by-product of a system of crafting recorded music, as it was created in the Hollywood movie lots devoted to making "B" Western films (Peterson 1997).

70. Ching 2001; Malone 2002.

71. Lovesey 2004.

72. Carney 1995, 18.

73. Talley 2005.

74. Middleton and Beebe 2002.

75. Middleton and Beebe 2002, 159.

76. Perhaps the most notable Avant-gardist circle grew out of the experiments of grunge-influenced artists who migrated to the Midwest and the southern United States. They mixed grunge sensibilities with the music and rural lyrical themes

of the country music and bluegrass of the 1950s. This genre, most often called "alternative country music," flowered in the last years of the twentieth century and has since lost its way while influencing mainstream country music, bluegrass, and the genre currently called "Americana" (Peterson and Beal 2001; Lee and Peterson 2004).

77. Kahn-Harris 2007. Christie (2004, 237–57) argues that the roots of death metal trace back to Venom's emergence in 1981, and that the style was actualized in a 1984 German compilation album and was maintained throughout the decade by the band called Slayer. During the late 1980s, bands working in this style eliminated most of the traces of rock felt in earlier works. Three bands, Death, Morbid Angel, and Decide, tended to avoid the blues scales employed by rock and earlier metal bands. Their sound combined fast, screaming guitar shredding and solo breaks with constant, fast, and polyrhythmic drumming. But the lyrical content set death metal apart from its rivals: "creatures like Glen Benton of Deicide tore out their larynxes to summon images of decaying corpses and giant catastrophic horrors. This created a nearly insurmountable barrier to entry for the casual listener" (Christie 2004, 239). Death metal lyrics routinely focused on occultist topics, including mythic interpretations of Satan. However, fans knew that the intensity of musical focus could not be sustained by a truly violent engagement: "Playing a form of music as difficult as death metal required discipline, artistic sensitivity, and physical endurance that was anything but an act of negation" (Christie 2004, 244). The music emerged from the tape-trading culture already established in metal, and although many artists (e.g., Death, Atheist, Cynic, Obituary, Brutality) worked from studios in Florida, the scene was truly global, with major artists located in San Francisco (Possessed), Chicago (Deathstrike), Ohio (Necrophagia), Toronto (Slaughter), Brazil (Sepultura), and Germany (Sodom).

78. McLeod 2001.

79. McLeod 2001, 60.

80. Reynolds 1998, 31–34; McLeod 2001, 66.

81. Fikentscher 2000.

82. Smith 1995, 95.

83. Reynolds 1998, 23; Rietveld 1998, 4.

84. Cosgrove 1988.

85. Rietveld 1998, 17.

86. Reitveld 1998; Reynolds 1998.

87. Reynolds 1998.

88. Reynolds 1998, 17.

89. Reynolds 1998, 18.

90. McLeod 2001.

91. McLeod 2001, 69.

92. Anand and Peterson 2000.
93. McLeod 2001, 70.
94. Thornton 1996, 74.
95. Bourdieu 1993.
96. McLeod 2001, 67.
97. Sinton and Huber 2007.
98. Shepherd, Horn, and Laing 2005, 15.
99. Shepherd, Horn, and Laing 2005, 309.
100. Greene 1992, 142.
101. Greene 1992, 142–43.
102. Greene 1992, 142–43.
103. Wilson and Portes 1980; Portes and Jensen 1987; Portes 1989.
104. Greene 1992, 141.
105. Greene 1992, 141.
106. Gans 1974, 41–44, 102–3.
107. Portes and Rumbaut 2001.
108. The debt of *conjunto* to polka is best demonstrated by the story of Narciso Mar-
tínez, a Mexican immigrant known as "the father of *conjunto* music," whose first
hit song was a polka called "La Chicharronera" (1935). Some of his many recordings from 1936 were issued by Victor Recording Company in its Polish catalog
under the pseudonym "Polish Kwartet" (Greene 1992, 147).
109. Bob Willis, credited with inventing western swing, picked cotton as a child
and sought to combine the Celtic and British fiddle tunes played by his father
with the blues and ragtime songs of their black coworkers (Townsend 1976).
By 1929, Willis launched his musical career traveling with a minstrel show and
soon formed a duo with the group's guitarist, Herman Arnspiger (Himes 1994,
87). The band played a radio show in Fort Worth and local house dances in the
evenings, and Willis spent the next several years forming and dissolving bands,
and working his way up to bigger radio station broadcasts. After the addition
of another fiddle, two guitars, bass, piano, banjo, and an amplified steel guitar,
Willis and his band crafted the classic western swing sound: country melodies,
and jazz rhythm and harmonies, punctuated by the "suitcase rhythm," produced
when Tulsa Dixieland drummer Smokey Dacus walloped his drum case (Himes
1994, 88). As a bandleader, Willis prized "feel" over musical precision and would
famously shout "a-ha!" when the band hit the right groove (Townsend 1976, 107;
Himes 1994). In late September 1935, the band recorded its first album in Dallas (although Willis had recorded several previous, unsuccessful singles with a
variety of bands and under several different names), and it sold well enough for
them to be invited to multiple other recording sessions. Over the next four years,
the band grew in size and introduced a mariachi sound into the mix of their first

bona fide hit, "New San Antonio Rose." This recording won Willis a gold record in 1940, and Bing Crosby's cover of the song hit number seven on the *Billboard* charts in 1941. Willis often remarked that it was "the song that took him from hamburgers to steaks" (Townsend 1976, 193). Many of Willis's sidemen (including Milton Brown, Leon McAuliffee, and Ashley Ashlock) led their own western swing bands, and the sound dominated the radio waves, recording studios, and dancehalls of the Southwest in the thirties, forties, and fifties.

Willis's band broke up with the outbreak of World War II, and Willis relocated to California, where he inspired another musical style, called the Bakersfield Sound. The Traditionalist genre of western swing was led by Merle Haggard, who reunited many of Willis's bandmates for his 1970 album, *A Tribute to the Best Damn Fiddler Player in the World*. Many country artists at the time were inspired by Willis, and his influence can be heard in songs by Hank Thompson, George Strait, Red Steagall, and Junior Brown. The revival really took off in the 1970s and 1980s, when folk revivalists began to emphasize country sounds, and artists like Commander Cody and his Lost Planet Airmen, Dan Hicks and His Hot Licks, Cowboy Jazz, and Asleep at the Wheel attributed their sound to Willis's influence.

110. Mackun 1964.
111. The history of doo-wop is a bit different. It began in the 1950s when young African American vocal groups began to use their voices to simulate contemporaneously popular black music. As the style became more popular, their vocal renditions were augmented by R&B bands of the day, and doo-wop merged into the black pop music stream (Pruter 1996).
112. Buerkle and Barker 1973, vii; Charters 2008, 82.
113. Charters 2008.
114. Charters 2008, 93.
115. Charters 2008, 94.
116. As related by historian Herbert Asbury (1936, 451–54), the murder of four sailors in Storyville in 1917, and the rise in incidence of venereal infections among soldiers, attracted the attention of the secretaries of both the Navy and War Departments in Washington, D.C. Newton D. Baker, secretary of war, issued an order forbidding prostitution within five miles of army barracks, and the secretary of the navy followed with a similar decree. They sent Bascom Johnson to inspect Storyville, and Johnson informed the mayor of New Orleans that brothels in the district would have to be closed for the city to be in compliance with these orders. Despite his opposition to the orders, Mayor Behrman was forced to introduce an ordinance to the city council in October 1917. By midnight on November 12, the secondhand furniture dealers and moving wagons and vans had emptied the district's brothels. The members of the Louisiana Federation of Women's Clubs

appointed a committee to help the prostitutes, but "none applied for succor. Few, in fact, needed it. They had simply moved from Storyville into various businesses and residential sections of New Orleans and were doing very well." While the prostitutes succeeded in surviving the closure of their business district, the jazz community foundered (Buerkle and Barker 1973; Charters 2008).

117. Jazz musician Danny Barker quoted in Buerkle and Barker 1973, 24.

118. Charters 2008, 163.

119. It appears to have been borrowed from a description of the pitcher for the San Francisco Seals baseball team, who threw a "jazz curve." A San Francisco dance band led by Art Hickman played the Seals training camp and was described in 1913 as a "jazz band," the earliest known description of the musical style. A drummer named Bert Kelley may have taken it with him to Chicago and then traveled to New Orleans with bandleader Tom Brown. Brown began to advertise his band as "Brown's Dixieland Jass Band, Direct from New Orleans, Best Dance Music in Chicago" as early as 1915 (Charters 2008, 116–17, 131). What is clear is that New Orleans musicians thought of their music as a modified form of ragtime.

120. Suhor 2001, 18.

121. Peterson 1967.

122. Suhor 2001, 18.

123. Quoted in Charters 2008, 148.

124. Suhor 2001, 19.

125. Roy 2004.

126. Charters 2008, 350.

127. Charters 2008, 349.

128. Don Marquis was among those who sought to define the history of the music and musicians, a journey he captured in a book appropriately titled *In Search of Buddy Bolden* (1978). Few records of Bolden's life and work remain, and accounts emphasize his genius and descent into mental illness, a condition that confined him to a sanatorium for the last twenty-four years of his life. These stories are known to have been embellished by fellow performers, most notably Jelly Roll Morton and Louis Armstrong, neither of whom was old enough to have reliable memories of Bolden. According to Charters (2008, 86), "The image of Bolden that was created in this search for any kind of biographical verification filled an emotional need to create a narrative about the early jazz decades around a figure larger than the little information that existed about him could actually support."

129. Buerkle and Barker 1973, 14.

130. A truly superb history of jazz music criticism can be found in Raeburn's *New Orleans Style and the Writing of American Jazz History* (2009).

131. Charters 2008, 144.

132. On Whiteman's nickname, see Raeburn 2009, 15. On the bitterness of jazzmen, see Charters 2008, 351.
133. Grazian 2003.
134. Buerkle and Barker 1973, 121.
135. Darden 2004, 170.
136. Darden 2004, 172.
137. Darden 2004, 173.
138. Jackson 2004, 51.
139. Darden 2004, 173; see also Shepherd, Horn, and Laing 2005, 193.
140. Cusic 1990, 91.
141. Heilbut 1997, 80.
142. Cusic 2001, 57.
143. Jackson 2004, 52.
144. Quoted in Jackson 2004, 60.
145. It is important to keep in mind that I focus here on market segments within the field of music production, rather than on the existence or viability of particular black-owned organizations. Of course, black-owned record labels have a venerable history, from the early successes of Harlem's Black Swan label to the crossover magic of Detroit's Motown label. These are, however, exceptions within the white-owned, major-label system that dominated production within relevant musical styles.
146. Lena 2003.
147. To the best of my knowledge, none of these "Robinsons" are related by blood.
148. Quoted in Rose 1994b, 129.
149. Lena 2003.
150. Lena 2003.
151. Rose 1994a, 7.
152. Basu and Werbner 2001, 248.
153. Chambers and Morgan 1992, 83.
154. The assertion that AgSIT is the predominant genre trajectory can be made only with caution. This trajectory roughly mirrors the story of genre development recounted in popular works and in many retrospective critical evaluations as well. There is a danger that this is as much a reconstructed myth as an accurate accounting of events. I have tried to avoid this potential bias as much as possible by relying on sources written close to the times that the events being described took place.
155. Nor were, for that matter, the variety of characteristics shared by virtually all contemporary American music. For example, most popular styles employ a similar song length, beat and tempo structure, and group size. When the Victor Recording Company introduced the twelve-inch disc in 1903, its playing time—

approximately 3.5 minutes—fixed the length of the popular song (Cusic 1990, 77). Although this is not the characteristic length of songs in all styles (consider, for example, that jazz solos are commonly twice that length), it is the form found on the pop charts. To the extent that producers seek mass profits, genre communities may adjust performance conventions toward the 3.5-minute format in order to place songs on the charts. Moreover, over the second half of the twentieth century, the tempo of music has increased dramatically, group sizes have decreased, and songwriters have adopted a more pronounced "backbeat," "a distinct off beat accent in common time usually hammered out as rim shots by the drummer on 2 and 4," a style noted in R&B and rock during the 1940s and 1950s (Goosman 2005, 8). These changes impacted many, but not all, American musical styles.

156. Peterson and Berger 1975; Lopes 1992; Dowd 2004.

157. Abbott 1988, 1992.

158. Abbott and Forrest 1986. Abell (1987), Heise (1988, 1989), and Griffin (1993) have completed comparable work using different methods.

159. Cantwell 1984; Lott 1995; Crouch 2007.

160. On the Booker Prize and the Grammys, see Anand and Jones 2008; Anand and Watson 2004. The "central tokens of value" are described in Appadurai 1986, 21.

161. By "legitimate," I mean to refer to those styles that have been repositioned or redefined as relevant and acceptable forms of art. Baumann (2007, 49), paraphrasing Zelditch (2001), argues that "Legitimation occurs when the unaccepted is made accepted through consensus." Other studies of artistic consecration include White and White 1965; DiMaggio 1982, 1992; Bourdieu 1990; Regev 1994, 2002; Baumann 2001; and Lopes 2002.

162. The first has also been referred to as "cultural consecration" (Allen and Lincoln 2004).

163. Crane 1976.

164. Baumann 2007, 56. On museums, see Zolberg 1997. On galleries, see Bowler 1997; Cherbo 1997; Rawlings 2001.

165. DiMaggio 1992 on modern dance, and Peterson 1972 on jazz.

166. Many scholars choose to define art worlds in these terms: Bourdieu views cultural fields as dominated by the power of cultural capital, or knowledge, skills, and habits associated with elite positions in society, and van Rees and Dorleijn (2001, 332) argue that a cultural field is structured around "agents producing belief in the value of goods in question."

167. Molnar (2005, 130) illustrates the role of "interpretative schemes and strategies . . . in the reception and legitimation" of modernist architecture as art within Hungary. DeNora (1991, 314) argues that aristocrats used a legitimating ideology to elevate great composers and "serious works" of classical music in eighteenth-

and early nineteenth-century Vienna. This ideology belongs among the three forms of critical discourse examined by van Rees (1983); it resembles the work that DiMaggio (1992, 44) argues Boston elites employed during their legitimation of high art (including theater, dance, and opera). Finally, Baumann (2001, 405) argues that a legitimating ideology was employed by film critics during the rise of this medium to the status of art in America. It remains rather difficult to match this legitimating ideology with other concepts that seek to describe similarly orienting beliefs. Social movements scholars in particular have sought to conceptualize the link between ideologies and group action and sentiment, offering discourses, ideologies, and frames as distinct organizing concepts. As Baumann (2007, 58) argues, discourses are the loosest of these, supplying a diffuse logic and the necessary tools for communication. Ideologies have a consistent and coherent logic that provides subscribers with both a general understanding of the world, and norms and values. Finally, frames are tight structures that direct specific forms of thinking, with respect to a concrete issue. One might argue that the general ideology of art (as distinct from craft) is most like an ideology, while the specific application of the concept of art to a specific genre or form (e.g., rap-as-art) resembles the practice of framing.

168. Lopes 2002, 177–78.
169. Baumann 2001.
170. Watt 2001.
171. Adams 2008.
172. White and White 1965; Clignet 1985; Crane 1987.
173. Lopes 2002.

Chapter 4
The Government-purposed Genre

1. Cantwell 1996; Lopes 2002.
2. Ryan 1985; Sanjek 1988; Peterson 1990.
3. On social movements and music, see Denisoff 1971; Cantwell 1996; Garofalo 1999; Brewster and Broughton 2000; Filene 2000; and Lipsitz 2007. On music censorship, see Weinstein 1991; Rose 1994a; Cantwell 1996; Garofalo 1999; and Lopes 2002.
4. Warren 1972; Vries 1996; Currid 2006; Pine 2007.
5. Edmonds 2004.
6. Jones 1992, 13–15.
7. Ho 2006.
8. Shepherd, Horn, and Liang 2005, 31.
9. Huang 2001, 2.

10. Huang 2001, 2.

11. Ho 2006, 443.

12. As a result of the Open Door Policy of 1978, Chinese students and business people traveled to the West and sent home care packages including audio cassettes
of rock and other music. Particularly in Shanghai, students were exposed to music by Bob Dylan, John Denver, and the Beatles. State factories began the mass
production of portable cassette players, and by 1988 more than 240 domestic
recording companies were producing and distributing over 100 million cassettes
per year (Brace and Friedlander 1992, 119).

13. Huang 2001.

14. Shepherd, Horn, and Liang 2005, 31.

15. Jones 1992; Huang 2001; Baranovitch 2003.

16. Jones 1992, 97–99.

17. Efird 2001, 75.

18. Quoted in de Kloet 2003, 43.

19. De Kloet 2003b, 46.

20. Quoted in de Kloet 2003, 35.

21. Hom 1998, 1016.

22. Jones 1992; Baranovitch 2003.

23. Jones 1992, 93–94. A closer examination of this title is revealing of its politics.
"Yi wu suo you," the title in Chinese, does not have a subject; the literal English
translation would be "To Have Nothing." Subject omission is common in col-
loquial Chinese, so English translations typically insert the subject "I," making
the English title, "I Have Nothing." However, when many Chinese translate the
title into English, they call the song "We Have Nothing." Brace and Friedlander
(1992, 121) conclude, "The political ramification of this interpretive move—of the
extension of 'I' to 'We'—are obvious and powerful."

24. Baranovitch 2003, 32.

25. Huang 2001, 5.

26. Mihalca 1992, 34.

27. Brace and Friedlander 1992, 120.

28. Jones 1992; Ho 2006.

29. Quoted in Jones 1992, 124–25.

30. Baranovitch 2003, 34.

31. Quoted in de Kloet 2003, 29.

32. Jones 1992, 2.

33. Laing and Stobbe 1993, 90–91.

34. De Kloet 2003, 31.

35. Jones 1992, 3.

36. On the operation of Chinese rock at the boundary of official culture, see Jones 1992, 149.
37. Steen 2000, 61.
38. Steen 2000, 49.
39. Huang 2001, 5–6.
40. Efird 2001, 79.
41. Quoted in Baranovitch 2003, 42.
42. Yan Jun 1999, 31.
43. Quoted in Efird 2001, 82.
44. Quoted in de Kloet 2001, 14.
45. Quoted in de Kloet 2001, 16.
46. On state-sponsored Chinese rock, see Barme 1995 and Huang 2001.
47. Ho 2006.
48. Linn 1984; Mattern 1998.
49. Linn 1984; Mattern 1998.
50. Quoted in Morris 1984.
51. Fruchtman 1975.
52. Quoted in Morris 1984.
53. I thank Iván Orosa Paleo for his insights on this issue.
54. Neustadt 2004, 128.
55. Mattern 1998, 40.
56. Quoted in Tumas-Serna 1992, 146.
57. Quoted in Mattern 1998, 41.
58. Quoted in Mattern 1998, 42.
59. Linn 1984, 61, 62.
60. Tumas-Serna 1992, 144.
61. Singer 1983.
62. Moreno 1986, 121.
63. Carrasco 1982, 23.
64. Neustadt 2004, 129.
65. Mattern 1998, 41.
66. Mattern 1998.
67. Mattern 1998, 63–64.
68. Inter alia Graham 1988, 598.
69. In fact, Fela's grandfather, Reverend J. J. Ransome-Kuti, recorded the first Yoruba-language hymns for the Zonophone Company, in 1914 (Waterman 1998, 4).
70. Quoted in Collins 1992, 77–78.
71. Stewart 1992, 117; Waterman 1998, 8.
72. Quoted in Collins 1992, 72.

73. Salamone 1998.
74. Quoted in Collins 1992, 74.
75. Quoted in Veal 2000, 4–5.
76. Amkpa 2003, 26.
77. Brooke 1988.
78. Waterman 1998; Amkpa 2003; Irobi 2003.
79. Brooke 1988; Salamone 1998.
80. Stewart 1992, 114.
81. Irobi 2003.
82. Salamone 1998, 12.
83. Veal 2000, 12.
84. Amkpa 2003, 26.
85. Ceribašić 2007, 4.
86. Prodger 2005.
87. Kronja 2004, 103.
88. Kronja 2004, 103.
89. On the region's pathological ethnocentrism, see Colovic 1993, 8; Barber-Kersovan 2002.
90. Gordy 1999.
91. Kronja 2004, 103.
92. Kronja 2004, 105.
93. Kronja 2004, 107.
94. Ceca paradoxically represented both the singer-as-sex-object image common among all female turbo-folk performers and the exemplary Serbian female patriot, "a symbolic 'mother of the nation'" (Kronja 2004, 108).
95. Itano 2008, 2; see also Steinberg 2004.
96. Quoted in Hudson 1997, 171.
97. Hudson 1997, 174.
98. Barber-Kersovan 2002.
99. Ceribašić 2007.
100. Manuel 1993.
101. Manuel 1993, xiv. In China, "cassette culture" has emerged in a new form called "dakou culture." In the United States unsold compact music discs are sawed or drill cut for sale to plastic garbage recyclers. Some are purchased by black market, Mafia-connected distributors, shipped through subdistributors located in towns in Guangdong Province, and then sold to the Chinese public. Since a CD player reads from the center to the margin, only a portion of the recording is irretrievable. According to rock critic Dundee (quoted in de Kloet 2001, 18): "This plastic rubbish dumped by foreign record companies becomes a major source of

pleasure for those discontented youths after they switch off their TV. When this plastic rubbish started flowing from the south to Beijing, it actually heralded a new rock era [after 1997]. All the new rock musicians in Beijing have grown up with dakou tapes."

102. Gellner 1983, 58–62.
103. Melly 1970.
104. Tumas-Serna 1992, 144.
105. Lent 1990.
106. Tumas-Serna 1992, 149.
107. Marett 2005.
108. Manuel 1993; Hayward 1998.
109. Shepherd, Horn, and Liang 2005.

Chapter 5
On Classification Systems

1. The industry categories also provide an interpretation of styles for listeners, including those at odds with (or not exactly sanctioned by) how performers within the style see their work. For example, Waksman (2009, 301) explains that "the musicians associated with grunge were more likely to stress opposition, and the industry more likely to stress symbiosis, [and this] speaks to the different investments in genre labels that these two groups had."
2. Espeland and Sauder 2007, 16.
3. Anand and Peterson 2000.
4. The racialization of music communities is commonplace and affects groups outside the white-black dichotomy. For example, the salsa community in New York was strongly Puerto Rican, and they defined the music as a form of nationalist sentiment against the specter of U.S. colonial domination, "although the music's scene was strongly interethnic . . . with Jewish and African-American musicians performing in several bands" (Waxer 2002, 4).
5. Vincent 1996, 20.
6. Hughes 2005 [1955].
7. George 1998.
8. Bolden 2008, 14.
9. Quoted in Vincent 1996, 270.
10. Kelley 2005, 7.
11. Quoted in Radano 2003, 237.
12. Reported in Brackett 2005, 101.
13. Garofalo 2002.

14. Ripani 2006, 4.

15. James Brown brought this approach to soul music, using the guitar as a percussion instrument. Even Brown's singing is rhythmic, arranged in repeated chants.

16. However, the roots of an anticorporatist taste in music are much deeper. In *American Quarterly*, then Harvard professor David Riesman (quoted in Denisoff 1975, 11) divided teenage fans into "majority" and "minority" taste groups. Of the minority group (whose affinity was for jazz and the blues), he wrote, "The rebelliousness of this group might be indicated in some of the following attitudes toward popular music: an insistence on uncommercialized, unadvertised small bands rather than name bands; the development of a private language and then a flight from it when the private language is taken over by the majority group; a profound resentment of the commercialization of radio and musicians." As a description of a particular group of fans, this points to a Scene-based community. However, as a description of a sensibility or taste disposition taken toward all consumption, it evidences an orientation toward genre forms, and not musical styles, to demarcate identities.

17. Lawrence (2003, 118) provides some historical details of this process: "Philadelphia International Records was set up in 1971, and in May of the following year Davis's strategy was validated when a special CBS-commissioned report, conducted by the Harvard University Business School, urged the company to enter into the soul market. 'The fact that 30 percent of the top 40 is composed of records which have "crossed over" from soul stations underscores the strategic importance of soul stations as one of the most effective vehicles for getting on to the top 40,' noted the report. 'What this means is that the competition among promoters for soul airplay involves far more than simply the prospect of record sales to black consumers.' The report warned CBS against attempting to acquire any of the big three specialized national companies—Atlantic, Motown, and Stax—and suggested instead that it could outmaneuver equally negligent majors such as Capitol, MCA, and RCA by developing a 'well-planned and well-financed initiative aimed at long-term market penetration' as well as raiding smaller independent companies. The creation of Philadelphia International constituted one such raid, and, just two months after the publication of what came to be known as the Harvard Report, Davis was able to bask in the glory of PIR's first hit, 'Back Stabbers' by the O'Jays."

18. Waksman 2009, 215.

19. Waksman 2009, 215.

20. Lena 2006.

21. Adapted from *Social Forces* vol. 85, no. 1. Copyright © 2006 by the University of North Carolina Press. Used by permission of the publisher. www.uncpress.unc.edu.

22. Star and Griesemer 1989, 393.

23. Thus it is important not to confuse boundary objects with music that can be classified but is not seen as legitimate. Take, as one example, the series of recordings produced by the KKK label of Indianapolis, Indiana, in the mid-1920s. With titles like "Why I Am a Klansman," "Cross in the Wildwood," "The Bright Fiery Cross," and "Wake Up America and Kluck, Kluck, Kluck," the label sought a distribution contract with Thomas Edison and his record label. Edison listened to the records on July 24, 1924, and pronounced that "'Why I Am a Klansman' had a 'fair tune,' but his final advice was, 'Don't bother with this trash'" (Tosches 1996, 215). The tune was classifiable, and the style undeniable, but the music was illegitimate.

24. Zuckerman 1999.

25. Urban, Weinberg, and Hauser 1996.

26. These specific examples are drawn from Levitin (2006, 141–42). Another example is the "salsa opera," including one version of the Who's *Tommy*, produced by Larry Harlow and Jenaro "Heny" Álvarez. *Hommy* was presented at Carnegie Hall on March 29, 1973, with Celia Cruz and Cheo Feliciano singing the leads (Roberts 1979, 187–88).

27. That is, the categorical imperative still obtains, but more than one legitimate category exists within the field. The concept of "typecasting" in the allocation of film roles may illuminate how this is possible (Bielby and Bielby 1992, 1996, 2001). While typecasting involves the curtailment of opportunities for particular actors based on age, sex, race, or previous role performances, it is not necessarily the case that only one "type" of role is available to any given actor. Older, white men can be comedic or romantic leads, and young Middle Eastern men may be villains or victims.

28. Rose 1994a.

29. We find one mention of such practices in Christe's (2004, 253) history of heavy metal: "a number of musicians abandoned the tightly wound structure of the [metal] music and experimented with abstractions of its founding elements. . . . In many cases these were some of the first metal bands to be seen wearing glasses. In other cases, as with Master's Hammer, the mixed-up metal influences were part of an exit strategy, the sign of metalheads leaving crumbs behind as they disappeared into strange new dark forests of experimentation."

30. Burt 1987; White 1988, 238.

31. White 1992.

32. Walker 2009.

33. Walker 2009.

34. I have also seen them referred to as "racial anthropologists" and "scientific racists."

35. Linnaeus also proposed a division of humans into taxa, reflecting a continental division of peoples (the Americans, Asians, Africans, Europeans) in addition

to a mythological race called the *Monstrosus*. Wildly stereotypic characteristics were attached to each: the *Asiaticus* race was yellow-skinned, avaricious, and easily distracted, and the *Americanus* had red skin, and were stubborn and easily angered.

36. Becker et al. 1961.
37. LeCompte and Goetz 1982.
38. Of course there are studies in which one seeks to understand how scientists are perceived, or how respondents interpret the purpose of scientific study, and in these cases, detecting the presence and effects of reactivity are the goals of the study. See Monahan and Fisher (2010) for an excellent argument in this regard.
39. Heimer 1985.
40. Callon 1998; see also Latour 1987; MacKenzie 2006.
41. Espeland and Sauder 2007.
42. Frickel and Gross 2005.
43. De Solla Price 1965; Crane 1972.
44. Crane 1972; Frickel and Gross 2005.
45. Peterson 1997.
46. Horowitz 2005.
47. Merton 1957; Gieryn 1998.
48. Fujimura 1996.
49. Mullins 1973 Frickel and Gross 2005.
50. Zuckerman et al. 2003, 1021; see also White 1970; Sørensen 1977; and Podolny 1993.
51. Zuckerman 1999. For a discussion of the success of innovations, see Schumpeter 1983 [1934]. For an accounting of the failure of most innovations because of their perceived illegitimacy, see Stinchcombe 1959; Hannan and Carroll 1992.
52. Meyer and Rowan 1977; DiMaggio and Powell 1983.
53. Zuckerman et al. 2003.
54. Fine 2001, 2–3.
55. Lang and Lang (1988, 80) note, "This shared image is made up not only of what people actually recall and then pass on but also of things that have somehow been revered, embellished, or even invented to serve some contemporary cause."
56. For one such example, see Gest et al. 2008.
57. Perhaps the best research on local reputations comes from organizational studies of niche competition (Bastedo and Bowman 2010). For an interesting study of the destructive effects of competition on reputations, see Anderson et al. 2007.
58. On celebrity, see Gamson 1994. On media frames in general, see Tuchman 1978. For a more recent review, see D'Angelo 2002. On the effect of the news on corporate reputations, see Meijer and Kleinnijenhuis 2006a. On the positive impact of

having a competitor criticize your company's reputation in the news (a "boomerang effect"), see Meijer and Kleinnijenhuis 2006b.

59. I refer to this elsewhere in the chapter as the "categorical imperative." On the link between arts and genres, see Becker 1982 and the unsuccessful example of the Pre-Raphaelites (Reitlinger 1961).

60. In addition to Lang and Lang's (1988) work on painter-etchers, interested readers may refer to Tuchman and Fortin (1989) on female novelists, or Connelly (1977) on the reputation of Robert E. Lee.

61. Lang and Lang 1988. See Haskell (1980) on the rediscovery of Botticelli, El Greco, and Vermeer. See Schwartz (1982, 1987) on the dependence of presidential reputations on perceived relevance to contemporary issues.

62. Salsa offers an interesting comparison case, since it was initially treated as a "domestic genre" (that is, as a product of Puerto Rico), yet "virtually all major companies, with the exception of EMI, farmed their Latin Music divisions out as subsidiaries of their international operations, with the resulting paradox that salsa became an 'international' or 'foreign' genre within the U.S. market" (Waxer 2002, 9).

63. Keil and Feld 1994, 239.

64. Collins 1992, 188.

65. Satizábal 2002.

66. Román-Velázquez 2002.

67. Collins 1992, 189.

68. Collins 1992, 190.

69. Roberts 1974, 245.

70. Appadurai 1990, 296.

71. Wicke 1992.

72. Wicke 1992, 86.

73. Bourdieu 1977. To illustrate the point, Wacquant explains: "Cumulative exposure to certain social conditions instills in individuals an ensemble of durable and transposable dispositions that internalize the necessities of the extant social environment, inscribing inside the organism the patterned inertia and constraints of external reality" (Bourdieu and Wacquant 1992, 13). Positions and dispositions thus describe individuals and groups in relation to one another and their embodied existence in that relational social space. Bourdieu (2002 [1991], 271) sums up the relationship as follows: "To each class of positions there corresponds a class of habitus (or *tastes*) produced by the social conditioning associated with the corresponding condition and, through the mediation of the habitus and its generative capability, a systematic set of goods and properties, which are united by an affinity of style."

74. Bourdieu 1984, 1993.

75. Before 1850, there were few distinctions between forms of entertainment—Mozart would be presented on the same stage as popular ballads. By 1910, a group of "cultural capitalists" in Boston established a new organizational form, the nonprofit cultural institution, allowing them, as board members influencing programming and art acquisition, to draw distinctions between art and popular entertainment. The aesthetic consequence was the institutionalization of so-called high culture: a strongly classified, consensually defined body of art distinct from "popular" fare. DiMaggio (1982, 38) argues that "the culture of an elite status group must be monopolized, it must be legitimate, and it must be sacralized."

76. On national and ethnic origin, see Ang 1985; Griswold 1987; Shively 1992; Liebes and Katz 1993. On social class, see Leal and Oliven 1988; Press 1991. On race, see DiMaggio and Ostrower 1990; Jhally and Lewis 1992. On gender and age, see Press 1991.

77. Fish 1980.

78. Ang 1985.

79. Liebes and Katz 1993.

80. Leal and Oliven 1988.

81. On the other hand, David Halle's (1993) study of artworks in upper- and working-class households concludes that class-based differences in cultural reception are less dramatic than is typically assumed. He finds that regardless of social class, most respondents displayed landscape paintings in their homes, and selected these because they "felt serene" and depicted a natural landscape that represented a relief or escape from modern society. Although elites were more likely to prefer images of foreign places, and abstract art, their reasons for doing so resembled the reasons all respondents gave for liking landscapes, in general. He ultimately questions Bourdieu's notion that taste is a symbolic means of social reproduction.

82. Peterson and Kern 1996, 904.

83. As Bettie (1995, 135) describes it, "class can be conceptualized as performative in that there is no [innate or] interior difference that is being expressed; rather, institutionalized class inequality creates class subjects who perform, or display, differences in cultural capital."

References

Abbott, Andrew. 1988. "Transcending General Linear Reality." *Sociological Theory* 6 (2): 169–86.

———. 1992. "From Causes to Events: Notes on Narrative Positivism." *Sociological Methods & Research* 20 (4): 428–55.

Abbott, Andrew, and John Forrest. 1986. "Optimal Matching Methods for Historical Sequences." *Journal of Interdisciplinary History* 16 (3): 471–94.

Abell, Peter. 1987. *The Syntax of Social Life: The Theory and Method of Comparative Narratives.* Oxford: Clarendon.

Abrahms, Roger D. 1970. *Deep Down in the Jungle: Negro Narrative Folklore from the Streets of Philadelphia.* Chicago: Adline.

Adams, John. 2008. *Hallelujah Junction: Composing an American Life.* New York: Farrar, Straus and Giroux.

Adams, Mary Louise. 1994. "Almost Anything Can Happen: A Search for Sexual Discourse in the Urban Spaces of 1940s Toronto." *Canadian Journal of Sociology* 19 (2): 217–32.

Ahlkvist, Jarl A. 2001. "Programming Philosophies and the Rationalization of Music Radio." *Media, Culture & Society.* 23 (3): 339–58.

Ahlkvist, Jarl A., and Robert Faulkner. 2002. "'Will This Record Work for Us?': Managing Music Formats in Commercial Radio." *Qualitative Sociology* 25 (2): 189–215.

Alberoni, Francesco. 1984. *Movement and Institution.* New York: Columbia University Press.

Albrecht, Milton C. 1970. "Art as an Institution." In *The Sociology of Art and Literature: A Reader,* edited by Milton C. Albrecht, James H. Barnett, and Mason Griff, 1–28. London: Duckworth.

Alexander, Victoria D. 1992. *The Production of Culture: Media and the Urban Arts.* New York: Sage.

———. 2003. *Sociology of the Arts: Exploring Fine and Popular Forms.* Oxford: Blackwell.

Allen, Michael Patrick, and Anne E. Lincoln. 2004. "Critical Discourse and the Cultural Consecration of American Films." *Social Forces* 82 (3): 871–93.

Aminzade, Ronald. 1992. "Historical Sociology and Time." *Sociological Methods & Research* 20 (4): 456–80.

Amkpa, Awam. 2003. "Nigeria: The Art of Neocolonial Dystopia and Postcolonial Utopias." *Black Renaissance/Renaissance Noire* 5 (2): 26–30.

Anand, N., and Brittany Jones. 2008. "Tournament Rituals, Category Dynamics, and Field Configuration: The Case of the Booker Prize." *Journal of Management Studies* 45 (6): 1036–60.

Anand, N., and Richard A. Peterson. 2000. "When Market Information Constitutes Fields: Sensemaking of Markets in the Commercial Music Industry." *Organization Science* 11 (3): 270–84.

Anand, N., and Mary R. Watson. 2004. "Tournament Rituals in the Evolution of Fields: The Case of the Grammy Awards." *Academy of Management Journal*. 47 (1): 59–80.

Anderson, Benedict. 1983. *Imagined Communities*. London: Verso.

Anderson, Melissa S., Emily A. Ronning, Raymond De Vries, and Brian C. Martinson. 2007. "The Perverse Effects of Competition on Scientists' Work and Relationships." *Science and Engineering Ethics*. 13 (4): 437–61.

Ang, Ien. 1985. *Watching Dallas: Soap Opera and the Melodramatic Imagination*. London: Routledge.

Appadurai, Arjun. 1986. "Introduction: Commodities and the Politics of Value." In *The Social Life of Things*, edited by A. Appadurai, 3–63. Cambridge University Press.

———. 1990. "Disjuncture and Difference in the Global Cultural Economy." In *Global Culture: Nationalism, Globalization and Modernity*, edited by Mike Featherstone, 295–309. London: Sage.

Apperley, Thomas H. 2006. "Genre and Game Studies: Toward a Critical Approach to Video Game Genres" *Simulation & Gaming*. 37 (1): 6–23.

Arian, Edward. 1971. *Bach, Beethoven and Bureaucracy*. Tuscaloosa: University of Alabama Press.

Artis, Bob. 1975. *Bluegrass*. New York: Hawthorne.

Asbury, Herbert. 1936. *The French Quarter*. New York: Alfred A. Knopf.

Attali, Jacques. 1985. *Noise: The Political Economy of Music*. Manchester: Manchester University Press.

Baker, Houston A. Jr. 1990 [1972]. *Long Black Song: Essays in Black American Literature and Culture*. Charlottesville: University Press of Virginia.

Baranovitch, Nimrod. 2003. *China's New Voices: Popular Music, Ethnicity, Gender, and Politics, 1978–1997*. Berkeley and Los Angeles: University of California Press.

Barber-Kersovan, A. 2002. "Popular Music in Ex-Yugoslavia: Between Global Participation and Provincial Seclusion." In *Global Repertoires: Popular Music within and beyond the Transnational Music Industry*, edited by A. Gebesmair and A. Smudits, 289–320. London: Ashgate.

Barme, G. 1995. "To Screw Foreigners Is Patriotic: China's Avant-Garde Nationalist." *China Journal* 34 (July): 209–34.

Barol, Bill. 1986. "Some Bad Raps for Good Rap." *Newsweek*, September, p. 85.

Bastedo, Michael N., and Nicholas A. Bowman. 2010. "*U.S. News & World Report* College Rankings: Modeling Institutional Effects on Organizational Reputation." *American Journal of Education* 116: 163–83.

Bastian, Vanessa, and Dave Laing. 2003. "Twenty Years of Music Censorship around the World." In *Policing Pop*, edited by Martin Cloonan and Reebee Garofalo, 46–64. Philadelphia: Temple University Press.

Basu, Dipannita, and Pnina Werbner. 2001. "Bootstrap Capitalism and the Culture Industries: A Critique of Invidious Comparisons in the Study of Ethnic Entrepreneurship." *Ethnic and Racial Studies* 24 (2): 236–62.

Bauck, Andrew. 1997. "Review." *Popular Music* 16 (2): 231–34.

Baumann, Shyon. 2001. "Intellectualization and Art World Development: Film in the United States." *American Sociological Review* 66: 404–26.

———. 2007. "A General Theory of Artistic Legitimation: How Art Worlds Are Like Social Movements." *Poetics* 35 (1): 47–65.

Bearman, Peter, Robert Faris, and James Moody. 1999. "Blocking the Future: New Solutions for Old Problems in Historical Social Science." *Social Science History* 23 (4): 501–33.

Becker, H., B. Geer, E. Hughes, and A. Strauss. 1961. *Boys in White: Student Culture in Medical School.* Chicago: University of Chicago Press.

Becker, Howard S. 1982. *Art Worlds.* Berkeley and Los Angeles: University of California Press.

———. 2004. "Jazz Places." In *Music Scenes*, edited by Andrew Bennett and Richard A. Peterson, 17–29. Nashville, TN: Vanderbilt University Press.

———. 2006. "The Work Itself." In *Art from Start to Finish*, edited by Howard S. Becker, Robert R. Faulkner, and Barbara Kirshenblatt-Gimblett, 21–30. Chicago: University of Chicago Press.

Bennett, Andrew. 1997. "'Going Down the Pub': The Pub Rock Scene." *Popular Music* 16 (1): 97–108.

———. 1999. "Subcultures or Neo-Tribes? Rethinking the Relationship between Youth, Style and Musical Taste." *Sociology* 33: 599–617.

———. 2004. "New Tales from Canterbury: The Making of a Virtual Scene." In *Music Scenes*, edited by Andrew Bennett and Richard A. Peterson, 205–20. Nashville, TN: Vanderbilt University Press.

Bennett, Andrew, and Richard A. Peterson, eds. 2004. *Music Scenes: Local, Translocal and Virtual.* Nashville, TN: Vanderbilt University Press.

Bennett, Tony. 2006. "Distinction on the Box: Cultural Capital and the Social Space of Broadcasting." *Cultural Trends* 15 (2–3): 193–212.

Bernard-Donals, Michael. 1994. "Jazz, Rock 'n' Roll, Rap and Politics." *Journal of Popular Culture* 28 (2): 127–38.

Bettie, Julie. 1995. "Class Dismissed? Roseanne and the Changing Face of Working-Class Iconography." *Social Text* 45: 125–49.

Biddle, Ian, and Vanessa Knights, eds. 2007. *Music, National Identity and the Politics of Location: Between the Global and the Local.* Aldershot: Ashgate.

Bielby, Denise D., and William T. Bielby. 1996. "Women and Men in Film: Gender Inequality among Writers in a Cultural Industry." *Gender and Society* 10: 248–70.

———. 2001. "Audience Segmentation and Age Stratification among Television Writers." Working paper. University of Santa Barbara, Department of Sociology.

Bielby, William T., and Denise D. Bielby. 1992. "Cumulative versus Continuous Disadvantage in an Unstructured Labor Market: Gender Differences in the Careers of Television Writers." *Work and Occupations* 19: 366–86.

Bikhchandani, Sushil, David Hirshleifer, and Ivo Welch. 1992. "A Theory of Fads, Fashion, Custom, and Cultural Change as Informational Cascades." *Journal of Political Economy* 11 (5): 992–1026.

Binder, Amy. 1993. "Constructing Racial Rhetoric: Media Depictions of Harm in Heavy Metal and Rap Music." *American Sociological Review* 58 (6): 753–67.

Bolden, Tony. 2008. "Theorizing the Funk: An Introduction." In *The Funk Era and Beyond: New Perspectives on Black Popular Culture*, edited by Tony Bolden, 13–32. New York: Palgrave Macmillan.

Bork, Robert H. 1996. *Slouching towards Gomorrah: Modern Liberalism and American Decline.* New York: Regan Books, Harper Collins.

Bourdieu, Pierre. 1977. *Outline of a Theory of Practice.* Translated by Richard Nice. New York: Cambridge University Press.

———. 1984. *Distinction.* Translated by Richard Nice. Cambridge, MA: Harvard University Press.

———. 1990. *Photography: A Middle-Brow Art.* Stanford: Stanford University Press.

———. 1993. *The Field of Cultural Production.* New York: Columbia University Press.

———. 2002 [1991]. "Social Space and Symbolic Space." In *Contemporary Sociological Theory, edited by Craig Calhoun et al.,* 259–66. Malden, MA: Blackwell.

———. 2003. "But Who Created the 'Creators?'" In *The Sociology of Art*, edited by Jeremy Tanner, 96–104. New York: Routledge.

Bourdieu, Pierre, and Loïc Wacquant. 1992. *An Invitation to Reflexive Sociology.* Chicago: University of Chicago Press.

Bowler, Anne. 1997. "Asylum Art: The Social Construction of an Aesthetic Category." In *Outsider Art: Contesting Boundaries in Contemporary Culture*, edited by

Vera L. Zolberg and Joni Maya Cherbo, 11–36. New York: Cambridge University Press.

Brace, Tim, and Paul Friedlander. 1992. "Rock and Roll on the New Long March: Popular Culture, Cultural Identity, and Political Opposition in the People's Republic of China." In *Rockin' the Boat: Mass Music & Mass Movements*, edited by Reebee Garofalo, 115–28. Cambridge: South End Press.

Brackett, David, ed. 2005. *The Pop, Rock, and Soul Reader: Histories and Debates*. New York: Oxford University Press.

Brewster, Bill, and Frank Broughton. 2000. *Last Night a DJ Saved My Life*. New York: Grove.

Brooke, J. 1988. "Lagos Journal." *New York Times*, November 18.

Brown, Scot. 2008. "A Land of Funk: Dayton, Ohio." In *The Funk Era and Beyond: New Perspectives on Black Popular Culture*, edited by Tony Bolden, 73–88. New York: Palgrave Macmillan.

Buerkle, Jack, and Danny Barker. 1973. *Bourbon Street Black: The New Orleans Black Jazzman*. New York: Oxford University Press.

Bukodi, Erzsébet. 2007. "Social Stratification and Cultural Consumption in Hungary: Book Readership." *Poetics* 35 (2–3): 112–31.

Burnett, Robert. 1995. *The Global Jukebox: The International Music Industry*. London: Routledge.

Burnett, Robert, and Robert Phillip Weber. 1989. "Concentration and Diversity in the Popular Music Industry 1948–1986." Paper presented at the Annual Meeting of the American Sociological Association, San Francisco, CA, August.

Burt, Ronald. 1987. "Social Contagion and Innovation: Cohesion versus Structural Equivalence." *American Journal of Sociology* 92: 1287–1355.

Callon, Michel, ed. 1998. *The Laws of the Markets*. Oxford: Blackwell.

Cantwell, Robert. 1984. *Bluegrass Breakdown: The Making of the Old Southern Sound*. Urbana: University of Illinois Press.

———. 1996. *When We Were Good: The Folk Revival*. Cambridge, MA: Harvard University Press.

Carney, George O. 1995. *Fast Food, Stock Cars, and Rock-n-Roll: Place and Space in American Pop*. Lanham, MD: Rowman & Littlefield.

Carrasco, Eduardo. 1982. *La nueva canción en America Latina*. Centro de Endagacion y Education Cultural y Artistica (CENECA).

Caves, Richard. 2000. *Creative Industries: Contacts between Art and Commerce*. Cambridge, MA: Harvard University Press.

Ceribašić, Naila. 2007. "Musical Faces of Croatian Multiculturality." *Yearbook for Traditional Music* 39: 1–26.

Cerulo, Karen A. 1995. *Identity Designs: The Sights and Sounds of a Nation*. New Brunswick, NJ: Rutgers University Press.

Chadbourne, Eugene. 1997. *I Hate the Man Who Runs This Bar: The Survival Guide for Real Musicians*. Emeryville, CA: Mix Books.

Chambers, Gordon, and Joan Morgan. 1992. "Droppin' Knowledge: A Rap Roundtable." *Essence Magazine*, September, pp. 83–85, 116–20.

Chang, Jeff. 2005. *Can't Stop Won't Stop: A History of the Hip-Hop Generation*. New York: Picador.

Charters, Samuel. 2008. *A Trumpet around the Corner: The Story of New Orleans Jazz*. Jackson: University Press of Mississippi.

Cheney, Charise. 1999. "Representin' God: Rap, Religion and the Politics of a Culture." *North Star* 3 (1): 1–12.

Cherbo, Joni Maya. 1997. "Pop Art: Ugly Duckling to Swan." In *Outsider Art: Contesting Boundaries in Contemporary Culture*, edited by Vera L. Zolberg and Joni Maya Cherbo, 85–97. New York: Cambridge University Press.

Chevigny, Paul. 1991. *Gigs: Jazz and the Cabaret Laws in New York City*. New York: Routledge.

Ching, Barbara. 2001. *Wrong's What I Do Best: Hard Country Music and Contemporary Culture*. New York: Oxford University Press.

Christe, Ian. 2004. *Sound of the Beat: The Complete Headbanging History of Heavy Metal*. London: Allison & Busby Limited.

Clignet, Remi. 1985. *The Structure of Artistic Revolutions*. Philadelphia: University of Pennsylvania Press.

Cloonan, Martin. 2003. "Call That Censorship? Problems of Definition." In *Policing Pop*, edited by Martin Cloonan and Reebee Garofalo, 13–29. Philadelphia: Temple University Press.

Cloonan, Martin, and Reebee Garofalo, eds. 2003. *Policing Pop*. Philadelphia: Temple University Press.

Cocks, Jay, Richard Stengel, and Denise Worrell. 1985. "Music: Rock Is a Four-Letter Word." *Time*, September 30, pp.70–72.

Cohen, Sara. 1991. *Rock Culture in Liverpool: Popular Music in the Making*. Oxford: Clarendon Press.

Cohen, Stanley. 2002 [1972]. *Folk Devils and Moral Panics*. 3rd ed. New York: Routledge.

Collins, John. 1992. *West African Pop Roots*. Philadelphia: Temple University Press.

———. 2009. "Ghana and the World Music Boom." In *World Music: Roots and Routes*, edited by Tuulikki Pietila, 57–75. Helsinki: Collegium.

Colovic, Ivan. 1993. *Bordel ratnika*. Belgrade: Vek.

Connelly, Thomas Lawrence. 1977. *The Marble Man: Robert E. Lee and His Image in American Society*. New York: Knopf.

Cosgrove, Stuart. 1988. Sleeve note to *The History of the House Sound of Chicago* (album). Kaarst, Diepholz, Basel, and Vienna: BCM Records.

Crane, Diana. 1972. *Invisible Colleges: Diffusion of Knowledge in Scientific Communities*. Chicago: University of Chicago Press.

———. 1976. "Reward Systems in Art, Science, and Religion." *American Behavioral Scientist* 19 (6): 719–34.

———. 1987. *The Transformation of the Avant-Garde*. Chicago: University of Chicago Press.

———. 1992. *The Production of Culture: Media and the Urban Arts*. New York: Sage.

———. 1999. "Diffusion Models and Fashion: A Reassessment." *Annals of the American Academy of Political and Social Science*. 566: 13–24.

Crouch, Stanley. 2007. *Considering Genius: Writings on Jazz*. New York: Basic Civitas Books.

Crowley, Daniel. 1977. *African Folklore in the New World*. Austin: University of Texas Press.

Currid, B. 2006. *National Acoustics*. Minneapolis: University of Minnesota Press.

Curtis, Jim. 1987. *Rock Eras: Interpretations of Music and Society, 1954–1984*. Bowling Green, OH: Popular Press.

Cusic, Don. 1990. *The Sound of Light: A History of Gospel Music*. Bowling Green, OH: Bowling Green State University Popular Press.

———. 2001. "The Development of Gospel Music" In *The Cambridge Companion to Blues and Gospel Music*, edited by Allan Moore, 44–60. Cambridge: Cambridge University Press.

D'Angelo, P. 2002. "News Framing as a Multiparadigmatic Research Program: A Response to Entman." *Journal of Communication* 52: 870–88.

Danielsen, Anne. 2006. *Presence and Pleasure: The Funk Groove of James Brown and Parliament*. Middletown, CT: Wesleyan University Press.

Dannen, Frederic. 1990. *Hit Men: Power Brokers and Fast Money inside the Music Business*. New York: Times Books.

Darden, Robert. 2004. *People Get Ready! A New History of Black Gospel Music*. New York: Continuum.

Davis, Mary E. 2006. *Classic Chic: Music, Fashion, and Modernism*. Berkeley and Los Angeles: University of California Press.

de Kloet, Jeroen. 2001. *Red Sonic Trajectories: Popular Music and Youth in Urban China*. Amsterdam: Amsterdam School for Social Science Research.

———. 2003. "Marx or Market: Chinese Rock and the Sound of Fury." In *Multiple Modernities: Cinemas and Popular Media in Transcultural East Asia*, edited by Jenny Kwok Wah Lau, 28–52. Philadelphia: Temple University Press.

De Solla Price, Derek. 1965. "Is Technology Historically Independent of Science? A Study in Statistical Historiography." *Technology and Culture* 6 (4): 553–67.

Decker, Jeffery L. 1993. "The State of Rap: Time and Place in Hip Hop Nationalism." *Social Text* 34: 53–84.

Denisoff, R. Serge. 1971. *Great Day Coming*. Urbana: University of Illinois Press.

———. 1975. *Solid Gold: The Popular Recording Industry*. New Brunswick, NJ: Transaction Publishers.

DeNora, Tia. 1991. "Musical Patronage and Social Change in Beethoven's Vienna." *American Journal of Sociology* 97: 310–46.

———. 1995. *Beethoven and the Construction of Genius: Musical Politics in Vienna 1792–1803*. Berkeley and Los Angeles: University of California Press.

———. 2000. *Music in Everyday Life*. New York: Cambridge University Press.

DeVeaux, Scott. 1997. *The Birth of Bebop: A Social and Musical History*. Berkeley and Los Angeles: University of California Press.

Devitt, Amy J. 2004. *Writing Genres: Rhetorical Philosophy and Theory*. Carbondale: Southern Illinois University Press.

DiMaggio, Paul. 1982. "Cultural Entrepreneurship in 19th Century Boston," pts. 1 and 2. *Media Culture and Society* 4: 33–50, 303–22.

———. 1987. "Classification in Art." *American Sociological Review* 52 (4): 440–55.

———. 1992. "Cultural Boundaries and Structural Change: The Extension of the High Culture Model to Theater, Opera, and the Dance, 1900–1940." In *Cultivating Differences: Symbolic Boundaries and the Making of Inequality*, edited by Michele Lamont and Marcel Fournier, 21–57. Chicago: University of Chicago Press.

DiMaggio, Paul, and Francille Ostrower. 1990. "Participation in the Arts by Black and White Americans." *Social Forces* 68: 753–78.

DiMaggio, Paul, and Walter W. Powell. 1983. "The Iron Cage Revisited: Institutional Isomorphism and Collective Rationality in Organizational Fields." *American Sociological Review* 48 (2): 147–60.

Dowd, Timothy J. 1992. "The Musical Structure and Social Context of Number-One Songs, 1955 to 1988: An Exploratory Analysis." In *Vocabularies of Public Life*, edited by Robert Wuthnow, 130–57. London: Routledge.

———. 2000. "Musical Diversity and the U.S. Mainstream Recording Market, 1955 to 1990." *Rassegna di Italiana di Sociologia* 41 (2): 223–63.

———. 2004. "Concentration and Diversity Revisited: Production Logics and the U.S. Mainstream Recording Market, 1940–1990." *Social Forces* 82 (4): 1411–55.

Dowd, Timothy J., and Maureen Blyler. 2002. "Charting Race: The Success of Black Performers in the Mainstream Recording Market, 1940 to 1990." *Poetics* 30 (1–2): 87–110.

Dowd, Timothy, Kathleen Liddle, Kim Lupo, and Anne Borden. 2002. "Organizing the Musical Canon: The Repertoires of Major U.S. Symphony Orchestras, 1842 to 1969." *Poetics* 30 (1–2): 35–61.

Drew, Paul, and John Heritage. 1992. "Analyzing Talk at Work: An Introduction." On *Talk at Work: Interaction in Institutional Settings*, edited by P. Drew and J. Heritage, 3–65. Cambridge: Cambridge University Press.

Dubrow, Heather. 1982. *Genre*. London: Methuen.

Dundes, Alan, ed. 1981. *Mother Wit from the Laughing Barrel: Readings in the Inter-pretation of Afro-American Folklore*. New York: Garland.

Edmonds, N. 2004. *Soviet Music and Society under Lenin and Stalin*. New York: Routledge.

Edwards, Richard. 1998. "Flexibility, Reflexivity and Reflection in the Contemporary Workplace." *International Journal of Lifelong Education* 17 (6): 377–88.

Efird, Robert. 2001. "Rock in a Hard Place: Music and the Market in Nineties Beijing." In *China Urban: Ethnographies of Contemporary Culture*, edited by Nancy N. Chen, Constance D. Clark, Suzanne Z. Gottschang, and Lyn Jeffery, 67–86. Chapel Hill, NC: Duke University Press.

Eliot, Marc. 1989. *Rockonomics: The Money behind the Music*. New York: Watts.

Ellis, Thomas Sayers. 2008. "From the Crib to the Coliseum: An Interview with Bootsy Collins." In *The Funk Era and Beyond: New Perspectives on Black Popular Culture*, edited by Tony Bolden, 89–103. New York: Palgrave Macmillan.

Ellison, Ralph. 1966. "The Golden Age, Time Past." In *Shadow and Act*. New York: Signet Books.

Ennis, Philip H. 1992. *The Seventh Stream: The Emergence of Rock-n-Roll in American Popular Music*. Middletown, CT: Wesleyan University Press.

Escott, Colin. 1991. *Good Rockin' Tonight: Sun Records and the Birth of Rock'n'Roll*. New York: St. Martin's Press.

Espeland, Wendy N., and Michael Sauder. 2007. "Rankings and Reactivity: How Public Measures Recreate Social Worlds." *American Journal of Sociology* 113 (1): 1–40.

Eyerman, Ron and Andrew Jamison. 1998. *Music and Social Movements*. Cambridge: Cambridge University Press.

Faulkner, Robert R. 2003. *Music on Demand: Composers and Careers in the Holly-wood Film Industry*. New Brunswick, NJ: Transaction Books.

Faulkner, Robert R., and Andy B. Anderson. 1987. "Short-Term Projects and Emer-gent Careers: Evidence from Hollywood." *American Journal of Sociology* 92 (4): 879–909.

Feather, Leonard. 1949. *Inside Bebop*. New York: Norton.

Ferguson, Priscilla Parkhurst. 2004. *Accounting for Taste: The Triumph of French Cuisine*. Chicago: University of Chicago Press.

Fernando, S. H., Jr. 1994. *The New Beats: Exploring the Music, Culture, and Attitudes of Hip-Hop*. New York: Anchor Books Doubleday.

Ferris, William. 1978. *Blues from the Delta*. New York: Doubleday.

Fikentscher, Kai. 2000. *"You Better Work!": Underground Dance Music in New York City*. Middletown, CT: Wesleyan University Press.

Filene, B. 2000. *Romancing the Folk*. Chapel Hill: University of North Carolina Press.

Fine, Gary Alan. 2001. *Difficult Reputations: Collective Memories of the Evil, Inept, and Controversial.* Chicago: University of Chicago Press.

Fischer, Paul D. 2003. "Challenging Music as Expression in the United States." In *Policing Pop,* edited by Martin Cloonan and Reebee Garofalo, 221–38. Philadelphia: Temple University Press.

Fish, Stanley. 1980. *Is There a Text in This Class? The Authority of Interpretive Communities.* Cambridge, MA: Harvard University Press.

Florida, Richard. 2002. *The Rise of the Creative Class: And How It's Transforming Work, Leisure, Community and Everyday Life.* New York: Basic.

Ford, Robert, Jr. 2004. "B-Beats Bombarding Bronx: Mobile DJ Starts Something with Oldie R&B Disks." In *That's the Joint!: The Hip Hop Studies Reader,* edited by Murray Forman and Mark Anthony Neal, 46–47. New York: Routledge.

Forman, Murray. 2002. *The Hood Comes First: Race, Space, and Place in Rap and Hip-Hop.* Middletown, CT: Wesleyan University Press.

Fornäs, Johan. 1995. "The Future of Rock: Discourses That Struggle to Define a Genre." *Popular Music* 14 (1): 111–25.

Fowler, Alastair. 1982. *Kinds of Literature: An Introduction to the Theory of Genres and Modes.* Cambridge, MA: Harvard University Press.

Fricke, Jim, and Charlie Ahearn. 2002. *Yes, Yes Y'all: Oral History of Hip-Hop's First Decade.* New York: Da Capo Press.

Frickel, Scott, and Neil Gross. 2005. "A General Theory of Scientific/Intellectual Movements." *American Sociological Review* 70 (2): 204–32.

Frith, Simon. 1983. *Sound Effects: Youth, Leisure and the Politics of Rock.* London: Constable.

———. 1987. "Towards an Aesthetic of Popular Music." In *Music and Society: The Politics of Composition, Performance and Reception,* edited by Richard Leppert and Susan McClary, 133–49. New York: Cambridge University Press.

———. 1988. "Video Pop: Picking Up the Pieces." In *Facing the Music,* edited by Simon Frith, 88–130. New York: Panetheon.

Frith, Simon. 1996. *Performing Rites: On the Value of Popular Music.* Oxford: Oxford University Press.

Frow, John. 2006. *Genre.* New York: Routledge.

Fruchtman, R. 1975. "Quilapayun: Ambassadors without a Country." *Ramparts* 13 (8): 30.

Fujimura, Joan H. 1996. *Crafting Science: A Sociohistory of the Quest for the Genetics of Cancer.* Cambridge, MA: Harvard University Press.

Gaines, Donna. 1994. "The Local Economy of Suburban Scenes." In *Adolescents and Their Music: If It's Too Loud, You're Too Old,* edited by Jonathon S. Epstein, 47–65. New York: Garland.

Gamson, Joshua. 1994. *Claims to Fame: Celebrity in Contemporary America*. Berkeley and Los Angeles: University of California Press.

Gans, Herbert. 1974. *Popular Culture and High Culture*. New York: Basic Books.

Garland, Phyl. 1970. *The Sound of Soul*. Chicago: Regnery.

Garofalo, Reebee. 1994. "Culture versus Commerce: The Marketing of Black Popular Music." *Public Culture* 7 (1): 275–87.

———. 2002. *Rockin' Out: Popular Music in the USA*. New York: Prentice Hall.

———. 2003. "I Want My MP3: Who Owns Internet Music?" In *Policing Pop*, edited by Martin Cloonan and Reebee Garofalo, 30–45. Philadelphia: Temple University Press.

Gates, Henry Louis, Jr. 1988. *The Signifying Monkey: A Theory of Afro-American Literary Criticism*. New York: Oxford University Press.

Gellner, Ernest. 1983. *Nations and Nationalism*. Oxford: Blackwell.

Gendron, Bernard. 2002. *Between Montmartre and the Mudd Club: Popular Music and the Avant-Garde*. Chicago: University of Chicago Press.

George, Nelson. 1998. *Hip Hop America*. New York: Penguin.

Gest, Scott D., Kelly L. Rulison, Alice J. Davidson, and Janet A. Welsh. 2008. "A Reputation for Success (or Failure): The Association of Peer Academic Reputations with Academic Self-Concept, Effort, and Performance across the Upper Elementary Grades." *Developmental Psychology* 44 (3): 625–36.

Gibson, David. 2008. "How the Outside Gets In: Modeling Conversational Permeation." *Annual Review of Sociology* 34: 359–84.

Giddens, Anthony A. 1979. *Central Problems in Social Theory*. Berkeley and Los Angeles: University of California Press.

Gieryn, Thomas F. 1998. *Cultural Boundaries of Science: Credibility on the Line*. Chicago: University of Chicago Press.

Gillett, Charlie. 1974. *Making Tracks: Atlantic Records and the Growth of a Multi-Billion-Dollar Industry*. New York: Dutton.

Gilroy, Paul. 1994. *Small Acts: Thoughts on the Politics of Black Cultures*. New York: Serpent's Tail.

Ginell, Cary. 1994. *Milton Brown and the Founding of Western Swing*. Urbana: University of Illinois Press.

Gitler, Ira. 1986. *Swing to Bop: An Oral History of the Transition to Jazz in the 1940s*. New York: Oxford University Press.

Glynn, Mary Ann. 2000. "When Cymbals Become Symbols: Conflict over Organizational Identity within a Symphony Orchestra." *Organization Science* 11 (3): 285–98.

Goff, James R., Jr. 2002. *Close Harmony: A History of Southern Gospel*. Chapel Hill: University of North Carolina Press.

Goldsmith, Thomas, ed. 2004. *The Bluegrass Reader*. Urbana: University of Illinois Press.

Goosman, Stuart L. 2005. *Group Harmony: The Black Urban Roots of Rhythm & Blues*. Philadelphia: University of Pennsylvania Press.

Gordy, E. D. 1999. *The Culture of Power in Serbia*. University Park: Penn State University Press.

Graham, R. 1988. *Stern's Guide to Contemporary African Music*. London: Pluto Press.

Grazian, David. 2003. *Blue Chicago: The Search for Authenticity in Urban Blues Clubs*. Chicago: University of Chicago Press.

———. 2004. "The Symbolic Economy of the Chicago Blues Scene." In *Music Scenes*, edited by Andrew Bennett and Richard A. Peterson, 31–47. Nashville, TN: Vanderbilt University Press.

Greene, Victor. 1992. *A Passion for Polka: Old-Time Ethnic Music in America*. Berkeley and Los Angeles: University of California Press.

Gribin, Anthony J., and Matthew M. Schiff. 1992. *Doo-Wop: The Forgotten Third of Rock 'n' Roll*. Iola, WI: Krause Publications.

Griffin, Larry J. 1993. "Narrative, Event-Structure Analysis, and Causal Interpretation in Historical Sociology." *American Journal of Sociology* 98 (5): 1094–1133.

Griswold, Wendy. 1987. "The Fabrication of Meaning: Literary Interpretation in the United States, Great Britain, and the West Indies." *American Journal of Sociology* 92 (5): 1077–1117.

Gronow, Pekka, and Ilpo Saunio. 1988. *An International History of the Recording Industry*. Translated by C. Moseley. New York: Cassell.

Guralnick, Peter. 1999. *Sweet Soul Music*. New York: Harper Collins.

Gustafson, James P., and Lowell Cooper. 1979. "Unconscious Planning in Small Groups." *Human Relations* 32 (12): 1039–64.

Gustafson, James P., Lowell Cooper, Nancy C. Lathrop, Karin Ringler, Frederic A. Seldin, and Marcia Kahn Wright. 1981. "Cooperative and Clashing Interests in Small Groups." *Human Relations* 34 (4): 315–39, 367–78.

Haenfler, Russ. 2006. *Straight Edge: Clean-Living Youth, Hardcore Punk, and Social Change*. Piscataway, NJ: Rutgers University Press.

Halle, David. 1993. *Inside Culture: Art and Class in the American Home*. Chicago: University of Chicago Press.

Hamm, Charles. 1983. *Yesterdays: Popular Song in America*. New York: Norton.

———. 1995. *Putting Popular Music in Its Place*. New York: Cambridge University Press.

Hannon, Michael T., and Glenn R. Carroll. 1992. *Dynamics of Organizational Populations*. New York: Oxford University Press.

Haskell, Francis. 1980. *Rediscoverings in Art: Some Aspects of Taste, Fashion, and Collecting in England and France*. 2nd ed. Oxford: Phaidon.

Hayward, Philip, ed. 1998. *Sound Alliances: Indigenous Peoples, Cultural Politics, and Popular Music in the Pacific.* London: Cassell.

Hebdige, Dick. 1979. *Subculture: The Meaning of Style.* New York: Methuen & Co.

Heilbut, Anthony. 1997. *The Gospel Sound: Good News and Bad Times.* 4th ed. New York: Limelight Editions.

Heimer, Carol. 1985. *Reactive Risk and Rational Action: Managing Moral Hazard in Insurance Contracts.* Berkeley and Los Angeles: University of California Press.

Heise, D. 1988. "Computer Analysis of Cultural Structures." *Social Science Computer Review* 6 (2): 183–96.

———. 1989. "Modeling Event Structures." *Journal of Mathematical Sociology* 14 (2–3): 139–69.

Henderson, Errol A. 1996. "Black Nationalism and Rap Music." http://www.nbufront.org/html/fvwin98/erroli.html.

Heritage, John, and David Greatbatch. 1991. "On the Institutional Character of Institutional Talk: The Case of News Interviews." In *Talk and Social Structure: Studies in Ethnomethodology and Conversation Analysis,* edited by Deirdre Boden and Don H. Zimmerman, 93–137. Berkeley and Los Angeles: University of California Press.

Hesmondhalgh, David. 1998. "Post-Punk's Attempt to Democratise the Music Industry: The Success and Failure of Rough Trade." *Popular Music* 16 (3): 255–74.

Himes, Geoffrey. 1994. "Regional Musics: Cajun, Western Swing, and the Bakersfield Sound." In *The Blackwell Guide to Recorded Country Music,* edited by Bob Allen, 70–118. New York: Blackwell.

Hirsch, Paul M. 1972. "Processing Fads and Fashions: An Organization-Set Analysis of Cultural Industry Systems. *American Journal of Sociology* 77 (4): 639–59.

Ho, WaiChung. 2006. "Social Change and Nationalism in China's Popular Songs." *Social History* 31(4): 435–53.

Holzman, Jac, and Gavan Daws. 1998. *Follow the Music: The Life and High Times of Elektra Records in the Great Years of American Pop Culture.* Santa Monica, CA: First Media Books.

Hom, Sharon K. 1998. "Lexicon Dreams and Chinese Rock and Roll: Thoughts on Culture, Language, and Translation as Strategies of Resistance and Reconstruction." *University of Miami Law Review* 53: 1003–18.

Horowitz, Joseph. 2005. *Classical Music in America: A History of Its Rise and Fall.* New York: W. W. Norton.

Hoskyns, Barney. 2006. *Hotel California: The True-Life Adventures of Crosby, Stills, Nash, Young, Mitchell, Taylor, Browne, Ronstadt, Geffen, the Eagles, and Their Many Friends.* Hoboken, NJ: John Wiley & Sons.

Hosokawa, Shuhei. 2002. "Salsa No Tiene Fronteras: Orquesta de la Luz and the Globalization of Popular Music." In *Situating Salsa: Global Markets and Local*

Meaning in Latin Popular Music, edited by Lise Waxer, 289–311. New York: Routledge.

Huang, H. 2001. Yaogun Yinyue: Rethinking Mainland Chinese Rock 'n' Roll. *Popular Music* 20 (1): 1–11.

Hudson, Robert. 1997. "Popular Music, Tradition and Serbian Nationalism." In *Music, National Identity and the Politics of Location: Between the Global and the Local*, edited by Ian Biddle and Vanessa Knights, 161–78. Burlington, VT: Ashgate.

Hughes, Langston. 2005 [1955]. "Highway Robbery across the Color Line in Rhythm and Blues." In *The Pop, Rock, and Soul Reader: Histories and Debates*, edited by David Brackett, 81–82. New York: Oxford University Press.

Hyon, Sunny. 1996. "Genre in Three Traditions: Implications for ESL." *TESOL Quarterly* 30 (4): 693–722.

Inglis, David, and Roland Robertson. 2005. "'World Music' and the Globalization of Sound." In *The Sociology of Art: Ways of Seeing*, edited by David Inglis and John Hughson, 156–70. New York: Palgrave Macmillan.

Irobi, Esiaba. 2003. "All Hail Atunda! Popularity and Anarchy in the Music of Fela Anikulapo Kuti." *Black Renaissance* 5 (2): 43.

Itano, Nicole. 2008. "Turbo-folk Music Is the Sound of Serbia Feeling Sorry for Itself." *Christian Science Monitor,* May 5. http://www.csmonitor.com/2008/0505/p20s01-woeu.html?page=1.

Jackson, Jerma A. 2004. *Singing in My Soul: Black Gospel Music in a Secular Age.* Chapel Hill: University of North Carolina Press.

Jensen, Joli. 1998. *Nashville Sound: Authenticity, Commercialization, and Country Music.* Nashville, TN: Vanderbilt University Press.

Jhally, Sut, and Justin Lewis. 1992. *Enlightened Racism: The Cosby Show, Audiences, and the Myth of the American Dream.* Boulder, CO: Westview Press.

Johnson, Cathryn, Timothy J. Dowd, and Cecilia L. Ridgeway. 2006. "Legitimacy as a Social Process." *Annual Review of Sociology* 32: 53–78.

Jones, Alan, and Jussi Kantonen. 2000. *Saturday Night Forever: The Story of Disco.* New York: A Cappella Books.

Jones, Andrew F. 1992. *Like a Knife: Ideology and Genre in Contemporary Chinese Popular Music.* Ithaca, NY: Cornell East Asia Series.

Jones, Leroi. 1963. *Blues People: Negro Music in White America.* New York: William Morrow and Company.

Kadushin, Charles. 1976. "Networks and Circles in the Production of Culture." *American Behavioral Scientist* 19 (6): 769–84.

Kahn-Harris, Keith. 2007. *Extreme Metal: Music and Culture on the Edge.* Oxford: Berg Publishers.

Keil, Charles, and Steven Feld. 1994. *Music Grooves*. Chicago: University of Chicago Press.

Kelley, Norman. 2005. "Notes on the Political Economy of Black Music." In *Rhythm and Business: The Political Economy of Black Music*, edited by Norman Kelley, 6–23. New York: Akashic Books.

Kelley, Robin D. G. 2004. "Looking for the 'Real' Nigga: Social Scientists Construct the Ghetto." In *That's the Joint! The Hip-Hop Studies Reader*, edited by Murray Forman and Mark Anthony Neal, 135–56. New York: Routledge.

Kennedy, Rick. 1994. *Jelly Roll, Bix, and Hoagy*. Bloomington: Indiana University Press.

Kibby, Marjorie. 2000. "Home on the Page: A Virtual Place of Music Community." *Popular Music* 19 (1): 91–100.

Kiley, David. 2005. "Hip Hop Gets Down with the Deals." *Bloomberg Businessweek*, May 16. http://www.businessweek.com/bwdaily/dnflash/may2005/nf20050516_5797_db016.htm.

King, Stephen A. 2002. *Reggae, Rastafari, and the Rhetoric of Social Control*. Jackson: University Press of Mississippi.

Kofsky, Frank. 1970. *Black Nationalism and the Revolution in Music*. New York: Pathfinder Press.

Kolodin, Irving. 1941. "The Dance Band Business: A Study in Black and White." *Harper's Magazine*. June, pp. 72–82.

Krasilovsky, M. William, and Sidney Schemel. 2000. *This Business of Music: The Definitive Guide to the Music Industry*. 8th ed. New York: Billboard Books.

Krims, Adam. 2000. *Rap Music and the Poetics of Identity*. New York: Cambridge University Press.

Kronja, Ivana. 2004. "Turbo-folk and Dance Music in 1990s Serbia: Media, Ideology and the Production of Spectacle." *Anthropology of East Europe Review* 22 (1): 103–14.

Kruse, Holly. 2003. *Sight and Sound: Understanding Independent Music Scenes*. New York: Peter Lang.

Laing, Dave. 1985. *One Chord Wonders: Power and Meaning in Punk Rock*. Milton Keynes, UK: Open University Press.

Lamont, Michèle, and Virág Molnár. 2002. "The Study of Boundaries in the Social Sciences." *Annual Review of Sociology* 28: 167–95.

Lang, Gladys Engel, and Kurt Lang. 1988. "Recognition and Renown: The Survival of Artistic Reputation." *American Journal of Sociology* 94 (1): 79–109.

Latour, Bruno. 1987. *Science in Action*. Cambridge, MA: Harvard University Press.

Lawrence, Tim. 2003. *Love Saves the Day: A History of American Dance Music Culture, 1970–1979*. Durham, NC: Duke University Press.

Leal, Odina Fachel, and Ruben George Oliven. 1988. "Class Interpretations of a Soap Opera Narrative: The Case of Brazilian Novella 'Summer Sun.'" *Theory, Culture, and Society* 5: 81–99.

LeCompte, Margaret D., and Judith Preissle Goetz. 1982. "Problems of Reliability and Validity in Ethnographic Research." *Review of Educational Research* 52 (1): 31–60.

Lee, Steve S., and Richard A. Peterson. 2004. "Internet-based Virtual Music Scenes: The Case of P2 in Alt.Country Music." In *Music Scenes*, edited by Andrew Bennett and Richard A. Peterson, 187–204. Nashville, TN: Vanderbilt University Press.

Lena, Jennifer C. 2003. "From 'Flash' to 'Cash': Producing Rap Authenticity, 1979 to 1995." Ph.D. diss., Columbia University.

———. 2004. "Meaning and Membership: Samples in Rap Music, 1979 to 1995." *Poetics* 32 (3–4): 297–310

———. 2006. "Social Context and Musical Content: Rap Music, 1979–1995." *Social Forces* 85 (1): 479–95.

Lent, John A. 1990. *Mass Communications in the Caribbean*. Ames: Iowa State University Press.

Levine, Lawrence. 1977. *Black Culture and Black Consciousness: Afro-American Folk Thought from Slavery to Freedom*. New York: Oxford University Press.

Levitin, Daniel J.. 2006. *This Is Your Brain on Music: The Science of a Human Obsession*. New York: Penguin.

Leymarie, Isabelle. 2002. *Cuban Fire: The Story of Salsa and Latin Jazz*. New York: Continuum.

Lewis, George E. 1996. "Improvised Music after 1950: Afrological and Eurological Perspectives." *Black Music Research Journal* 16 (1): 91–122.

Liang, H., and U. Stobbe. 1993. "Cui Jian and the Birth of Chinese Rock Music." In *China Avant-Garde*, edited by J. Noth, W. Pohlmann, and K. Reschke, 88–92. New York: Oxford University Press.

Lieberson, Stanley. 2000. *A Matter of Taste: How Names, Fashions, and Culture Change*. New Haven: Yale University Press.

Liebes, Tamar, and Elihu Katz. 1993. *The Export of Meaning*. Oxford: Oxford University Press.

Light, Alan. 1992. "Ice-T." *Rolling Stone*, August 20, p. 32.

Linn, Karen. 1984. "Chilean *Nueva Canción*: A Political Popular Music Genre." *Pacific Review of Ethnomusicology* 1: 57–64.

Linnaeus, Carl. 1767. *Systema Naturae*. 12th ed. Stockholm.

Lipsitz, George. 2007. *Footsteps in the Dark: The Hidden Histories of Popular Music*. Minneapolis: University of Minnesota Press.

Lloyd, Richard. 2006. *Neo-Bohemia: Art and Commerce in the Postindustrial City*. New York: Routledge.

Lomax, Alan. 1959. "Blue Grass Background: Folk Music with Overdrive." *Esquire* 52 (October): 108.

Lopes, Paul. 1992. "Innovation and Diversity in the Popular Music Industry, 1969 to 1990." *American Sociological Review* 57 (1): 56–71.

———. 2002. *The Rise of a Jazz Art World*. New York: Cambridge University Press.

Lorenzen, Mark, and Lars Frederiksen. 2005. "The Management of Projects and Product Experimentation: Examples from the Music Industry." *European Management Review* 2 (3): 198–211.

Lornell, Kip, and Charles C. Stephenson, Jr. 2001. *The Beat: Go-Go's Fusion of Funk and Hip-Hop*. New York: Billboard Books.

Lott, Eric. 1995. *Love and Theft: Blackface Minstrelsy and the American Working Class*. New York: Oxford University Press.

Lott, Thomas. 1992. "Marooned in America: Black Urban Youth Culture and Social Pathology." In *The Underclass Question*, edited by Bill E. Lawson, 71–89. Philadelphia: Temple University Press.

Lovesey, Oliver. 2004. "Anti-Orpheus: Narrating the Dream Brother." *Popular Music* 23 (3): 331–48.

Lydon, Michael. 2004. *Ray Charles: Man and Music*. New York: Routledge.

MacKenzie, Donald. 2006. *An Engine, Not a Camera: How Financial Models Shape Markets*. Cambridge, MA: MIT Press.

Mackun, Stanley. 1964. "The Changing Patterns of Polish Settlement in the Greater Detroit Area: Geographical Study of the Assimilation of an Ethnic Group." Ph.D. diss., University of Michigan.

Maffesoli, Michael. 1996. *The Time of Tribes: The Decline of Individualism in Mass Society*. Translated by Don Smith. London: Sage.

Magee, Jeffrey. 2005. *The Uncrowned King of Swing: Fletcher Henderson and Big Band Jazz*. New York: Oxford University Press.

Mahoney, James. 2000. "Path Dependence in Historical Sociology." *Theory and Society* 29: 507–48.

Malone, William C. 1968. *Country Music, U.S.A.* Austin: University of Texas Press.

———. 2002. *Don't Get above Your Raisin': Country Music and the Southern Working Class*. Urbana: University of Illinois Press.

Mann, Geoff. 2008. "Why Does Country Music Sound White? Race and the Voice of Nostalgia." *Ethnic and Racial Studies* 31 (1): 73–100.

Manns, Patrico, Catherine Boyle, and Mike Gonzalez. 1987. "The Problems of the Text in Nueva Canción." *Popular Music* 6 (2): 191–95.

Manuel, Peter. 1993. *Cassette Culture: Popular Music and Technology in North India*. Chicago: University of Chicago Press.

Marable, Manning. 2002. "The Politics of Hip Hop—Check II." BRC Radical Congress list-serv: "Along the Color Line." worker-brc-news@lists.tao.ca.

Marett, Allan. 2005. *Songs, Dreamings and Ghosts: The Wangga of North Australia.* Middletown, CT: Wesleyan University Press.

Marshall, Wayne. 2006. "The Rise of Reggaeton: From Daddy Yankee to Tego Calderón, and Beyond." *Boston Phoenix,* January 19.

———. 2007. "Kool Herc." In *Icons of Hip Hop: An Encyclopedia of the Movement, Music, and Culture,* edited by Mickey Hess, 1–26. Westport, CT: Greenwood Press.

Martinez, Theresa A. 1997. "Popular Culture as Oppositional Culture: Rap as Resistance." *Sociological Perspectives* 40 (2): 265–86.

Mattern, Mark. 1998. *Acting in Concert: Music, Community, and Political Action.* New Brunswick, NJ: Rutgers University Press.

May, Clifford. 1985. "On L.I., Fights Follow a Film on Rap Music." *New York Times,* November 6, p. B1.

McCarthy, John D., and Mayer N. Zald. 1977. "Resource Mobilization and Social Movements: A Partial Theory." *American Journal of Sociology* 82 (6): 1212–41.

McLeod, Kembrew. 2001. "Genres, Subgenres, and More: Musical and Social Differentiation within Electronic/Dance Music Communities." *Journal of Popular Music Studies* 13 (1): 59–76.

McNeil, Legs, and Gillian McCain. 1996. *Please Kill Me: The Uncensored Oral History of Punk.* New York: Penguin.

Meijer, May-May, and Jan Kleinnijenhuis. 2006a. "The Effects of Issue News on Corporate Reputation: Applying the Theories of Agenda Setting and Issue Ownership in the Field of Business Communication." *Journal of Communication* 56 (2): 543–59.

———. 2006b. "News and Corporate Reputation: Empirical Findings from the Netherlands." *Public Relations Review* 32: 341–48.

Melly, George. 1970. *Revolt into Style.* London: Penguin Press.

Merton, Robert K. 1957. *Social Theory and Social Structure.* New York: Free Press.

Merwe, Peter van der. 1989. *Origins of Popular Style: The Antecedents of Twentieth-Century Popular Music.* Oxford: Clarendon Press.

Meyer, J. W., and B. Rowan. 1977. "Institutionalized Organizations: Formal Structure as Myth and Ceremony." *American Journal of Sociology* 83: 340–63.

Middleton, Jason, and Roger Beebe. 2002. "The Racial Politics of Hybridity and 'Neo-Eclecticism' in Contemporary Popular Music." *Popular Music* 21 (2): 159–72.

Mihalca, Matei P. 1992. "Chinese Rock Stars." *Far Eastern Economic Review* 155 (19): 34.

Modleski, Tania. 1982. *Loving with a Vengeance: Mass-Produced Fantasies for Women.* Hamden: Shoestring Press.

Mohr, John W., and F. Guerra-Pearson. 2010. "The Duality of Niche and Form: The Differentiation of Institutional Space in New York City, 1888–1917." *Research in the Sociology of Organizations* 31: 321–68.

Molnar, Virag. 2005. "Cultural Politics and Modernist Architecture: The Tulip Debate in Postwar Hungary." *American Sociological Review* 70: 111–35.

Monahan, Torin, and Jill A. Fisher. 2010. "Benefits of 'Observer Effects': Lessons from the Field." *Qualitative Research* 10 (3): 357–76.

Moore, Ryan. 2005. "Alternative to What? Subcultural Capital and the Commercialization of a Music Scene." *Deviant Behavior* 26 (3): 229–52.

Moreno, Albrecht. 1986. "Violeta Parra and La Nueva Canción Chilena." *Studies in Latin American Popular Culture* 5: 108–26.

Morris, Nancy E. 1984. "Canto Porque Es Necesario Cantar: The New Song Movement in Chile, 1973–1983." Research Paper Series No. 16, University of New Mexico.

Mullins, Nicholas C. 1973. *Theories and Theory Groups in Contemporary Sociology*. New York: Harper & Row.

Murray, David Bruce. 2006. *Murray's Encyclopedia of Southern Gospel Music*. Charleston, SC: BookSurge Publishing.

Neal, Mark Anthony. 2008. "Sly Stone and the Sanctified Church." In *The Funk Era and Beyond: New Perspectives on Black Popular Culture*, edited by Tony Bolden, 3–12. New York: Palgrave Macmillan.

Neale, Steve. 1980. *Genre*. London: British Film Institute.

Negus, Keith. 1999. *Music Genres and Corporate Cultures*. New York: Routledge.

Neustadt, Robert. 2004. "Music as Memory and Torture: Sounds of Repression and Protest in Chile and Argentina." *Chasqui* 33 (1): 128–37.

Nidel, Richard O. 2005. *The Basics: World Music*. New York: Routledge.

Nonaka, I., and R. Toyama. 2003. "The Knowledge-Creating Theory Revisited: Knowledge Creation as a Synthesizing Process." *Knowledge Management Research & Practice* 1 (1): 2–10.

Nusbaum, Philip. 1993. "Bluegrass and the Folk Revival: Structural Similarities and Experiential Differences." In *Transforming Tradition: Folk Music Revivals Examined*, edited by Neil V. Rosenberg, 203–19. Urbana: University of Illinois Press.

Ogbar, Jeffrey O. G. 1999. "Slouching toward Bork: The Culture Wars and Self-criticism in Hip-Hop Music." *Journal of Black Studies* 30 (2): 164–83.

Olavarria, Margot. 2002. "Rap and Revolution: Hip-Hop Comes to Cuba." *NACLA Report on the Americas* 35 (6): 28–30.

Olson, Ted. 1999. "Hippie Hootenanny: Gram Parsons and the Not-Quite-Nashville Cats." *Journal of Country Music* 20 (3): 26–36.

Osumare, Halifu. 2001. "Beat Streets in the Global Hood: Connective Marginalities of the Hip Hop Globe." *Journal of American & Comparative Cultures* 24 (1–2): 171–81.

Paniccioli, Ernie. 2004. *Who Shot Ya? Three Decades of Hip-Hop Photography*. New York: Amistad.

Parker, Marc T. 1999. "An Analysis of Rap Music as the Voice of Today's Black Youth." Senior Thesis, Gannon University.

Pearson, Fred M. 1987. *Goin' to Kansas City*. Urbana: University of Illinois Press.

Perkins, William Eric. 1996. "The Rap Attack: An Introduction." In *Droppin' Science: Critical Essays on Rap Music and Hip Hop Culture*, edited by William Eric Perkins, 1–45. Philadelphia: Temple University Press.

Peterson, Richard A. 1967. "Market and Moralist Censors of a Rising Art Form: Jazz." *Arts in Society* 4 (2): 253–64.

———. 1972. "A Process Model of the Folk, Pop and Fine Art Phases of Jazz." In *American Music: From Storyville to Woodstock*, edited by Charles Nanr, 13–51. New Brunswick, NJ: Transaction Books.

———. 1973. "The Unnatural History of Rock Festivals: An Instance of Media Facilitation." *Popular Music & Society* 2 (2): 97–123.

———. 1990. "Why 1955? Explaining the Advent of Rock and Roll." *Popular Music* 9 (1): 97–116.

———. 1997. *Creating Country Music: Fabricating Authenticity*. Chicago: University of Chicago Press.

Peterson, Richard A., and B. A. Beal. 2001. "Alternative Country: Origins, Music, World-View, Fans and Taste in Genre Formation." *Popular Music and Society* 25 (1–2): 233–49.

Peterson, Richard A., and David Berger. 1975. "Cycles in Symbolic Production: The Case of Popular Music." *American Sociological Review* 40 (2): 158–73.

Peterson, Richard A., and Roger Kern. 1996. "Changing Highbrow Taste: From Snob to Omnivore." *American Sociological Review* 61 (5): 900–907.

Peterson, Richard A., and Gabriel Rossman. 2008. "Changing Arts Audiences: Capitalizing on Omnivorousness." In *Engaging Art: The Next Great Transformation of America's Cultural Life*, edited by Steven Tepper and Bill Ivey, 307–42. New York: Routledge.

Peterson, Richard A., and John Ryan. 2003. "The Disembodied Muse: Music in the Internet Age." In *Culture and Socialization Online*, edited by P. Howard and S. Jones, 233–36. Newbury Park, CA: Sage.

Peterson, Richard, and Albert A. Simkus. 1992. "How Musical Tastes Mark Occupational Status Groups." In *Cultivating Differences: Symbolic Boundaries and the Making of Inequality*, edited by Michele Lamont and Marcel Fournier, 152–86. Chicago: University of Chicago Press.

Pine, Lisa. 2007. *Hitler's "National Community": Society and Culture in Nazi Germany*. London: Hodder Arnold.

Pinn, Anthony B. 1999. "'How Ya Livin'?': Notes on Rap Music and Social Transformation." *Western Journal of Black Studies* 23 (1): 10–21.

Podolny, J. M. 1993. "A Status-Based Model of Market Competition. *American Journal of Sociology* 98: 829–72.

Portes, Alejandro. 1989. "The Enclave and the Entrants: Patterns of Ethnic Enterprise in Miami before and after Mariel." *American Sociological Review* 54 (6): 929–49.

Portes, Alejandro, and Leif Jensen. 1987. "What's an Ethnic Enclave? The Case for Conceptual Clarity." *American Sociological Review* 52 (6): 768–71.

Portes, Alejandro, and Rubén G. Rumbaut. 2001. *Legacies: The Story of the Immigrant Second Generation.* Berkeley and Los Angeles: University of California Press.

Potter, Mitch. 1989. "Rap Music of the Street Has Come Uptown, with Major Record Labels That Once Ignored It Eager to Sign the Hot New Acts." *Toronto Star,* July 8, p. F1.

Powell, Catherine Tabb. 1991. "Rap Music: An Education with a Beat from the Street." *Journal of Negro Education* 60 (3): 245–59.

Press, Andrea. 1991. *Women Watching Television: Gender, Class, and Generation in the American Television Experience.* Philadelphia: University of Pennsylvania Press.

Price, Steven D. 1975. *Old as the Hills: The Story of Bluegrass Music.* New York: Viking.

Prodger, Matt. 2005. "Serbs Rally to 'Turbo-folk' Music." *BBC News,* January 11. http://news.bbc.co.uk/go/pr/fr/-/2/hi/europe/4165831.stm.

Pruter, Robert. 1996. *Doo Wop: The Chicago Scene.* Urbana: University of Illinois Press.

Radano, Ronald. 2003. *Lying Up a Nation: Race and Black Music.* Chicago: University of Chicago Press.

Raeburn, Bruce Boyd. 2009. *New Orleans Style and the Writing of American Jazz History.* Ann Arbor: University of Michigan Press.

Rawlings, Craig. 2001. "'Making Names': The Cutting Edge Renewal of African Art in New York City, 1985–1996." *Poetics* 29: 25–54.

Redhead, Steve. 1999. *The End-of-the-Century Party Youth and Pop towards 2000.* Manchester: Manchester University Press.

Regev, Motti. 1994. "Producing Artistic Value: The Case of Rock Music." *Sociological Quarterly* 35 (1): 85–102.

———. 2002. "The 'Pop-Rockization' of Popular Music." In *Studies in Popular Music,* edited by Dave Hesmondhalgh and Keith Negus, 251–64. London: Arnold.

Reitlinger, Gerald. 1961. *The Economics of Taste: The Rise and Fall of the Picture Market, 1760–1960.* New York: Holt, Rinehart & Winston.

"Review: Parliament's Clones of Dr. Funkenstein." 1979. *Melody Maker* 52 (May 28).

Reynolds, Simon. 1998. *Generation Ecstasy: Into the World of Techno and Rave Culture.* New York: Little, Brown and Company.

Rietveld , Hillegonda C. 1998. *This Is Our House: House Music, Cultural Spaces and Technologies*. Brookfield, VT: Ashgate.

Ripani, Richard. 2006. *The New Blue Music: Changes in Rhythm & Blues, 1950–1999*. Jackson: University of Mississippi Press.

Roberts, John Storm. 1974. *Black Music of Two Worlds*. New York: William Morrow.

———. 1979. *The Latin Tinge: The Impact of Latin American Music on the United States*. New York: Oxford University Press.

Rochon, Thomas. 1998. *Culture Moves: Ideas, Activism, and Changing Values*. Princeton, NJ: Princeton University Press.

Román-Velázquez, Patria. 2002. "The Making of a Salsa Music Scene in London." In *Situating Salsa: Global Markets and Local Meaning in Latin Popular Music*, edited by Lise Waxer, 259–88. New York: Routledge.

Rose, Tricia. 1994a. *Black Noise: Black Music and Black Culture in Contemporary America*. Hanover, NH: Wesleyan University Press.

———. 1994b. "Contracting Rap: An Interview with Carmen Ashhurst-Watson." In *Microphone Fiends: Youth Music & Youth Culture*, edited by Andrew Ross and Tricia Rose, 122–44. New York: Routledge.

Rosenberg, Neil V. 1985. *Bluegrass: A History*. Urbana: University of Illinois Press.

Rosenthal, David. 1992. *Hard Bop*. New York: Oxford University Press.

Rossman, Gabriel. 2004. "Elites, Masses, and Media Blacklists: The Dixie Chicks Controversy." *Social Forces* 83 (1): 61–79.

Roy, William G. 2004. "'Race Records' and 'Hillbilly Music': Institutional Origins of Racial Categories in the American Commercial Recording Industry." *Poetics* 32 (3–4): 265–79.

Rubinstein, Ruth P. 1995. *Dress Code: Meanings and Messages in American Culture*. Boulder, CO: Westview Press.

Ryan, John. 1985. *The Production of Culture in the Music Industry*. Lanham, MD: University Press of America.

Salaam, Kalamu ya. 1995. "It Didn't Jes Grew: The Social and Aesthetic Significance of African American Music." *African American Review* 29 (2): 351–75.

Salamone, F. A. 1998. "Nigerian and Ghanaian Popular Music: Two Varieties of Creolization." *Journal of Popular Culture* 32 (2): 11–25.

Salganik, Matthew J., Peter S. Dodds, and Duncan J. Watts. 2006. "Experimental Study of Inequality and Unpredictability in an Artificial Cultural Market." *Science* 311 (5762): 854–56.

Sanjek, Russell. 1988. *American Popular Music and Its Business*. Vol. 3. New York: Oxford University Press.

Santelli, Robert. 1980. *Aquarius Rising: The Rock Festival Years*. New York: Delta.

Satizábal, Medardo Arias. 2002. "Se Prohibe Escuchar 'Salsa y Control': When Salsa Arrived in Buenaventura, Colombia." Translated by Lise Waxer. In *Situating*

Salsa: Global Markets and Local Meaning in Latin Popular Music, edited by Lise Waxer, 247–58. New York: Routledge.

Schilt, Kristen. 2004. "'Riot Grrrl is . . .': Contestation over Meaning in a Music Scene." In *Music Scenes*, edited by Andrew Bennett and Richard A. Peterson, 115–30. Nashville, TN: Vanderbilt University Press.

Schumpeter, J. 1983 [1934]. *The Theory of Economic Development: An Inquiry into Profits, Capital, Credit, Interest, and the Business Cycle.* Cambridge, MA: Harvard University Press.

Schwartz, Barry. 1982. "The Social Context of Commemoration; A Study in Collective Memory." *Social Forces* 61: 374–402.

———. 1987. *George Washington: The Making of an American Symbol.* New York: Free Press.

Seabrook, John. 2010. "Relics: The Back Room." *New Yorker*, August 30, pp. 26–27.

Sewell, William. 1996. "Historical Events as Transformations of Structures: Inventing Revolution at the Bastille." *Theory and Society.* 25 (6): 841–81.

Shank, Barry. 1994. *Dissonant Identities: The Rock 'n' Roll Scene in Austin, Texas.* London: Wesleyan University Press.

Shepherd, John, David Horn, and Dave Laing, eds. 2005. *Continuum Encyclopedia of Popular Music of the World.* New York: Continuum.

Shipton, Alyn, 2001. *A New History of Jazz.* London: Continuum.

Shively, JoEllen. 1992. "Cowboys and Indians: Perceptions of Western Films among American Indians and Anglos." *American Sociological Review* 57: 725–34.

Shusterman, Richard. 1991. "The Fine Art of Rap." *New Literary History* 22 (3): 613–32.

Simmons, Russell. 2001. *Life and Def: Sex, Drugs, Money and God.* New York: Crown.

Singer, Roberta L. 1983. "Tradition and Innovation in Contemporary Latin Popular Music in New York." *Revista de Musica Latinoamericana* 4 (2): 183–202.

Sinton, Diana, and William A. Huber. 2007. "Mapping Polka and Its Ethnic Heritage in the United States." *Journal of Geography* 106 (2): 41–47.

Smelser, Neil. 1963. *Theory of Collective Behavior.* New York: Free Press.

Smith, Mayne. 1965. "An Introduction to Bluegrass." *Journal of American Folklore* 78: 245–56.

Smith, Richard. 1995. *Seduced and Abandoned.* New York: Cassell.

Smitherman, Geneva. 1977. *Talkin' and Testifyin': The Language of Black America.* Boston: Houghton Mifflin.

———. 1997. "'The Chain Remain the Same:' Communicative Practices in the Hip Hop Nation." *Journal of Black Studies* 28 (1): 3–25.

Sørensen, Aage B. 1977. "The Structure of Inequality and the Process of Attainment." *American Sociological Review* 42 (6): 965–78.

Spring, Ken. 2004. "Behind the Rave: Structure and Agency in a Rave Scene." In *Music Scenes, Local, Translocal and Virtual*, edited by Andy Bennett and Richard A. Peterson, 48–63. Nashville, TN: Vanderbilt University Press.

Star, Susan Leigh, and James R. Griesemer. 1989. "Institutional Ecology, 'Translations' and Boundary Objects: Amateurs and Professionals in Berkeley's Museum of Vertebrate Zoology, 1907–39." *Social Studies of Science* 19 (3): 387–420.

Steen, Andreas. 2000. "Sound, Protest and Business: Modern Sky Co. and the New Ideology of Chinese Rock." *Berliner China-Hefte* 19: 40–64.

Steinberg, Marc W. 2004. "When Politics Goes Pop: On the Intersections of Popular and Political Culture and the Case of Serbian Student Protests." *Social Movement Studies* 3 (1): 3–29.

Stewart, Gary. 1992. *Breakout: Profiles in African Rhythm*. Chicago: University of Chicago Press.

Stewart, Kathleen. 1988. "Nostalgia—a Polemic." *Cultural Anthropology* 3 (3): 227–41.

Stinchcombe, Arthur L. 1959. "Bureaucratic and Craft Administration of Production: A Comparative Study." *Administrative Science Quarterly* 4:168–87.

Stokes, W. Royal. 1991. *The Jazz Scene: An Informal History from New Orleans to 1990*. New York: Oxford University Press.

Suhor, Charles. 2001. *Jazz in New Orleans: The Postwar Years through 1970*. Vol. 38 of *Studies in Jazz*. London: Scarecrow Press; New Brunswick, NJ: The Institute of Jazz Studies, Rutgers University.

Swales, John M. 1990. *Genre Analysis*. Cambridge: Cambridge University Press.

Talley, Tara. 2005. "Grunge and Blues, a Sociological Comparison: How Space and Place Influence the Development and Spread of Regional Musical Styles." *Chrestomathy: Annual Review of Undergraduate Research, School of Humanities and Social Sciences*, 4:228–40. College of Charleston.

Tepper, Steven. 2009. "Stop the Beat: Quiet Regulation and Cultural Conflict." *Sociological Forum* 24 (2): 276–306.

———. 2010. *Not Here, Not Now, Not That: Protesting Art and Culture in America*. Chicago: University of Chicago Press.

Thornton, Sarah. 1996. *Club Cultures: Music, Media, and Subcultural Capital*. Hanover, NH: Wesleyan University Press.

Tilly, Charles. 1997. *Roads from Past to Future*. Lanham, MD: Rowman & Littlefield.

Tosches, Nick. 1996. *Country: The Twisted Roots of Rock 'n' Roll*. New York: Da Capo Press.

Townsend, Charles R. 1976. *San Antonio Rose: The Life and Music of Bob Wills*. Urbana: University of Illinois Press.

Toynbee, Jason. 2000. *Making Popular Music: Musicians, Creativity and Institutions*. London: Arnold.

Traugott, Mark, ed. 1995. *Repertoires and Cycles of Collective Action*. Durham, NC: Duke University Press.

Tsitsos, William. 1999. "Rules of Rebellion: Slamdancing, Moshing, and the American Alternative Scene." *Popular Music* 18 (3): 397–414.

Tuchman, Gail. 1978. *Making News*. New York: Free Press.

Tuchman, Gaye, and Nina Fortin. 1989. *Edging Women Out: Victorian Novelists, Publishers, and Social Change*. New Haven: Yale University Press.

Tumas-Serna, Jane. 1992. "The '*Nueva Canción*' Movement and Its Mass-Mediated Performance Context." *Latin American Music Review* 13 (2): 139–57.

Urban, Glen L., Bruce D. Weinberg, and John R. Hauser. 1996. "Premarket Forecasting of Really-New Products." *Journal of Marketing* 60: 47–60.

Urquía, Norman. 2004. "'Doin' It Right': Contested Authenticity in London's Salsa Scene." In *Music Scenes*, edited by Andrew Bennett and Richard A. Peterson, 96–114. Nashville, TN: Vanderbilt University Press.

Vaccaro, Valerie L., and Deborah Y. Cohn. 2004. "The Evolution of Business Models and Marketing Strategies in the Music Industry." *International Journal on Media Management* 6 (1–2): 46–58.

van Eijck, Koen. 2000. "Richard A. Peterson and the Culture of Consumption." *Poetics* 28 (2–3): 207–24.

van Rees, C. J. 1983. "How a Literary Work Becomes a Masterpiece: on the Threefold Selection Practiced by Literary Criticism." *Poetics* 12: 397–417.

van Rees, Kees, and Gillis J. Dorleijn. 2001. "The Eighteenth-Century Literary Field in Western Europe: The Interdependence of Material and Symbolic Production and Consumption." *Poetics* 28: 331–48.

Veal, Michael E. 2000. *Fela: The Life & Times of an African Musical Icon*. Philadelphia: Temple University Press.

Vincent, Rickey. 1996. *Funk: The Music, the People, and the Rhythm of the One*. New York: St. Martin's Griffin.

Vries, Willem de. 1996. *Sonderstab Musik*. Amsterdam: Amsterdam University Press.

Wahl, Greg. 1999. "I Fought the Law (and I Cold Won!): Hip-Hop in the Mainstream." *College Literature* 26 (1): 98–112.

Waksman, Steve. 2009. *This Ain't the Summer of Love: Conflict and Crossover in Heavy Metal and Punk*. Berkeley and Los Angeles: University of California Press.

Walker, Michael. 2006. *Laurel Canyon: Rock-and-Roll's Legendary Neighborhood*. New York: Faber and Faber.

Walker, Rob. 2009. "The Song Decoders." *New York Times*, October 14, p. MM48.

Walser, Robert. 1993. *Running with the Devil: Power, Gender, and Madness in Heavy Metal Music*. Hanover, NH: Wesleyan University Press.

Warren, Ronald L. 1972. "The Nazi Use of Music as an Instrument of Social Control."
    In *The Sounds of Social Change*, edited by R. S. Denisoff and R. A. Peterson, 72–
    78. Chicago: Rand McNally.
Warrick, Mancel, Joan R. Hillsman, and Anthony Manno. 1977. *The Progress of Gos-
    pel Music: From Spirituals to Contemporary Gospel*. New York: Vantage Press.
Waterman, Christopher A. 1998. "Chop and Quench." *African Arts* 31 (1): 1–9.
Watson, Mary, and N. Anand. 2006. "Award Ceremony as an Arbiter of Commerce
    and Canon in the Popular Music Industry." *Popular Music* 25 (1): 41–56.
Watt, Ian. 2001. *The Rise of the Novel*. Berkeley and Los Angeles: University of Cali-
    fornia Press.
Waxer, Lise, ed. 2002. "Situating Salsa: Latin Music at the Crossroads." In *Situating
    Salsa: Global Markets and Local Meaning in Latin Popular Music*, edited by Lise
    Waxer, 3–22. New York: Routledge.
Weber, Max. 1978 [1924]. *Economy and Society*. Vols. 1 and 2. Edited by Gunther
    Roth and C. Wittich. Berkeley and Los Angeles: University of California Press.
Weinstein, Deena. 1991. *Heavy Metal*. New York: Macmillan.
Weisbard, Eric. 2008. "'Me in the R&B Charts?': Elton John's 'Bennie and the Jets'
    and the British Invasion-Soul-Top 40 Nexus." Paper presented at the EMP Pop
    Music Conference, Seattle, WA, April 12.
Weller, Sheila. 2008. *Girls Like Us: Carole King, Joni Mitchell, Carly Simon—and the
    Journey of a Generation*. New York: Atria Books.
Wepman, Dennis, Ronald Newman, and Murray Binderman. 1976. *The Life: The Lore
    and Folk Poetry of the Black Hustler*. Philadelphia: University of Philadelphia
    Press.
West, Cornel. 1988. *Prophetic Fragments: Illuminations of the Crisis in American Reli-
    gion and Culture*. Grand Rapids, MI: William B. Eerdmans Publishing.
Whitburn, Joel. 1996. *Top R&B Singles 1942–1995*. Menomonee Falls, WI: Record
    Research.
White, Harrison C. 1970. *Chains of Opportunity*. Cambridge, MA: Harvard Univer-
    sity Press.
———. 1988. "Varieties of Markets." In *Social Structures: A Network Approach*, ed.
    Barry Wellman and Stephen D. Berkowitz, 226–60. New York: Cambridge Uni-
    versity Press.
———. 1992. *Identity and Control: A Structural Theory of Social Action*. Princeton, NJ:
    Princeton University Press.
White, Harrison C., and Cynthia White. 1965. *Canvasses and Careers: Institutional
    Change in the French Painting World*. New York: Wiley.
Wicke, Peter. 1992. "The Times They Are a-Changin': Rock Music and Political
    Change in East Germany." In *Rockin' the Boat: Mass Music and Mass Move-
    ments*, edited by Reebee Garofalo, 81–92. Cambridge, MA: South End Press.

Williams, Caroline. 2006. "Genre Matters: Response." *Victorian Studies* 48 (2): 295–304.

Williams, J. Patrick. 2006. "Authentic Identities: Straightedge Subculture, Music, and the Internet." *Journal of Contemporary Ethnography* 35 (2): 173–200.

Williams, Raymond. 1981. *Culture*. London: Fontana.

Wilson, Kenneth, and Alejandro Portes. 1980. "Immigrant Enclaves: An Analysis of the Labor Market Experiences of Cubans in Miami." *American Journal of Sociology* 86 (2): 295–319.

Wolff, Kurt H., trans. and ed. 1950. *The Sociology of Georg Simmel*. New York: Free Press.

Wright, Amy Nathan. 2008. "A Philosophy of Funk: The Politics and Pleasure of a Parliafunkadelicment Thang!" In *The Funk Era and Beyond: New Perspectives on Black Popular Culture*, edited by Phillip D. Beidler and Gary Taylor, 33–50. New York: Palgrave Macmillan.

Yan Jun, Beijing Xinsheng. 1999. "New Sound of Beijing: A Sonic China Project." Changsha.

Zelditch, Morris. 2001. "Processes of Legitimation: Recent Developments and New Directions." *Social Psychological Quarterly* 64: 4–17.

Zolberg, Vera L. 1997. "African Legacies, American Realities: Art and Artists on the Edge." In *Outsider Art: Contesting Boundaries in Contemporary Culture*, edited by Vera L. Zolberg and Joni Maya Cherbo, 53–70. New York: Cambridge University Press.

Zuckerman, Ezra W. 1999. "The Categorical Imperative: Securities Analysts and the Illegitimacy Discount." *American Journal of Sociology* 104 (5): 1398–1438.

Zuckerman, Ezra W., Tai-Young Kim, Kalinda Ukanwa, and James von Rittman. 2003. "Robust Identities or Nonentities? Typecasting in the Feature-Film Labor Market." *American Journal of Sociology* 108 (5): 1018–74.

Index